TOWNS & VILLAGES
OF BRITAIN:
CHESHIRE

Ron Scholes

Series editor: Terry Marsh

Published by Sigma Leisure – an imprint of
Sigma Press, 1 South Oak Lane, Wilmslow, Cheshire SK9 6AR, England.

British Library Cataloguing in Publication Data
A CIP record for this book is available from the British Library.

ISBN: 1-85058-637-3

Series Editor: Terry Marsh

Typesetting and Design by: Sigma Press, Wilmslow, Cheshire.

Cover Design: MFP Design & Print

Cover photographs: main photograph – Beeston Castle; smaller photographs, from top – Shutlingsloe from Berry Bank, Marbury village, Peckforton Castle.

Photographs: by the author, except where otherwise acknowledged

Map: Morag Perrott

Printed by: MFP Design & Print

Acknowledgement: Many thanks to Mrs Freda Murphy for the word processing work involved in the preparation of the manuscript for this book.

Contents

Introduction   1

    Explanatory Notes   1

    County Information Centres   2

Cheshire   3

    Peak and Plain   3

    The Landscape of Cheshire   3

    A Potted History   4

    Place Names   5

    Turbulent Times   5

    Agriculture and Urbanisation   7

The Towns and Villages   9

Bibliography   175

Index   176

CHESHIRE

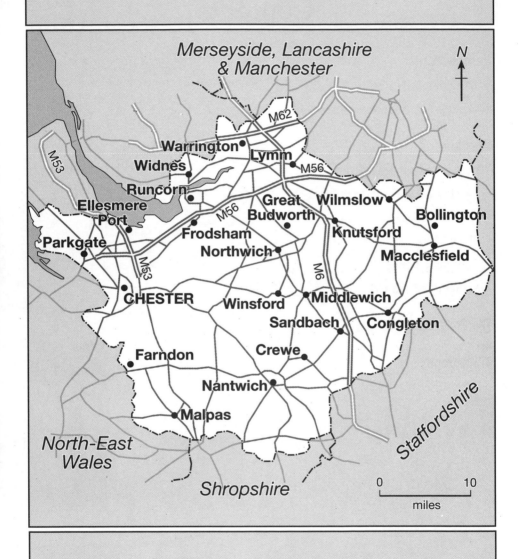

Merseyside, Lancashire & Manchester

N

M62

M53

M56

Warrington
Lymm
M56
Widnes
Runcorn
Great Wilmslow
Ellesmere Port
Budworth
Bollington
Parkgate
Frodsham
Knutsford
M56
Northwich
Macclesfield
M53
M6
CHESTER
Winsford
Middlewich
Sandbach
Congleton
Farndon
Crewe
Nantwich
Staffordshire
Malpas
North-East Wales
Shropshire

0   10
miles

Introduction

The 'Towns and Villages of Britain' is a series of titles detailing a county-by-county approach to the many delights and fascinations of our country's cities, towns, villages and hamlets. There is much of interest and value throughout our towns and villages, but not all of it is widely documented, and some of it, particularly local customs, folklore and traditions, is in danger of being lost forever. By bringing all this information together, county-by-county, it becomes possible to build a unique and substantially comprehensive library of knowledge.

All of the books in the series are compiled to the same specification and in gazetteer format, and include information about the way or the reason a town or village evolved; references to anything associated with the preservation of the past, such as museums, heritage centres, historic or prehistoric sites, battle sites, places of worship and other locally or architecturally important buildings. Landscape features are also detailed, including important natural history sites, geological sites, water features, etc. as is information about important local people, and details of local events. There are also notes about any significant present-day informal amenity/recreational features, such as country parks, open access land, Areas of Outstanding Natural Beauty, nature reserves, and Sites of Special Scientific Interest. Finally, information is given on any significant Roman or prehistory context, and any anecdotal or endemic folklore references associated with the town or village which might illustrate a particular way of life or social development. The books are therefore eminently suitable for anyone interested in their own locality or in local history; students of history, folklore and related subjects; professional journalists wanting up-to-date and comprehensive information; public relations and similar businesses; photographers and artists, and, of course, the tourists and visitors to the counties.

Explanatory Notes

It has been suggested that to qualify as a village, a 'community' must possess a school, a pub, a post office and a church. Such a requirement, however, excludes a large number of places that are of immense interest, many having important historical associations, and which have played a vital part in the development of the county and its people. So, for the purposes of the books in this series, the criteria for inclusion have been kept deliberately simple: there must be something of interest about the place; or it must have associations with events and people of countywide or wider significance.

Often, the 'something of interest' will simply be the village church (its history, contents or architecture), or its green or a river bridge. In addition, the village may be important to the heritage of the county because it maintains the traditions, ways and beliefs of local culture, or has played a key role in the social, economic or political history of the county or the country as a whole.

Only occasionally, however, is the village pub of special interest in this context, and often the development of large supermarkets within easy travelling distance of the villages has, sadly, signalled the demise of the traditional village shop. Local schools have often been swallowed up by larger schools, and far too many post offices are proving difficult to sustain as viable concerns. So, while that 'classic' definition of a village has much to commend it, in reality it is today too restrictive.

Quite what makes a town is another, arguable, matter. But the precise definition is not too important here; it's the place and its people, not its status, that matters. As a very broad distinction, that no-one should take seriously, a 'hamlet' (a few of which appear in these books) is a distinct community, while a 'village' could be said to be a hamlet with a church, and a 'town' is a village with a market.

In many cases, the historical development of the community, whether a tiny village, a town or a city, is fascinating in itself, and so it is that each entry gradually builds up a picture of the county that is unique. That is what this book endeavours to portray, in a logical and easily accessible way, as well as being a source of reference.

Inevitably, there will be places that have been omitted that others might argue should have been included. But the value each community has to bring to a work of this nature has been carefully weighed; invariably, borderline cases have been given the benefit of the doubt and included.

It is equally clear that, taken to its logical conclusion, this book would be ten times larger, and there has had to be a considerable degree of selective editing to make it of manageable size. One day, perhaps, there could be one book that says everything there is to say about the county, but could we afford to buy it? Could we carry it? Would we want it, when part of the beauty of what does exist is the range of voices and shades of opinion so many different authors can bring?

Following the General Introduction, the book becomes a gazetteer, listing the towns and villages of the county in alphabetical order.

After each town or village name there appears, in square brackets, [ ], the name of the relevant district council (see below).

Next appears a two-letter, four-figure grid reference, which will pinpoint the settlement to within half a mile (one kilometre). This is followed by an approximate distance from some other, usually larger, settlement, together with an equally approximate direction indicator.

Those features or people 'of interest' directly associated with the settlement are highlighted in bold text, while an index lists other features or people only incidentally associated.

County Information Centres

Where information is given about events, such as agricultural shows, or facilities, such as museums, details of dates and hours of opening are usually available from any of the Tourist Information Centres listed below.

Chester: 01244 402111
Congleton: 01260 271095
Knutsford: 01565 632611
Macclesfield: 01625 504114
Nantwich: 01270 610983
Poynton: 01625 874225
Runcorn: 01928 575776
Warrington: 01925 442180
Wilmslow: 01625 522275
Winsford: 01606 815055

Also, most of the public libraries in larger Cheshire towns have an "information point". Outside of library opening hours, dial 03456-03456 for the Cheshire County Council information network. Finally, there is the county's internet web site at htttp://www.cheshire.gov.uk.

Cheshire

Cheshire is often thought of as a predominantly rural county which is mostly flat and scenically uninspiring. Certainly, the Cheshire Plain covers a large part of the county, although it is more in the nature of a shallow basin that extends southwards into Shropshire. On its eastern edge, in proportion to the bulk of lowland, Cheshire is a sliver of high land abutting the foothills of the South Pennines and the Staffordshire Moorlands. This is millstone grit country; a landscape of upland slopes, villages with swift-flowing watercourses and rough grassland with rush and heather.

Peak and Plain

However, not to be outdone, the Cheshire Plain has its heights in the form of the Mid-Cheshire Ridge, which combines wooded slopes and sandstone cliffs. Bickerton, Peckforton and Beeston Hills line up with Frodsham and Helsby in the north. Certainly, these vantage points, overlooking the lowland forests and swamps, were effectively used by early man for settlements and security.

Gradually the forests were cleared and, in time, the area became the Cheshire we know today, a tapestry of rich farmland, lush meadows and riverside pastures, hedgerows and copses of trees.

Much use was made of local building materials: clay for daub and brick making, oak for timber-framed buildings, reeds for thatch and red sandstone and fine-grained Carboniferous gritstone for walls and roofs. These materials have influenced the appearance of the villages and towns in this man-made landscape. Cheshire is rightly famous for its 'black and white' buildings and this attractive architecture is an integral part of the county's heritage.

The Landscape of Cheshire

The physical character of the landscape of Cheshire bears a close relationship to what lies in layers beneath the surface. Like the colours and tints on an artist's canvas, the geology of the rocks has shaped the foundations of the landscape's scenic picture. From pre-Cambrian times, a geological period that may have lasted some 4000 million years, sediments were laid down under marine, deltaic and freshwater conditions. Throughout their long history, the deposits of sandstone, conglomerates, grits, shales, limestones, clays, coal-seams and sands have been affected by earth movements as the strata were uplifted, squeezed, folded and faulted.

These events have been partnered through time by climatic changes from tropical to arid temperature to glacial. In the Permo-Triassic period the area experienced the full rigours of conditions typical of the Sahara desert. Bounded by high land, the basin was subsequently filled by sediments carried along by violent storms and desert winds. Salt deposits formed due to solar evaporation and flash floods carried vast quantities of rounded pebbles to create great thicknesses of Bunter Pebble Beds. For millions of years winds carried dust to dry ground or into standing water, eventually to become consolidated into Keuper Marl which provides the surface soil over much of the area today.

During the Pleistocene geological era, four major Ice Ages were separated by periods of fluctuating climatic conditions. Primitive men existed as nomadic hunters, living in the open air and camping beside rivers or in the mouths of caves. From 11,000BC onwards, following the rise in temperature after the retreat of the final ice sheet, the tundra-like vegetation of sedge, grass and moss gave way to prairie-like grassland with patches of hazel and alder. A milder and damper climate induced the growth of woodland with great forests of birch, pine, oak, lime and elm.

The immense mass of water resulting from the melting ice gradually rose to cover the remaining land bridge, possibly about 6500BC, and thus Britain became separated from the mainland of Europe.

A Potted History

The Neolithic (New Stone Age) practice of communal burial was established at an early date in parts of continental Europe. The burial custom began with the use of natural features such as caves and then progressed to earthen long barrows and chambered tombs. Eventually, huge blocks and slabs of stone called megaliths were raised forming sectional or chambered passages.

The hill fort idea developed from the principal of a refuge easily defended by an earthen bank with a deep external ditch and superbly sited to give a wide field of vision. Circular huts were built, constructed of spaced posts interwoven with laths and covered in clay. In some regions, rough stone walls were used instead of wattle and daub. Many of these long-lasting features of the Bronze and Iron Ages have survived as part of the present landscape, in the form of grass-grown ditches and weathered earthworks.

Gnaeus Julius Agricola, who arrived in AD78, is the best known governor of Roman Britain. He placed the seal on the occupation of the country. Firstly he moved into Wales, completely defeated the Ordovices and established forts to control the main routes. With the establishment of Chester, the military control of the area was now complete. The great legionary fortress at Chester (Deva) was later rebuilt in stone but there is evidence that an auxiliary fortress was established in AD60. The Twentieth Legion garrisoned the base until they were replaced by the Second Legion (Adiutrix). Later the Twentieth returned and remained at Chester until the end of the Roman occupation.

Much is known about the fortress from excavation, and the Grosvenor Museum, Chester has a fine collection of Roman remains, including a remarkable number of inscribed tombstones. Comparatively little is known about the development of the area during the Roman period, but their main roads crossed the county from Chester to Wroxeter, and there were routes linking Warrington, Northwich and Manchester. The salt industry was developed near Middlewich and Northwich and evidence of metalworking and glass-making was discovered at Wilderspool near Warrington.

When the Romans left Cheshire, the native British carried on their lives. At the same time, Christianity was also making converts from paganism. In the west, the early Celtic church extended its influence into Cheshire, with even a recorded synod at Chester in AD610.

It was only after the death of Penda, the pagan king of Mercia, that a greater number of the scattered population began to accept the new religion. The number of pre-Norman crosses erected between the seventh and 11th centuries illustrates the spread of the Christian faith in Cheshire; these were either Mercian or Anglo-Norse (Northumbrian influences). Some were plain; some were beautifully carved and both types were set in socketed stone bases. These monuments served as preaching crosses, gravestones, signposts or boundary markers.

Place Names

The interpretation of place names has played an important role in the understanding of landscape history in Cheshire and elsewhere in the country. It is essential to know the earliest surviving form of the place to make an interpretation with some degree of certainty.

Even though there are examples of Welsh, Celtic influence in certain Cheshire place names, for example, Tarvin (Welsh *terfyn*, meaning 'a boundary'); it was the time when Mercian power developed. At the end of the seventh century, Cheshire was certainly part of Anglian Mercia. In a general sense, place names in many localities give clues regarding their former woodland cover. The first Saxon settlers, who made clearings in the dense forests, gave the names. The places cleared of trees and undergrowth were named 'leah', and these settlements can be recognised by names ending in the modern form 'ley'. To confuse matters, however, the name could also mean a glade or an open space in the forest that required little clearing. For example, in the area of Delamere Forest: Kingsley - 'The King's leah'; Norley - 'Northern Leah'; Manley - 'Common wood leah'.

In some cases the name contains a personal element: Alvanley – 'Aelfwald's leah'; [Nether] Alderley – 'Aldred's leah'.

Other present-day names that have some connection with former woodland end in 'leigh', 'hurst' and 'stock'. Anglian settlers continued to move into the area, exploring the river valleys and making use of the Roman roads. The later groups preferred more open ground above the flood levels of the valleys and their enclosed homesteads developed into village settlements with the suffix element 'tun'. The meaning of the word 'tun' may well have denoted an outlying farm attached to an original homestead. These settlements can now be recognised by names ending in 'ton'. In many cases, the name contains a personal element. For example: Shavington – 'the tun of Sceafa's people'; Cuddington – 'the tun of Cuda's people'; and Marton – *Maer-tun*, 'the tun by a lake'.

Another common element found in place names is the ending 'ham'. The original meaning is thought to refer to flat land close to a river or stream, or in the bend of a river, where the type of land would be pasture or water meadow. For example: Weaverham – 'a homestead close to a winding river'; Swettenham – 'Sweta's ham'; and Warmingham – 'the ham of Waermund's people'.

Turbulent Times

Until the end of the eighth century, England was still divided into the four great kingdoms of East Anglia, Wessex, Northumberland and Mercia. A dark cloud appeared over the development of Anglo-Saxon civilisation in the shape of the Vikings. Between AD865 and 880 the Danes conquered Northumbria, eastern Mercia and East Anglia.

At the beginning of the 11th century a new Scandinavian invasion began with the landing of Norsemen from Ireland and the Isle of Man. The Wirral area in particular was colonised by the Norwegian Vikings, whilst the Danes infiltrated east Cheshire. The density of Norse settlement in the Wirral is clearly reflected in the place names in the area. For example: Irby – 'the by of the Irish' was Irabyr in Old Scandinavian. The element 'by' represents a homestead or settlement. Thingwall was an 'assembly field', as in Tynwald in the Isle of Man; Neston meant 'headland'; and [West] Kirby is from the Norse *kirkiubyr* 'a village with a church'.

In east Cheshire, Danish influence extends to the Hulme group of places; this is derived from 'holm' meaning a small island or a piece of land partly surrounded by a stream or streams.

After the Norman Conquest, it was the north and west of England that gave William a great deal of trouble. He subjected Yorkshire, in particular, to a scorched earth policy, before marching across the Pennines to subdue Cheshire. At that time, most of Cheshire was a rather wild, remote area, where most of the inhabitants lived in the river valleys outside the thickly wooded parts of the region. Systematic wasting occurred in Cheshire as, indeed, in neighbouring Staffordshire and Shropshire.

William completed his campaign by building a castle at Chester then another at Stafford. By February 1071, William had granted all Cheshire barring only the bishop's lands to Hugh d'Avranches. His task was the final suppression of the remaining English and Welsh resistance.

The Domesday Survey of 1086 provides us with a picture of 11th century England. It gives documentary evidence of another stage in this country's evolving landscape. In Cheshire, a great number of existing village names are to be found in the Domesday Book. The clerks engaged in the survey were referring to the taxable estates and did not differentiate between a farmstead, a hamlet, a village or a group of villages. Nevertheless, it does give a good picture of the countryside at that time, including farmland, meadowland and woodland.

Later castles were built at Beeston and Halton and little has remained of the domestic architecture. Even ecclesiastical buildings are limited with only chapels at Shocklach and Prestbury remaining to the present day.

After the Norman Conquest, William ordered the creation of royal forests and chases. In Cheshire there were two such forests in 1086, Delamere Forest and Macclesfield Forest. Today, Delamere Forest is a very shrunken version of the Forest of Mara and the Mondrum Forest, which were spread over the now rich agricultural area between the Bickerton Hills, Acton near Nantwich and Malpas. The term 'forest' did not necessarily mean woodland but also referred to heathland and upland.

With the arrival of the Normans, most of the earlier religious houses were replaced by others based on the continental pattern of order. An early foundation was the Benedictine Abbey of St Werburgh at Chester in 1093. In fact, the church of St John in Chester held the position of Cathedral in the time of the first Norman Bishop of Lichfield.

Norton Priory was founded in 1210 as a religious centre for Augustinian Canons, and troubled Vale Royal was the largest Cistercian house in the land. Combermere Abbey, the other large Cistercian house, was founded in 1133 and had five churches appointed to it. A number of these religious houses had extensive possessions in the form of lands, farms and mineral wealth. Some attached granges lay a considerable distance from the mother house. Cheshire's security lay in the hands of Earl Hugh and his barons. In the early days of Norman rule, defensive positions were established in the form of the motte and bailey castle. Even so, Cheshire is not rich in castles. In the early 13th century the King took over this powerful earldom which included the castles of Beeston and Chester.

Agriculture and Urbanisation

In much of England, from the south to the Vale of York, the agricultural routine of farmed strips in two or three open fields continued through the Middle Ages. This system of cultivating the land and pasturing the stock in common meadows and unenclosed rough pasture continued in one form or other until the parliamentary enclosures of the 19th century. Generally, throughout the Midlands and the south of England, the village had its church, manor house and peasant dwellings sited close to each other.

In the 14th century, there may well have been an open area or green with trackways radiating from it. These headed out to the fields, some connecting with routes to neighbouring settlements. However, communications at that time would be very difficult with muddy holloways and deeply grooved tracks. In Cheshire, as in many other areas of the country, these old ways now constitute a remarkable heritage of present-day rights of way through the countryside.

During the Middle Ages, responsibility for highways devolved on the manor, but with greater traffic and inadequate maintenance, the condition of the roads became worse and worse. After the Highways Act of 1555, the parish became responsible for highway maintenance. But really there was no effective highway authority and often the parishes neglected their duties. The solution for this problem in Cheshire, as elsewhere, was vested in the Turnpike Trusts. From the early 18th century onwards, turnpike roads were constructed in Cheshire, together with the erection of toll bars and the charging of fees. From 1864, the Turnpike Trusts were phased out and all the turnpikes became main roads; this was followed by the creation of county councils in 1888 who undertook the responsibility for highway maintenance.

Until the mid-18th century, transport of heavy goods throughout this country was generally by sea or by navigable rivers. Cheshire began to develop her inland waterways in order to transport agricultural products, cattle, salt, stone and coal. The first important construction work was the Weaver Navigation to connect the salt-producing area to the Mersey; this was authorised in 1720. This was followed by the Bridgewater Canal in 1761, which ultimately connected Worsley with Runcorn. In 1793 it was proposed to link the Dee with the Severn at Shrewsbury but problems of a late scheme and competition from the railways caused the canal to be constructed through Whitchurch. The famous canal engineer James Brindley worked on a number of these projects and, with the Trent and Mersey Canal, he connected the Mersey with the Birmingham area; this was authorised in 1766.

The development of railways in Cheshire is linked with the expanding towns in the county and the need to provide links with Holyhead and with routes to London, the Midlands and Northern England. Between 1840 and 1860, the towns of Crewe and Chester became route centres of national importance. Crewe in particular became a focal point for routes going to all points of the compass. Various railway companies provided lines to Derbyshire, Yorkshire, Lancashire and Staffordshire, and a tunnel link was opened between Liverpool and Birkenhead in 1886.

In 1921, all the many companies operating the country's railways were grouped under the Railway Act. The four main railways formed were the London,

Midland and Scottish (LMS), London and North Eastern (LNER), Great Western (GWR) and the Southern Railway (SR). In Cheshire the London and North Western Railway and the Midland Railway became part of the LMS. The LNER absorbed the Great Central Railway. In March 1963, the 'Beeching Plan' decimated Cheshire's branch lines so that only the original trunk routes remained. The plan had similar effects in every region in the country.

Electrification came to the main routes and they are now connected with Eurostar and the Channel Tunnel. But what is the future? One day, who knows, there will be a resurrection of many of these 'lost' branch lines; when the railway transportation needs of the new century have been effectively, economically and environmentally thought out.

It is believed that salt has been extracted from the salt deposits underneath the Cheshire Basin since Roman times. The Roman name for Middlewich was Salinae. It lay on King Street, part of the Roman route thought to have run from Sandbach to Wilderspool (Warrington). The rock salt occurs naturally in thick layers amongst beds of Keuper Marl. The present extraction methods used are by natural brine pumping, controlled brine pumping and rock salt mining. In the controlled brine pumping method water is pumped into a layer of rock salt, which then forms a cavity as the salt dissolves. Most of the brine is used in the chemical industry. The Winsford rock salt mine has been in existence since 1844. However, the increased demand for rock salt for keeping roads ice-free in winter has led to sophisticated mining operations.

Cheese is the other famous product of Cheshire, and one of those items associated with the country's dairy industry. Cheese has been made for centuries in this part of England but a considerable number of farms have ceased making it due to factory production. However, there are still about ten farms making this cheese in the traditional manner.

Today, there are parts of Cheshire that have changed in many ways because of industrial development and urbanisation. But Cheshire is still a county of dramatic contrasts: embracing the stark industrial landscape of Stanlow, the banks of the Mersey and Winnington, as well as the green hills around Rainow and Wildboarclough.

Its people have contributed to the landscape through the centuries and they have left their marks in many ways. However, towns and villages have seen high levels of growth and there is much concern about long-distance commuting. The county has the same problem as any other shire of combining attractive rural landscapes and urban areas eager for expansion. The two key points here are strong planning control and the imposition of green belts.

Cheshire has had an illustrious past, a prosperous present and is playing its part towards the future. Good motorway links enable people and manufactured products to be moved around easily and the main line railways give access to the Channel Tunnel and continental markets. But the planners and guardians of this fragile landscape should be increasingly vigilant as Cheshire moves into the next century.

The Towns and Villages

ACTON [Crewe]

SJ6353: 1½ miles (2km) W of Nantwich

The parish of Acton, in the heart of south Cheshire, is typical of the softly undulating landscape that lies between the Peckforton and Bickerton hills to the west and the moors of the Pennines to the east. The area is still predominantly used for agriculture and the villages, scattered hamlets and large farmhouses are linked by a network of winding roads and lanes.

Acton was listed in Domesday as 'Actune'. In Old English this means 'tun by the oaks', or oak homestead. The whole area seems to have been under the control of William Malbank and Earl Morcar owned the lands.

The village lay in the Hundred of Warmundestrou. Hundreds were the divisions of a shire, each 'hundred' being an area capable of supporting 100 families. They were especially important in Norman times, although they were probably Saxon in origin.

Domesday left us a picture of the landscape by recording the presence of a considerable tract of woodland, a sizeable acreage of meadow and a mention of a hawk's eyrie – a feature very close to Norman hearts. The Domesday window illustrates a prosperous, well-endowed settlement with two priests; it also states that there was one house exempt of tax in Wich (Nantwich) for the making of salt. The **church of St Mary** is one of the finest ecclesiastical buildings in Cheshire. Until the end of the 16th century, Acton's church was more important church than that of Nantwich, which was a mere chapel in the parish of Acton.

Due to a great storm in 1757, the upper part of the tall tower crashed down, wrecking the ancient roof and the clerestory. After restoration, only the two lower stages remained of the 13th-century work, together with the 13th-century lower arches and the nave arcades of four bays. The lancet windows of the tower display fine Early English work. The north aisle was built in the Decorated style towards the end of the 14th century.

The Mainwaring Chapel lies at the east end of the north aisle; it contains the richly carved, canopied wall **tomb** in alabaster and sandstone of Sir William Mainwaring who died in 1399. He was Lord of Baddiley and Peover. The effigy is shown wearing plate armour and there are still some traces to be seen of the original rich colour.

At the east end of the south aisle is a beautifully sculptured ancient **piscina**. Another important **monument** is the marble tomb of Sir Richard Wilbraham, (1578-1643), his son, Sir Thomas Wilbraham, (1601-1660), and their wives. The splendid figures of Sir Thomas and his wife are very fine indeed. He dressed in plate armour, with long hair and a short, pointed beard; she beautifully attired in a long dress with a hood. The Mainwarings and the Wilbrahams were representatives of the main lines of two of the greatest families in the county.

An unusual feature of the church is the **stone seating** built against the inner walls; this was specifically intended for the weak and the infirm when wooden chairs or benches were not provided – hence the expression, 'The weakest go to the wall.' The Norman **font** has a round bowl carved with figures and simple ornamentation.

A prominent feature in the churchyard is a 17th-century **sundial** comprising a tall shaft rising from three stone steps. It carries a square stone head with a dial on each face. The top is surmounted by a globe.

A well-known grave in the churchyard at Acton is that of a **famous local sportsman**, A.N. Hornby. At the end of the 19th century he was the first man to captain English teams at cricket and rugby. His gravestone is in marble with the prominent carving of a wicket, bat and ball.

During the Civil War, in 1643 and 1644, there was considerable fighting between the Royalist and Parliamentarian forces around Acton during the siege of Nantwich.

Dorfold Hall lies half a mile (1km) south of Acton and is approached by an impressive drive lined with lime trees. At the far end are **ornamental iron gates** bought at the Paris Exhibition of 1855.

The present house was begun in 1616 by Ralph Wilbraham, a member of the junior branch of the Wilbrahams of Woodhey. There was a possible completion date of 1621. It is a brick, two-storey Jacobean country mansion with large **mullioned and transomed windows**. The lodge, drive and paved forecourt were added in Victorian times.

The Jacobean interiors are found only on the first floor, which is reached by the original oak staircase in the west cross wing. One half-panelled room contains a large **plaster frieze** over the fireplace depicting the arms of James I. The central part of the upper floor is occupied by the splendid **Great Chamber** with its panelled walls and spectacular plasterwork – one of the finest Jacobean ceilings in the country. A magnificent Spanish chestnut, thought to be a survivor of the Forest of Delamere, stands near the entrance to the house.

ACTON BRIDGE [Vale Royal]
SJ5875: 4 miles (6km) W of Northwich

Acton Bridge, once named Acton-in-Delamere, is a pleasant rural village set in a predominantly farming area. The name Acton is a common name and is generally derived from the Old English 'actun' meaning 'a tun by the oaks'.

The village lies on the west bank of the Weaver Navigation Waterway and also close to the Trent and Mersey Canal. Nowadays, both waterways are mainly used by pleasure craft and visitors can enjoy watching boats in the marina, as well as in the building and renovating area. The new bridge was built in 1932 and was the first swing-bridge on a floating pontoon in the country.

The canalisation of the River Weaver, authorised in 1720, was the first major canal work in Cheshire. These improvements to the River Weaver played a significant part in the growth of the Cheshire salt industry. Salt was shipped out and coal was brought in from Lancashire.

The Trent and Mersey Canal, which was opened in 1777, was styled the Grand Trunk by its builder, James Brindley. It connected the Mersey with the Humber and later with the Birmingham area via the Cheshire salt field and the Potteries. Its Cheshire terminal was Preston Brook.

From the early days, the normal loads on most canals were carried in boats that must have been very similar to the wooden craft still seen today in waterway museums and adapted for tourist traffic. The long-distance carriers were relatively light, all-timber constructions.

The early craft were clinker-built of overlapping planks but later carvel-built boats with the planks flush were used. The latter being more suited to canal use, as well as being cheaper to build. A cabin was built to accommodate the crew. The boats were horse-drawn and were capable of carrying about 20 tons (19.4 tonnes).

The first railway line in Cheshire was opened in 1837. It formed part of the Grand Junction route from Birmingham to Warrington via Crewe, and was thus a route of national as well as local importance. Today, a modest number of trains stop at Acton Bridge Station to pick up local passengers. This is the main route to Liverpool, the North West of England and Scotland.

The village is still fortunate to have a blacksmith's forge – an important facility in a farming community. There is an excellent village hall, a Methodist chapel and a Baptist chapel. Other features include a fine thatched cottage, and a neighbouring barn with circular windows and splendid drystone walling. Along Acton Cliff is a beautiful residence called The White House. It formerly belonged to the Whitleys (of brewery fame) and was later owned by the Lyles of Tate and Lyle (sugar manufacturers).

A number of footpaths pass through the environs of the village. One route follows the banks of the Weaver Navigation and is part of the Cheshire Ring Canal Walk. This pedestrian way crosses the river at Dutton Lock and passes under the imposing railway viaduct. It is a fine stone structure of 20 arches by George Stephenson, supervised by Joseph Locke, and was opened in 1837.

ADLINGTON [Macclesfield]

SJ9181: 4 miles (6km) N of Macclesfield

Adlington is a scattered village nestling amidst undulating countryside just north of Macclesfield. Small-scale coal mining took place in the area, and from the middle of the 18th century the lords of the manor, the Legh family, leased the mining rights to individual companies.

The completion of the Macclesfield Canal in 1831 enabled the coal to be transported more easily. The coming of the railway in 1845 also provided an impetus for the local dairy farming industry in the production of milk for the nearby towns and urban areas.

For well over six hundred years, the Legh family of Adlington Hall has been closely linked with the village and its activities.

In the Domesday Survey, Adlington was listed as 'Edulvin tune'. Earl Edwin held the settlement and the lands were owned by Earl Hugh. According to Domesday, the locality contained extensive ploughland, meadowland and woodland; there were several enclosures and four hawk's eyries.

The name 'Adlington' is derived from 'the tun of Eadwulf's people'. The settlement was described as 'Adelvinton' in 1248.

Adlington Hall has been the home of the Leghs from 1315 to the present day. The house was built on the site of a hunting lodge in the Forest of Macclesfield. Originally, Adlington was moated, and had timber-framed buildings in the typical 'black and white' Cheshire style round two sides of a courtyard and the east wing. The Great Hall is dated 1505 inside, but the porch was added in 1581 according to the inscription carved on its lintel.

'Thomas Leyghe Esquyer who married Sibbell daughter of Sr Urian Brereton of hondeforde Knighte and by her had Issue foure sonnes & fyve doughters made this buyldinge in the yeare of Or lorde god

1581 And in the raigne of our soveraigne Lady Queene Elizabeth the xxiijth'.

In the late 17th century, the Great Hall, except for the porch, was encased in brick, and tall, mullioned windows were put in on the south side.

Colonel Thomas Legh the younger inherited the hall in 1644, but Adlington was a Royalist garrison and was twice besieged in the Civil War. The estate was confiscated and heavy fines imposed and it was not returned to him until 1656.

Two great oak trees, part of the original building, still remain with their roots in the ground and support the east end of the Great Hall. The hall roof is of the hammerbeam type with (later) angels against the hammers.

At the west end of the Great Hall is the coved canopy, which is divided into sixty compartments, each one painted with Cheshire family arms. At the east end of the Great Hall is the large organ installed in the 17th century by Colonel Thomas Legh. It has two tiers of pipes arranged between carved grilles, and is one of the earliest instruments to have survived. The organ was almost certainly the work of Bernard Smith, whose other major organs included Westminster Abbey and St Paul's. Those instruments have either been altered or destroyed so the Adlington organ is one of the few remaining 17th-century pieces in the country.

George Frederick Handel played on the organ in 1741 or 42. He also set to music a hunting song written by Charles Legh. This hand-written manuscript was given to Charles Legh in 1751, and is kept at the house.

Charles Legh, who was probably his own architect, was responsible for a programme of modernisation at Adlington – the south front and west wings that were added between 1749 and 1757. The south front has an impressive stone portico with a pediment and four great pillars.

The gardens were landscaped in the style of Capability Brown in the middle of the 18th century. There are areas of rhododendrons and azaleas, various follies, walks along avenues of trees, a rose garden and maze.

ALDERLEY EDGE
[Macclesfield]

SJ8378: 2 miles (3km) S of Wilmslow

Until the middle of the 19th century, Alderley Edge was called Chorley or Corleigh. In Domesday it is listed as 'Cerlere', which is derived from 'ceorla-leah' or 'the leah of the peasants'.

Alderley Edge takes its name from a long, wooded, sandstone escarpment, nearly 2 miles (3km) long and rising some 600ft (182m) above the Cheshire Plain. It also provides some superb views towards the Pennine hills on the eastern edge of the county. Alderley Edge is now under the care of the National Trust.

Traces of Iron Age settlement have been found on the Edge and the Romans are believed to have mined copper here. In fact, the whole area of the Edge is riddled with pits, caverns and tunnels as a result of mining activities over the centuries. Before 1640, the Edge was an open heathland and, because of its fine viewpoint, it was used as a beacon site. One of its important functions was signalling the approach of the Armada. This great sandstone bluff was once a desolate heath of gorse and brushwood. However, in the early 17th century, Thomas Stanley planted hundreds of beech trees. One hundred years later, Scots pine were added and today the National Trust is carrying on the good work.

Nether Alderley Mill – a restored flour mill near to the village of Alderley Edge and now in the care of the National Trust *(Graham Beech)*

The Stanleys had acquired the Alderley Park estate in 1602. Sir Thomas Stanley built the Old Hall, which stood close to Nether Alderley Mill in the 17th century. The house was extended and destroyed by fire in 1779. It was rebuilt in the plain classical style. Fire struck again in 1931 and the house was demolished.

The mines were worked for about 130 years from 1790, being opened and closed by various owners over the time of operation. Veins of copper and lead were found near the surface, but there was also cobalt, which was at first discarded until it was analysed. There were three mines – the Engine Vein Mine, the West Mine and the Wood Mine.

The West Mine started in 1857 but was exhausted after only 20 years. However, for a mineral not particularly common in this country, the mine yielded a total of 4000 tonnes of copper. Cobalt was extracted from the deep, opencast Engine Vein Mine that was last worked during the First World War. Cavers now use

Wood Mine and underground explorations are organised by the Derbyshire Caving Club. Apart from the padlocked entrance leading to the passages and caverns of Wood Mine, all other shafts have been sealed.

Alderley Edge is linked with interwoven tales of history and legend. One particular story describes a Wizard and his sleeping warriors who are meant to be knights of King Arthur. It appears that the warriors will awake in their underground caverns and sally forth at times of great national danger. This legend, which has been associated with many locations, inspired Alan Garner's novel *The Wierdstone of Brisingamen*.

A farmer crossing the Edge to sell a fine white mare at Macclesfield market was stopped by an old man dressed in a cloak who offered to buy the horse. The farmer refused and then the old man told him that he would fail to sell the animal and that he would wait for him on his return.

The farmer did not receive a single enquiry or a bid for the horse and, as he was returning over the Edge, the old man suddenly confronted him. Now considerably unnerved, the farmer agreed to sell the horse and the old man led him to a rock buttress. He tapped the rock with his staff and an entrance appeared flanked by two iron gates.

Leading his horse, the farmer followed the old man into a huge cavern. The interior was full of sleeping warriors and all but one had a white steed. The farmer was taken to a second cave that was crammed with gold and precious gems and told to take what he thought was a fair price for the horse. The old man then told the farmer that one day, when the country needed them, the warriors would awake and ride forth to do battle. As the farmer left, he was told that he would never see the cave and its occupants again and when he looked back, the wizard, the entrance and the gates had disappeared.

The railway arrived in Alderley Edge in 1842 and this convenient transportation attracted wealthy Mancunian merchants and businessmen. In the mid-19th century and early 20th century, an impressive variety of villas and houses were built. Some were classical and picturesque, some were to be later enlarged and altered. One edifice was even castellated and complete with tower.

In absolute contrast to the early Victorian style of dwelling, a medieval manor house is tucked away down a side lane. **Chorley Hall** is the oldest inhabited country house in Cheshire. Dating from the 14th century, it stands in a cobbled courtyard approached by a narrow stone bridge across a moat.

The stone house can probably be dated to around 1330 and is thought to have been built by Robert de Chorley during the reign of Edward III. Robert de Chorley was a yeoman farmer. Another member of the de Chorley family was keeper of the park of Macclesfield. The family supplied horses to the Crown for the Hundred Years War. Standing next to the hall is a superb Elizabethan, busily patterned, half-timbered building. The house stands on a sandstone foundation and was constructed by the Davenports in the 16th century.

The Davenports were one of Cheshire's great families of landed gentry, dating from the 12th century, with many branches, notably of Davenport, of Marton, of Calveley, of Woodford and of Capesthorne.

Chorley is a typical medieval house; it was built with a Great Hall with a two-storey wing set at right angles to it and separated from it by a screened passage. Right at the beginning of the 17th century, the estate passed to the Stanleys of Alderley. In 1915, the house was fully restored the east wall has recently been rebuilt in stone.

ALDERSEY GREEN [Chester]
SJ4656: 7½ miles (12km) SE of Chester

This small community, ringed by patches of sheltering woodland, lies to the west of the Peckforton Hills in a secluded area of low-lying farmland. Between the village and the River Dee, numerous brooks and small watercourses drain the lush water-meadows and hedged pastures. The surrounding countryside is dotted with numerous ponds and crossed by a small number of lanes, farm tracks, bridleways and footpaths that link the isolated farmsteads.

The settlement's name was recorded as 'Aldrisey' in 1284, meaning 'a piece of firm land between streams, belonging to Aldhere'.

Winding country roads reach quiet

Aldersey. There is a local belief that the spectral Dogs of Odin haunt the byroad from the village to Chowley.

The family of Aldersey takes its name from the village, the first member of the family being Hugh who lived here in the 13th century. In 1594 Thomas Aldersey, a wealthy merchant and haberdasher from Spurstow, founded the Aldersey Free Grammar School for Boys in Bunbury.

Aldersey Hall was a plain block-like house of stucco with classical interiors. It was built in 1805 to replace the earlier home of the Aldersey family but was demolished around 1958. The site is now occupied by a small housing estate set in the middle of the former parkland. The evidence of the former estate lies in two pairs of gate-piers, two lodges and a section of walled garden with a gate dated 1901.

The Manor Farmhouse at Aldersey Green, 1630, is a black and white building with lattice and herringbone decoration.

Records of school admissions from the mid-1800s indicate that many children walked the three or four miles from Aldersey and Coddington to attend school in Tattenhall. The cane was used frequently for bad behaviour and the timetable always started with Scripture. Other subjects included Reading, Writing, Arithmetic, Needlework and some Music.

ALDFORD [Chester]

SJ4159: 5 miles (8km) S of Chester

Aldford lies in the west of the county and is situated on a wedge of land between the River Dee and the Aldford Brook. The River Dee emerges from its mountains and hills at the Vale of Llangollen and wriggles past wooded slopes before turning north. East of Wrexham it meanders through quiet pastoral countryside and forms the natural boundary between England and Wales. Just south of Aldford the border veers away westwards and the River Dee flows towards Chester and on through its silted estuary to the open sea.

The border country has, in the past, been fiercely disputed and has been adjusted many times. Prior to the Norman Conquest, the Mercian kings ruled over much of modern-day Clwyd; hence the mixture of English and Welsh names dotted across the area.

When Edward I conquered Wales he did not extend the English county system to the whole of the country but left it under the control of the Marcher lords. Their powers were not terminated until 1540 when Henry VIII made additional Welsh counties out of their lands. The land near Malpas belonged to the Welsh princes who had supported Llywelyn ap Gruffudd against Edward I and was, therefore, annexed to the new county of Flint.

That is why the confused traveller used to enter a piece of detached Flintshire in this border country. At least the 1974 boundary changes ended the confusion by placing those particular areas of Denbighshire and Flint into the new creation of Clwyd.

Aldford is not mentioned in Domesday. The settlement was described as 'Aldeford' in 1253 and its name means 'old ford'. In the two centuries before 1350, a large number of new markets were authorised by charter. The manorial lord with an eye to business realised the commercial potential of a market. Aldford dates from 1253 but competition from the existing large market at Chester soon put paid to Aldford and it failed.

Aldford lies on the route of the Roman road that ran south from Chester. The road followed the line of the present road to Eccleston and Eaton Hall through Eaton Hall Park, where it crossed the Dee to the north of Aldford church. South of the river, the road is marked by a track between two rows of old thorn trees up to the south side of the Norman castle motte close to the church.

The agger runs up to the churchyard. At the church, which is on relatively high ground, there is a change of alignment to south-south-east. This is clearly marked on first leaving the village by a line of hedgerows and traces of the agger. It then followed the route of the present green lane, continued by more hedgerows with clear remains of an agger some 24ft (7m) wide and 1ft (0.3m) high.

At Aldford, the conspicuous earthworks called Blobb Hill are the remains of a Norman motte and bailey castle. They comprise one of the best examples of the locality and date from at least the 12th century. The fortification's principal role was to defend the border against Welsh attacks, a constant threat at that time.

Aldford village has a considerable amount of the characteristic Eaton estate housing, much of it dating from the time of the first Duke of Westminster. The houses were designed largely by his architect, John Douglas. Some of the cottages are of the 1850s and 1860s and are typical of those built in the time of the second Marquess. Main features are the use of common bricks, low-pitched roofs and diamond patterned windows.

The **church of St John the Baptist** was built at the expense of Sir Richard Grosvenor, the second Marquess, in 1866. The architect was John Douglas. This sandstone building is in the late 13th-century style, with a fine square tower, buttressed at the corners. It has a recessed shingled spire and a stair-turret with a conical roof in the south-west corner. The interior of the church contains polished granite pillars, a marble and granite font and pulpit, and a tiled floor.

The north transept has a brightly coloured rose window. The reredos is of mosaics made by Salviati. Inside the south doorway is a carved stone with a medieval Latin inscription recording the foundation of the church. The previous 1866 church was of stone with a low chancel and nave without side aisles and a squat square tower with a small steeple.

The cast-iron bridge over the Dee lies on the Aldford approach to Eaton Hall. This graceful structure was built in 1824 for Robert Grosvenor, first Marquess of Westminster of Eaton Hall. Its single span measures 151ft (46m) and the name of its builder, William Hazeldine, appears in raised lettering on the carriageway band at the east end of the bridge. This bridge is more or less a copy of one which Hazeldine had built to Telford's design at Atcham near Shrewsbury in 1818. This important bridge at Aldford will continue to be protected because traffic across it is very light.

The Grosvenor family of Eaton Hall is of Norman descent through Hugh Lupus Earl of Chester. The first Eaton Hall appears on an estate map as a gabled, moated manor house a little way south of the present hall.

The first house, built on the present site, was built between 1675 and 1682 by Sir Thomas Grosvenor, third Baronet, who in 1677 married Mary Davies of Ebury. The second Earl Grosvenor (later first Marquess) employed William Porden as his architect between 1804 and 1812. The building was an array of buttresses, pinnacles, battlements and turrets.

The house was extended between 1823 and 1825, with remodelling and alterations completed in 1851; it was then completely transformed by Alfred Waterhouse between 1870 and 1882. There was even a lofty clock tower modelled on Manchester Town Hall next to the chapel. The first Duke of Westminster was an improving landlord: he initiated extensive building programmes throughout the estate for the welfare of his tenantry. The hall was wrecked during army occupation in the 1950s and everything except the chapel, clock tower and stables were demolished. The new Eaton Hall was built between 1971 and 1973. It is a stark, rectangular, concrete block faced with white travertine.

ALLGREAVE [Manchester]

SJ9769: 6 miles (9km) SE of Macclesfield

This small isolated community lies on the A54 Congleton to Buxton road. The Clough Brook starts from its high moorland sources near to the lonely Cat and Fiddle Inn, which at 1690ft (515m) is the second highest inn in England. It then flows south past the shapely hill of Shuttlingsloe, the sequestered village of Wildboarclough, and on below Allgreave to its confluence with the River Dane.

The surrounding gritstone hill country of heather moorlands, deeply cut valleys and upland pastures is predominantly sheep country. Just across the Dane, in neighbouring Staffordshire, is the popular Grandbach Youth Hostel. Hidden away on the flanks of Back Forest, at the north end of an escarpment known as The Roaches, lies the narrow, sinister cleft of **Lud's Church**. Formed from a major landslip, the sheer gritstone walls are 60ft (18m) high and only 8ft (2m) apart.

Lud's Church gets its name from Walter de Lud-Auk, one of **Wycliffe's Lollards** (precursors of the Reformation during the reign of Henry V). They worshipped here in secret when the sect was persecuted.

Tales abound about this place; it was supposedly the Green Chapel of the classic poem *Sir Gawain and the Green Knight*. Also at Lud's Church is Trafford's Leap, where a squire of Swythamley leapt the chasm while hunting.

ALPRAHAM [Crewe]

SJ5860: 3 miles (5km) SE of Tarporley

Alpraham is a small village closely associated with the village of Calveley along the Shropshire Union Canal and the River Gowy. The surrounding area is largely farmland.

Alpraham is mentioned in the Domesday Survey. The Saxon Earl Edwin had held it but the lands passed to Gilbert of Venables. The settlement was listed as 'Alburgham'. There is land for four ploughs. Three villagers with six smallholders have one plough. Domesday records woodland and meadowland. The value before 1066 was 20 shillings, but it had fallen to 8 shillings. The settlement was described as 'Alpram' in 1259; the name is derived from 'the ham of Alhburg' (a woman), or 'Alhburg's homestead'.

As a result of the Puritan movement in the Bunbury area, its leader, Richard Cawley of Moat Farm, Alpraham, invited **John Wesley** to visit the group in 1749. He also made subsequent visits and preached at Moat Farm. A commemorative plaque marks the spot in the orchard where Wesley and his followers assembled.

Wesley did not inaugurate these meetings; he encouraged them and then joined them into a great national movement.

The village hall, formerly the Alpraham and Calveley reading room, serves the community. It was erected in about 1882 with money raised by public donations.

There used to be two chapels in Alpraham, one Wesleyan Methodist and the other a Primitive Methodist, but they are now both demolished. At nearby Calveley, a radio telescope now stands on the site of a Second World War airfield.

ALSAGER [Congleton]

SJ7955: 6 miles (10km) E of Crewe

Alsager lies close to the Staffordshire border and the large conurbation of Stoke-on-Trent. The mainly residential area is situated between the M6 and the Trent and Mersey Canal; it is surrounded by farmland and open countryside. Alsager Station lies on the Crewe to Derby line.

The settlement was listed in Domesday as 'Eleacier'. Originally in Midestivic Hundred, it later became part of Warmundestrou Hundred. Wulfric, a free man, held the settlement. Earl Hugh owned the lands. There was land for one plough. Its value before 1066 was 3 shillings, but it had fallen to waste.

The name is described as 'Alisacher' in 1288, and is derived from 'Aelle's field'. In Old English the word *aecer* means 'a field' or 'plough land'. The Old Norse *akr* is used in 'acre' and is the second element of the word Alsager.

Christ Church (built 1789-90), is a Georgian church built at the expense of the Misses Alsager. Designed by Thomas Stringer, it has a west tower with a slightly projecting centre and doorway with Tuscan columns. There are six bays

of arched windows along the sides, separated by large pilasters. The font is 18th century with an octagonal bowl.

The church of **St Mary Magdalene** was built between 1894 and 1898 by Austin and Paley. This large church, was planned with a west tower that was never built. The chancel has an aisle of two high arches to the north but no aisle to the south. Instead, there are three tall, decorated windows.

The **Manchester Metropolitan University**, Crewe and Alsager Faculty; formerly the Cheshire College of Education, with extensive playing fields, lies on the western side of Alsager.

ALVANLEY [Vale Royal]

SJ4974: 6½ miles (10km) NE of Chester

The village of Alvanley is situated on rising ground just to the south of Helsby. The settlement existed in Saxon times and later came into the ownership of the Arderne family. The estate was sold in 1922. The surrounding land is mainly agricultural, and farmhouses still occupy positions at the heart of the village.

The building materials used are a delightful mixture of sandstone, brick and thatch, and many of the dwellings have been well restored. Commonside Farm has a thatched roof and is built with a mixture of sandstone and brick. Church House Farm is late Georgian, with an attractive brick frontage; it has three bays with a three-bay pediment. An unusual event locally was the transportation of a complete brick and timber-framed house from Nantwich to a new site under the lee of Alvanley Cliff.

Alvanley is recorded in the Domesday Survey as 'Elveldelie' in Roelau Hundred. This settlement was held by Leofric from the earl. Ernwy held it; he was a free man. There was land for four ploughs. In Lordship one the survey lists one villager and two smallholders. Domesday mentions some woodland. There is no reference to its value. The settlement was described as 'Alvaldeleh' in 1220, and the name is derived from 'Aelfwald's leah', or 'the clearing in the forest belonging to Aelfwald'.

The **church of St John Evangelist** was built in 1861 in the style of 1300. Both the church and school building have good architectural character. The west front has three pitched roofs and a diagonally set bellcot. In the chancel there is a four-light **open stone screen** with tracery, similar to a large window, which separates the chancel from the organ chamber.

There is a network of interconnecting footpaths in the area, plus the Sandstone Trail. This walking route links Beacon Hill, near Frodsham, with the Shropshire Way at Grindley Brook, near Whitchurch. The path hugs the base of wooded Alvanley Cliff, where once were several sandstone quarries. One in the vicinity produced a fine pale stone used for the rebuilding of Chester Castle.

ANTROBUS [Vale Royal]

SJ6480: 2 miles (3km) NW of Great Budworth

The township of Antrobus was formed from the mother parish of Great Budworth in 1848. It lies just off the A559, Northwich to Warrington road, and the surroundings are mainly agricultural with dairy and arable farming.

Antrobus is recorded in the Domesday Survey as 'Entrebus' in Tunendune Hundred. Woodland is mentioned. In 1282 the settlement's name was 'Anterbus', and it may be derived from the Old

French, *'entre buis' (bois)* for 'between the thickets'.

The **church of St Mark** (1847-8) was the design of Sir George Gilbert Scott. This is a Commissioners' church in the Decorated style with a combined nave and chancel. It has a bellcot on the east end of the nave and there is a priest's doorway in a south buttress. The interior contains a **screen** that is partly of wood and partly of iron.

A Friends' Meeting House in Frandley, 1726, is a plain brick building with an outer stairway. George Fox, 1620-91, is reputed to have preached at an outdoor meeting nearby.

Most of the houses in the village were built in the 19th century. A Methodist chapel was built in 1838 and continued in use until 1937 when a new chapel took its place. The oldest building is one of cruck construction called Broom Cottage.

The Cheshire naturalist, **Arnold Boyd** (1885-1959), lived in the village and was well known for books on the natural history of the area. He helped to revive the Soul-Caking Play which is still performed every year on or near All Souls' Day in local hostelries. The horse's head used in the performances is over 100 years old.

APPLETON THORN [Warrington]

SJ6383: 3 miles (5km) SSE Warrington

The village of Appleton Thorn is a small residential area south of Warrington. The surroundings are mainly farmland with dairy farming and arable farming. A variety of crops are grown, including turnips, kale, oats, wheat, barley, grass and potatoes. The M56 passes along the southern side of the village.

Appleton is recorded in the Domesday

Survey as 'Epletune' in Tunendune Hundred. Dot held it; he was a free man. The lands were owned by Osbern, son of Tezzo. There was land for four ploughs. Domesday mentions woodland and also states that it was and is waste. The value before 1066 was 16 shillings.

In 1178 the lord of the manor was Adam de Dutton, an ancestor of the Egerton Warburton family of Arley. It is said that he brought and planted the original thorn tree, which was believed to be an offshoot from the Holy Glastonbury thorn, which grew from the staff of Joseph of Arimathea.

The custom of '**Bawming** (adorning or anointing) **the Thorn**' is one of England's oldest customs. The day starts with a procession through the streets of the village. Children, themselves garlanded, carry their posies of flowers and ribbons to the hawthorn tree and 'bawn' both it and the iron railings which protect it. Then they dance round the tree.

Tree worship is of great antiquity. Our ancestors believed that a tree could contain a god who would protect the village. The custom of Bawming the Thorn takes place in the middle of June, having been revived in 1973.

The **church of St Cross** was built in the Decorated style in 1887. It has a dominant central tower and an aisleless nave. The west baptistery has a large rose window. The chancel has an organ loft on the north side with access to a stone pulpit.

A large industrial estate has been established on the site of a Second World War airfield. Also on this site stands a HM Detention Centre for Young Offenders; it is known as Thorn Cross Youth Custody Centre.

ARLEY [Macclesfield]

SJ6780: 4 miles (6km) N of Northwich

Arley is a small hamlet with a few charming cottages, a park and the great house of Arley Hall. The original mansion was built in 1469, enlarged in the 16th century and encased in brick in 1758. An unknown local architect, George Latham, was engaged by Rowland Egerton-Warburton, and a new mansion and chapel were built between 1832 and 1845 in the Jacobean style.

The house contains fine plasterwork and panelling, together with family furniture and pictures. There is also a very fine library. Beautiful parkland and gardens surround the hall.

ASHLEY [Macclesfield]

SJ7784: 2 miles (3km) S of Altrincham

Ashley is a small village situated south of the River Bollin, the county boundary adjoining Greater Manchester and the area of land comprising Tatton Park. The surroundings are mainly agricultural with dairy and arable farming. The railway came in 1841 and the village station is on the line between Altrincham and Northwich.

Ashley is recorded in Domesday as 'Ascelie', in Bochelau Hundred. Alfward held it as a free man and the lands were owned by Hamo de Mascy. There was land for two oxen. It was and remained waste. The settlement's name is derived from the Old English 'aescleah' or 'ash wood'.

The Greyhound Inn, situated at the central crossroads of the village, was a farm at the end of the 19th century. Initially, the inn was called the Orrell Arms after Robert Orrell of nearby Arden House. In 1841 the hostelry became part of the Tatton estate and was renamed The Greyhound after Lord Egerton's favourite dog.

Ashley Hall was built in the late 15th century and was partly demolished in

1972. The remaining section includes a 16th-century chimney stack and some timber framing. On the approach are a 17th-century carriage house and later stables.

Ashley Hall is famous for the Cheshire gentlemen who met there in 1715 to consider whether to support the Stuarts or the Hanoverians. They decided to support the latter, and to commemorate this meeting they commissioned a set of portraits in 1720. These paintings are now displayed at Tatton Park.

At Coppice Farm, Ashley, there is a tithe barn of cruck construction, with fine, weathered oak boarding.

The church of St Elizabeth, 1880, was built by Lord Egerton of Tatton Park; it is of red brick and red terracotta with some pleasant decorative details in the windows.

ASHTON [Chester]

SJ5169: 6 miles (9km) ENE of Chester

ge lies on the fringes of Delamere Forest and is overlooked by Longley Hill. It is a compact rural community surrounded by farmland, with agriculture the main occupation.

Ashton is listed in Domesday as 'Estone' in Risedon Hundred. Thored held it as a free man; the lands were owned by Richard of Vernon. There is land for five ploughs. Woodland was recorded, and its value before 1066 was 16 shillings. This had risen to 20 shillings although it was found to be waste.

The settlement is described as 'Asshton' in 1408, and is derived from the Old English 'Aesctun', 'a tun where ash grew'.

In 1933, a **medieval pottery kiln** was unearthed in the garden of a house in the village. The kiln measured 7ft (2m) by 7ft

(2m). The availability of suitable materials, such as water, clay and firewood led to a thriving local industry. Examples of Ashton pottery may be seen in the Grosvenor Museum, Chester.

The remains of a defensive fortification, **a motte**, lie to the south of the village.

The remaining parts of **Peel House** indicate that it was a Jacobean house of some importance. Above one of the doorways the date of its erection is recorded as 1637. Its builder was probably Henry Hardware IV. The Hardwares were successful traders in Chester.

The name of Peel Hall derives from a former pele tower built as part of the defence of the Welsh border. The present L-shaped house is only a third of the original rectangular building. A tall parapet conceals the roof, which looks out over a walled garden. At one time the building was moated. It is a fine example of a Jacobean Artisan house erected by Cheshire merchants. There is a possibility that Peel House was never completed, for in 1639 both Henry Hardware and his only child died. On 2 June 1690, King William III visited the house on his way to Ireland.

The **church of St John Evangelist**, was built in 1849 by Shellard of Manchester. Its benefactor, William Atkinson of Ashton Hayes, a textile manufacturer, gave the church and school to the village. The church has a west tower, a recessed spire and two transepts. The chancel was altered in 1900. In a beautiful little chapel are windows showing the Annunciation, John the Baptist kneeling at the feet of Christ, and the scene at Pentecost. There is a splendid Art Nouveau pulpit, a carved oak altar and a frontal of brass covering the front of the altar. The old school is now the village hall.

The nearest station is at Mouldsworth on the Manchester to Chester line, one mile north of Ashton.

ASTBURY [Congleton]

SJ8461: 2 miles (3km) SW of Congleton

Astbury is situated on the eastern edge of the Cheshire Plain just south of Congleton. Its attractive dwellings are grouped round a small village green within sight and sound of the busy main road. There are still a number of timber-framed black and white buildings, in particular, one very appealing cottage next to the church. Astbury is not listed in the Domesday Survey, but its name in 1100 was 'Esteburi', which became 'Asteburi' in 1180. Its name means 'eastern burg'.

The village still retains its rural atmosphere, with a number of interesting farms in the vicinity – for example, Glebe Farm, its name showing that income from the land was part of the priest's stipend.

A little distance from the church is **Peel Farm**, which occupies the ancient site of Newbold Manor. It seems that the manor of Newbold and the manor of Astbury were given as one holding to the Earl of Chester. The manorial rights were then passed on to Baron Gilbert Venables. The old manor house was pulled down in the 16th century, then replaced by a fortified homestead, which in turn was succeeded by the present farm. However, there is still evidence of the protecting moat behind the farm.

The **church of St Mary** dominates the surroundings, as it stands proudly above the houses and cottages of the village. This magnificent and exciting building was once the mother church of Congleton. It was built in the Perpendicular style; although the tower and spire, which stand apart from the nave, were probably built in the 13th century. The stone is hard millstone grit with some particularly fine carved gargoyles on the aisles.

The lofty nave and chancel are separated by a screen and the tall columns lead upward to a splendid roof of the low-pitched camber-beam type. This is richly decorated with many bosses and copious gilding. The interior furniture includes box pews, a Jacobean font cover and pulpit and a fine chancel screen of the 16th century. The south chapel contains an effigy of a late 14th-century knight, and a tomb-chest lid with an inscription and date of 1654.

There is an early 14th-century canopied tomb to the Brereton family in the churchyard, the only one of its kind surviving in the county, which is entered through an impressive round-arched gateway. The effigies under the canopy represent a knight, Sir Ralph Brereton, and his lady. The other two weatherworn figures outside the canopy are Richard de Venables de Newbold, c1342, and William de Venables who was Rector in the latter part of the 13th century.

Sir William Brereton of Handforth was an important parliamentary commander during the Civil War. He defeated the Royalist troops at the battle of Nantwich in 1643. During the siege of Biddulph Hall his troop of Roundheads stabled their horses in Astbury church. They smashed the medieval stained glass windows and destroyed the organ.

ASTON [Crewe]

SJ6146: 5 miles (8km) SW of Nantwich

Aston in Newhall is an extended rural community adjoining the River Weaver and largely surrounded by farmland. It lies between two arms of the Shropshire Union Canal, the Llangollen branch and the Nantwich and Market Drayton section. Wrenbury Station, on the Crewe to Shrewsbury line, is situated one mile to the west of Aston.

The settlement was mentioned in Domesday as 'Estune'. Dot, a free man, held it. The lands were owned by William Milbank for Earl Hugh. There was land for two ploughs. Domesday records a large area of woodland. The value before 1066 was 10 shillings but that had halved and it was found waste.

The settlement was described as Aston in 1287; the word is commonly derived from the Old English 'East-tun' meaning 'eastern tun' or 'eastern homestead'.

The Methodist **chapel of St Andrew** was built in 1865. The building has been modernised and a community room installed upstairs.

The local hostelry, the Bhurtpore Inn, is named after the battle of Bhurtpore in India. Sir Stapleton Cotton was made 1st Baron Combermere in 1814 in recognition of his leadership in battle and elevated to Viscount Combermere in 1830. The Field Marshall celebrated his two greatest victories at Bhurtpore and Salamanca in Spain by building two inns to be named after the battles. The latter, in Wrenbury, is now closed.

Aston is in the parish of Newhall, which was part of the Combermere estate. This was the Abbey of Combermere in pre-Reformation times.

The **Aston mill**, built in the 19th century, was owned by the Sumner family for many years. It is now Dalgety Spillers Agriculture Limited. The mill provides much employment in the area.

ASTON-BY-SUTTON [Vale Royal]

SJ5578: 3 miles (5km) SE of Runcorn

Aston-by-Sutton is a scattered rural community of farms and cottages in the valley of the winding River Weaver, and on the north side of the Weaver Navigation Canal.

Aston is mentioned in the Domesday Survey as 'Estone' in Tunendune Hundred. Odard held it from William, son of Nigel Leofnc, a free man. There was land for two and half ploughs. There were three ploughmen and one villager and one smallholder with one plough. A mill served the Court and there was a fisherman. Domesday records one acre of woodland.

Aston is a common name, mostly derived from Old English 'East-tun' meaning 'eastern tun' or 'homestead'.

Aston Hall was situated about a quarter of a mile to the south-west of Aston Church. The hall was built in 1668 by Sir Willoughby Aston to replace an earlier house. It was a tall, classical brick dwelling with twin-hipped roofs and a raised central attic. The grounds were landscaped by Humphry Repton, c1793. The hall was demolished in 1938, except for a **brick dovecote** of 1696, a Georgian dower house, two lodges and a large area of walled garden.

Sir Willoughby's father, Sir Thomas Aston, was the royalist general in command against Sir William Brereton at the beginning of the Civil War. After two defeats, as well as losing a whole army, he was removed from the scene.

The **church of St Peter** was remodelled in the 17th and 18th centuries. Unfortunately, on the night of 28 November 1940, a German landmine exploded close to the east end of the church. After much delay, the work of restoration and repair began in May 1949 and was completed in June 1950.

Built of sandstone, the building plan consists of a chancel of 1697 and a nave of 1736, with a north porch dated 1736 and a rebuilt south porch. Sir Willoughby Aston, whose written records contain various references to Vanbrugh, did the work of 1697. The north porch is reminiscent of the architectural style of Sir John Vanbrugh.

The nave has arched windows with pilasters and an open bell cupola in the west font. The east wall of the chancel has a circular window and the south wall has three round-headed windows. Over the south doorway is a fine example of the **royal arms,** painted on a wooden panel dated 1664. The font, panelling and pews are of 1857.

Memorials, particularly those in the chancel to the Aston family, occupy much of the interior wall space of the nave and chancel. There are two painted tablets to the Aston family, probably early 18th century, with many coats of arms. Memorials were erected to Sir Thomas Aston and John Aston in 1697, when the chancel was built. Another tablet records Sir Willoughby Aston, died 1702, and his wife Mary, who died 1752.

ASTON JUXTA MONDRUM [Crewe]

SJ6457: 4 miles (6km) W of Crewe

This is a scattered community where farming is still of major importance, particularly dairy farming. The neighbourhood is now developing into a dormitory village. The Crewe to Chester railway line passes through the parish but there is no station.

The settlement is mentioned in Domesday as 'Estone' in Warmundestrou Hundred. Ravenkel, a free man, held it. There was land for one plough and one rider with half a plough with two smallholders. The Survey lists meadowland and woodland.

The name is derived from the Old English 'East-tun' meaning 'eastern tun' or 'homestead' and the ancient forest of Mondrum.

The **church of St Oswald** is referred to as Worleston Church. It is a low, well-proportioned building of cruciform shape (1872) designed by C. Lynam of Stoke-on-Trent. There are no aisles but there is a slender spire on the centre of the roof over the crossing. The church is built of rough rubble blocks. There is stained glass by Kempe, 1872 and 1882, also a late Morris & Co window.

Nearby, the Worleston Dairy Institute was closed in 1926 and transferred to the Cheshire College of Agriculture at Reaseheath near to Nantwich.

AUDLEM [Crewe]

SJ6643: 6 miles (9km) N of Market Drayton

Audlem is situated in the south of Cheshire close to the county boundary of Shropshire and Staffordshire, in the centre of an important dairy farming area.

Audlem was listed in Domesday as 'Aldelime'. The Forest of Lyme included Macclesfield Forest. Lyme is a British name derived from the word for elm. Audlem is 'Old Lyme' or 'the part of Lyme belonging to Alda'.

In Domesday the settlement was held by Osmer and the lands were owned by Richard of Vernon. Domesday paints a picture of ploughland, meadowland and a sizeable area of woodland. Also recorded was a hawk's eyrie. Edward I granted a Market Charter in 1295.

The church commands a prominent position on a mound overlooking the village. At the foot of the church steps stands the **Buttercross** or the Shambles – an open structure on eight columns erected in 1733. The **stone** now situated between the Buttercross and the church steps was once used for bear baiting. The boulder is an erratic of granite deposited in the Ice Age.

The **church of St James the Great** dates from the 14th century and has a typical Perpendicular appearance. The first building to occupy the site was probably the one given by Thomas de Aldelim to the Priory of St James at Stafford in the reign of Edward I. The 14th-century plan of nave, north aisle, narrow south aisle and a two-bay chancel has remained, despite later alterations.

The Lady Chapel is the oldest part of the building and was the chancel of the 14th-century church. The church was remodelled in the 15th century with the work principally confined to the upper walls of the nave. The nave is now high with large windows and a splendid clerestory. The **nave roof** is of the cambered beam type of massive construction. The square **tower** has walls 4ft (1m) in thickness, and contains six bells cast as a ring in 1736.

Interesting items inside the church include an iron-bound **parish chest** with three locks and with three different keys; three **decorated wooden panels** dated 1611, 1622 and 1708 in the north aisle; a brass candelabrum of 1751 suspended in the middle of the nave; and 17th-century **Flemish wood carvings**, notably the foliage panels on the choir stalls, and a Jacobean pulpit.

In Audlem Ecclesiastical Parish there were the remains of five watermills and evidence of others in 1980. They were Brooks Mill on the River Weaver, Audlem Old Mill on Audlem Brook, Audlem New Mill or Swanbach near the confluence of Audlem Brook and the River Weaver, Hankelow on the River Weaver and Kingbur at the canal wharf. A sixth was Buerton Windmill.

The Audlem Wesleyan Chapel was opened in 1833. The building has a façade with lancet windows that are decoratively edged in yellow brick.

The picturesque **Shropshire Union Canal** runs through the village. The inclusion of fifteen locks takes the water level from the Shropshire heights down some 93ft (28m) to the Cheshire Plain.

The Nantwich and Market Drayton railway line was opened in 1863 with a station at Audlem. It became part of the Great Western Railway but was closed in 1967.

BACKFORD [Chester]

SJ3972: 3 miles (5km) N of Chester

Backford is a small, widespread village north of the Shropshire Union Canal and situated between the conurbations of Chester and Ellesmere Port.

Although not mentioned in Domesday, a ford was shown on early maps and a 13th-century record mentions 'a bridge over the water of Backford'. Until the River Dee was canalised in 1734, the marshes reaching up to the road at Backford were tidal. Backford, as its name suggests, was the 'back ford', which was probably the most reliable.

The first leg of the Ellesmere Canal was an easy eight miles through the 'Backford Gap', the valley between the Hundreds of Broxton and Wirral. This section was a success, not for the amount of goods carried, but because of the brisk passenger traffic en-route to Ellesmere Port and Liverpool.

The **church of St Oswald**, which stands on high ground, was rebuilt between 1877 and 1879 by Ewan Christian. The chancel is of the early 14th century and in it is preserved one of the county's remaining **aumbries**. In the days before safes, items such as church plate, registers and vestments would be stored in cupboards or wall niches.

The tower is Perpendicular with pinnacles and fine gargoyles. Some of the latter are carvings of rural scenes, such as a goose and a fox. The nave walls have **decorative paintwork** by Edward Frampton, which dates from the rebuilding period. The church contains several heraldic memorials by the **Randle Holme** family, the earliest is 1624. This decorative work was part of their services as carpenters and undertakers.

Backford Hall is an attempted neo-Tudor style house of 1863. Designed by John Cunningham in red brick, it has a symmetrical centre, shaped gables and twisted chimneys. The house replaced a brick mansion, which in turn replaced the 16th-century hall of the Birkenhead family. This was the home of **George Birkenhead**, the poet, who founded a professorship of poetry at Oxford in 1707.

In 1811 the hall was sold to **George Ormerod**, the author. It was here that he wrote the famous definitive work *The History of Cheshire*. The hall is now used for Council offices.

BARNTON [Vale Royal]

SJ6375: 1 mile (2km) NW of Northwich

Barnton lies on the northern outskirts of Northwich in a loop of the Trent and Mersey Canal and the **Weaver Navigation**, with an impressive view over the Winnington ICI chemical works. Not only does Barnton have these famous local canals, but only a short distance to the east lie other large stretches of water: namely, Marston Flashes, Budworth Mere and Pick Mere.

In 1873, Brunner Mond's new ammo-nia process proved to be more efficient and cleaner than the old sulphur process. These famous industrialists boasted that they had filled more stomachs then the Cheshire gentry. Previously, there was a claim that Barnton used to be known as 'Jam Town', because its residents were so poor that they ate only jam butties.

Christ Church was built of large, square-cut stone in 1842 and enlarged in 1900. The elaborate pulpit was brought from St Helen's Church, Witton at Northwich.

At the eastern corner of Barnton, the **Anderton Boat Lift** was built in 1875 by E. Leader Williams. This example of Victorian ingenuity and engineering skill was constructed to connect the Trent and Mersey Canal with the Weaver Navigation.

The Friends of Anderton Boat Lift, formed in May 1996, are a group of people dedicated to supporting the restoration of the structure.

BARTHOMLEY [Crewe]

SJ7552: 4 miles (6km) SE of Crewe

The village lies close to the Staffordshire border and not far from Alsager, Crewe and Newcastle-under-Lyme. Here the land rises slightly from the Cheshire Plain, and it is among the first undulations approaching the Pennines.

The church stands on a mound known as Barrow Hill, so-called because it is an ancient burial ground. It is a good vantage point for the village with its huddle of Jacobean cottages and its thatched, timber-framed black and white inn, the White Lion. The inn was built in 1614, but it is mostly 19th century and was built for the Crewe estate.

During the Civil War, in December 1643, a number of villagers who had fired on the Royalists retired to the church for safety and were smoked out by the Royalist troops who had set fire to the rushes and pews. On surrendering, the hapless villagers were stripped and twelve of them were massacred.

In the Domesday Survey, Barthomley was listed as 'Bertemelev'; the settlement was held by Siward and the lands were owned by William Milbank. According to Domesday, the locality contained ploughland, woodland, meadowland and an enclosure. A priest is mentioned as well as a hawk's eyrie. The name of the place is derived from the Old English 'Beorhtwynn's leah' – 'Beorhtwynn' being a woman's name. The settlement was described as 'Bertumleg' in 1260 and 'Berthoneleg' in 1296.

The **church of St Bertoline** , which stands well above the road, has a fine west tower built in the Perpendicular style. This beautiful church is dedicated to an eighth-century Mercian prince turned hermit who lived on an island in the River Sow near Stafford. The church once served the whole of Crewe. The tower is battlemented and pinnacled and the clerestory and the nave are also battlemented. Inside the church, part of the wall of the south aisle between the windows appears to be 12th century. In the 15th century, the wall was raised by four courses. The nave is covered by a fine cambered roof, also 15th century.

The main roof timbers are massively strong and have intricate tracery on each side, carved shields and bosses. The north aisle roof is fine, late 16th-century work. A new chancel was built between 1925 and 1926 by the Marquess of Crewe as a memorial to his son and heir, the Earl of Madeley. On the north side of the Crewe chapel is a splendid Norman doorway with clear zigzag mouldings.

This church has a beautiful parclose screen (a screen separating a chapel or aisle from the body of the church) of the early 16th century. The decorated altar dates from the late 16th century.

The Crewe chapel houses a number of memorials, including an alabaster effigy of a knight in full armour. Sir Robert de Foulshurst was one of the squires to Lord Audley at the Battle of Poitiers in 1356. Note the representations on the tomb chest of Sir Robert's relations, six males and six females. There is also an altar tomb in alabaster of the reclining figure of a priest. Of very high technical merit is the altar tomb of Lady Sibyl Houghton, 1857-1887. This beautiful example of 19th-century sculpture depicts a graceful, serene figure in white.

Englesea-Brook lies one mile south-west of Barthomley. This small community is home to the **Museum of Primitive Methodism**, the breakaway movement that took the religion back to its working-class roots.

The chapel that houses the museum is the only monument in England to Primitive Methodism. The movement began around the Cheshire-Staffordshire border when North Staffordshire-born, Hugh Bourne, and potter, William Clowes, turned away from the established Wesleyan Methodists.

The chapel, built to resemble local cottages, contains many fascinating **exhibits and artefacts**, including the first pipe organ to be used in a Primitive Methodist Chapel. One of the most emotive relics of the museum could easily be missed. Under the carpet of the central aisle lies the burial place of a 12-year-old boy. This is very unusual as underfloor burials are rarely found in chapels.

BEESTON [Chester]

SJ5459: 3 miles (5km) S of Tarporley

The village lies at the foot of Beeston Crag on the eastern side of the

Peckforton Hills. These undulating wooded slopes comprise the southern half of the sandstone Mid-Cheshire Ridge.

Most of the cottages date from the 17th century and there is a good example of a cruck-framed half-timbered dwelling.

Listed in the Domesday Book as 'Buistan' in Broxton Hundred, it was held by Wulfwy and the lands owned by Robert, son of Hugh. The settlement's name became Bestan in 1282 and probably means 'a stone where commerce took place'.

Overlooking the village, **Beeston Castle** stands on the steep-sided isolated hill that rises abruptly from the flat plain.

The castle, now maintained by English Heritage, was built about 1220 by Rannulf de Blundeville, earl of Chester. The ruins that now occupy the site lie on the probable location of an Iron Age fort. Little survives of the castle buildings, but originally they lay along the walls of an outer and an inner bailey. The inner bailey in the north-west corner is separated from the outer bailey by a rock-cut ditch. The 13th-century **inner gatehouse** is moderately well preserved with two semi-circular projecting towers. A steep but rather elegant concrete causeway now crosses the ditch.

East of the gatehouse is another tower with a semi-circular front, and north-east of that yet another. The outer bailey has much curtain walling and the remains of an outer gatehouse, with guardroom and latrines. There are seven towers with semi-circular fronts. There are no towers on the precipitous west and north sides.

The inner bailey contains a deep well cut 370ft (113m) into the solid rock. The lost treasure of Richard II was supposed to have been hidden in its depths. However, excavations in 1842 and 1935 revealed only rubbish.

The castle fell into a ruinous condition after the Wars of the Roses. In the Civil War, the crumbling defences were repaired and the castle occupied by Parliamentarian soldiers during 1643. It was later captured by Royalists who, in turn, gave up the fortress after the Battle of Rowton Moor in 1645.

BICKERTON [Crewe]

SJ5052: 4 miles (6km) NE of Malpas

The neighbourhood is characterised by the hills of Peckforton and Bickerton that rise abruptly from the Cheshire Plain.

Bickerton is a scattered community set along winding leafy lanes beneath the wooded eastern slopes of the Bickerton Hills. In Domesday the settlement was listed as 'Bicreton'. It was held by Drogo and Dot, Edwin and Ernwin, who held it as three manors. Robert, son of Hugh, owned the lands. An area of woodland was recorded. In 1260 the settlement's name became 'Bikirton', 'the tun of the bee-keepers'. It is interesting to note that Domesday lists a settlement in the area called 'Lavorchedone', which became 'Laverketon' in 1282, 'the tun frequented by larks'.

Although no such settlement of that name now exists, there remains Larkton Hill, Larkton Hall and Larkton House. Larkton is also the name of the civil parish. It is possible that the site of the Domesday village may lie in the area of Larkton Hall.

The **church of Holy Trinity** (1839) nestles between two hills and is set within its own well-tended graveyard. The burial area now extends across to the other side of the lane. The building has a nave and chancel with bellcot and slender arched windows. The chancel was added between 1875 and 1876 and the baptistery in 1911.

There is a neat wall clock, black with gold figures, sited at the north-east end of the church. A post in the churchyard displays three plaques awarded in previous Best Kept Village competitions.

Nearby is Galantry (Gallow Tree) Bank, a site of more scattered dwellings set in the gap between the hills. The route of the A534 is thought to follow the line of an ancient 'salters' route' along which salt from Nantwich was transported into Wales.

The **chimney** standing tall against the hillside, and easily seen from the A534, is from a copper mine pumping house. The mine was worked intermittently from 1764 to 1802 by the Cheshire Mining Corporation. However, the return was poor and eventually the mine fell into disuse.

BICKLEY [Chester]

SJ5247: 2 miles (3km) E of Malpas

The small hamlets of Bickley Moss, Bickley town and Bickleywood make up a small scattered rural community to the east of Malpas. To the north lie the wooded sandstone hills of Bickerton and Peckforton. The infant River Weaver flows south at first, through the grounds and past Cholmondeley Castle. The whole area consists of quiet country lanes, farms, farmland and tracts of woodland.

Bickley was mentioned in Domesday as 'Bichelei' in Dudestan Hundred. Fulk held the settlement from Earl Hugh. There was land for three ploughs. In lordship, one plough with a reeve and two smallholders. The settlement was described as 'Bikeleg' in 1259 and is probably derived from 'Bica's or Bicca's leah'.

The **church of St Wenefrede**, Bickley Moss, was built in 1892 for the fourth Marquess of Cholmondeley; it was designed by Douglas and Fordham. The building is attractive in appearance with a very broad, low west tower, crowned by a spire.

An interesting feature inside the church is the timber passage aisle on the north side. The supporting posts carry a long beam running lengthwise and above it is a hammerbeam roof.

BLAKENHALL [Crewe]

SJ7247: 6 miles (9km) SE of Nantwich

The village of Blakenhall lies near to the main Crewe to London railway line on the Staffordshire border. The surroundings consist of an undulating landscape of small valleys and their attendant streams. In this farming area the pastures and fields are dotted with ponds.

The settlement is recorded in Domesday as 'Blachenhale' in Warmundestrou Hundred. Amongst items listed are woodland, an enclosure and a hawk's eyrie. In 1260 it was described as 'Blake Halch' which is derived from 'Black Halh'. The Old English word 'halh' usually means a quiet recess or remote valley.

On the death of Henry de Delves in 1390, the King took possession of the Blackenhall estates and Henry's heir, John Delves, could not recover them until he had served the sovereign. He fought in Normandy against the French and thus recovered the Manor of Blakenhall.

During the Civil War, at the time of the battles for Nantwich, the village was plundered by troops who were quartered nearby.

The village was part of the estate of the

Delves Broughton family of Doddington Hall until 1917.

Towards the north-west, on the fringe of Blakenhall, lies Doddington Old Mill on the banks of the Forge Brook. It was working until 1925. Sir Thomas Delves used this ancient site as a furnace where the hammers and anvil were cast. Records state that in 1677, 500 tons of pig iron were produced here.

BOLLINGTON [Macclesfield]

SJ9277: 3 miles (5km) NE of Macclesfield

One of the delightful features of Bollington is its location at the foot of the surrounding hills. Situated in the valley of the River Dean, its position acts as a natural gateway to the south Pennines. In the 18th century, Bollington was a quiet agricultural community, composed of a number of hamlets along the road from Macclesfield to Pott Shrigley.

The effect of the Industrial Revolution on the area was dramatic and reflected in the community's rapid growth in the first half of the 19th century. A number of water-powered mills were packed into this little corner of the Dean Valley for cotton spinning. This led to the construction of many of the terraced houses that survive today. In Ingersley Road, one can observe the pattern of accommodation for the cotton workers, since the houses were built progressively from 1820 to 1865.

The **Macclesfield Canal** was the last of the waterways to be built in England. It was surveyed by Telford and engineered by Crosley in 1831. It runs from Marple to Kidsgrove in Staffordshire. The purpose was to transport cotton and silk as well as coal and stone. However, it was overtaken by events and served little industrial purpose. A serious problem faced by the canal engineers was the crossing of the marshy valley at Bollington. Before the embankment and soaring aqueduct were constructed, the streams had to be diverted through a rock-drilled tunnel. Credit for this scheme, according to local sources, should go to a local canal engineer, Charles Nichol.

Today, the canal is used by holiday craft and is considered to be one of the prettiest waterways in the country. Those who travel on its meandering route will be taken along the edge of the hills, at times some 518ft (158m) above sea level.

The **Adelphi Mill** and the **Clarence Mill** stand sentinel over Bollington. They were built at the height of the cotton industry in the town, or as the locals prefer to call it, the village. The mills are magnificent examples of 19th-century industrial buildings. The Adelphi was operated until closure in 1974. It became part of the Courtaulds group, processing artificial fibres, in 1964. It now has a new lease of life as offices, leisure facilities and a hotel.

The former railway from Macclesfield to Marple was opened in 1869 as a route for passengers and textile goods. The viaduct, built between 1866 and 1868, was one of the line's major works. It closed in 1970. The former trackbed is now a route for walkers and cyclists – the **Middlewood Way**.

The best place to view Bollington is from **Kerridge Hill** (920ft, 280m), with its distinctive landmark called White Nancy. The Gaskell family of Ingersley Hall built this folly in 1820 by to commemorate the Battle of Waterloo in 1815. The hilltop is an excellent vantage point that affords wide panoramas of the surrounding countryside.

The **Kerridge quarries** on the west side of the ridge are famous for their buff-coloured sandstone. The rock is

Bollington from White Nancy, with Nab Hill beyond *(Graham Beech)*

easily split into thin sheets suitable for roofing and paving. Coventry Cathedral is paved with Kerridge stone.

It is the predominance of local stone-built houses and cottages which gives Bollington its characteristic atmosphere. Coal was mined on Kerridge, with three seams rising to outcrop one above the other on the lower part of the hill. Drift mines were driven into the hillside and drained by soughs. In the 19th century, small-scale operators worked them.

The **church of John the Baptist** (1832-4) is a Commissioners' church with a west tower. The slender pointed-arch windows have a Y-tracery. There are no aisles but galleries instead.

BOSLEY [Macclesfield]

SJ9166: 5 miles (8km) S of Macclesfield

Bosley lies close to the Staffordshire border on the A523, Leek to Macclesfield road. The River Dane is the county boundary in a landscape of hills and delightful wooded valleys. Soft red sandstone and lush pastures give way to the Pennine foothills, where hedges almost imperceptibly give way to gritstone walls.

South-west of the village rises the prominent escarpment prow of The Cloud, 1125ft (343m). From the summit there are wide-ranging views across central Cheshire. To the north-east rises the rounded height of Bosley Minn, 1260ft (384m). This summit offers a contrasting panorama to the east of rolling hills, steep-sided wooded valleys, gritstone escarpments and moorland slopes.

Bosley was mentioned in Domesday as 'Boselega' in Hamestan Hundred. Godric, a free man, held it. The lands were owned by Hugh, son of Norman, who held them for the Earl. There was land for four ploughs. Domesday records an extensive tract of woodland. The settlement was described as 'Boseleg' in 1278, derived from 'Bosa's leah'.

The earl's Forest of Macclesfield

stretched as far south as Bosley, with the settlement of Macclesfield being the capital of eastern Cheshire.

The **church of St Mary** has a stone west tower with battlements, which belonged to a former medieval church of about 1300. After being destroyed by fire, the nave and chancel were rebuilt in brick. The nave (1777) and the chancel (1834) are by James Green. The nave windows are arched and the building has an open timber roof.

There is a mid-17th-century pulpit with unusual detached small columns and a monument to John Williams Newell who died in 1851. The tower contains six bells, the first installed in 1756 before the fire. The font went missing after the rebuilding of the church, but decades later it turned up in a local farmyard. It was returned to the church in 1848.

Just to the west of the village, in the valley of the Dane, are the Wood Treatment works. Charles Roe originally built the factory as a copper rolling and hammering works. A number of cottages were also built for the workers. With the help of James Brindley the river was harnessed to power the machinery. Later, the works were converted into cotton mills, and then around 1860 the buildings were utilised by corn millers and even a silk throwster. From the early 1920s the factory complex has been a wood flour treatment works. The factory tug-of-war team has become quite famous having achieved many successes at home and abroad.

Also in the valley, the former railway from Leek followed the River Dane towards its junction with the main line to Macclesfield. Nearby is the impressive flight of twelve locks and aqueduct on the Macclesfield Canal.

Bosley reservoir, built by Messrs. Tredwell in 1832, is a large stretch of water that supports abundant wildlife. It was constructed in order to act as a feeder for the Macclesfield Canal. Thomas Telford engineered the canal, which opened in 1831.

To the north-east of Bosley crossroads rises the high land of Sutton Common and Croker Hill 1325ft (404m), which is adorned by a Radio Telecommunication Mast.

The village usually holds its annual Rose Queen festival on the third Saturday in June.

BOSTOCK GREEN [Vale Royal]

SJ6769: 3 miles (5km) NW of Middlewich

This small community situated on the Middlewich to Northwich road lies just to the west of the River Dane and the Trent and Mersey Canal. It claims to be the centre of Cheshire and an oak tree marking the spot was planted in 1887 to commemorate the Golden Jubilee of Queen Victoria. Bostock Green is also at the centre of a farming area with attendant estate farms and cottages. These local buildings are conspicuous by their distinctive red brick and pleasing black and white gables. Since 1976, the village has been declared a conservation area.

The settlement is mentioned in Domesday as 'Botestoch' in Mildestwich Hundred. The Survey lists meadowland and woodland. The name was described as 'Bostoc' in 1260, which is derived from 'Bota's Stoc', 'the dairy farm or cattle farm belonging to Bota'.

The half-timbered Bostock Old Hall, which was reputed to have many rooms and a large hall or gallery, was demolished in 1803. Some of the timber was used in the building of Oldhall Farm.

Bostock New Hall is a large brick house with an early Georgian core that was completely rebuilt in 1775. The house is L-shaped in plan with two main fronts. In 1792 it was purchased by the France family of Liverpool, who lived there until 1950. The house was extensively remodelled in the mid-19th century, and further extensions were added in 1875 for Lt Col C.H. France Hayhurst. The interiors were decorated in a series of styles such as neoclassical and Italianate. Between 1950 and 1980 the house was used as a school, but it is now privately owned.

In the early 20th century, land was given to the village by Col W.H. Hayhurst to provide facilities for the community. These included a bowling green, sports pavilion and tennis courts. Opposite the village green is the workshop of a modern-day blacksmith; an agricultural engineer who caters for the needs of the surrounding farms.

BRERETON HEATH
[Congleton]

SJ8064: 4 miles (6km) W of Congleton

Brereton Heath is a scattered community amongst farmland to the south of the River Dane. **Brereton Heath Park** is well wooded and consists of 32 hectares (80 acres) which once belonged to the Brereton family. In 1959, pure silica sand was extracted from the site, with the quarrying operations finishing in 1973. Congleton Borough Council managed the area then and laid out paths around a small lake. This is an excellent venue for birdwatching, picnicking and water sports.

A short distance to the west, **Brereton Hall**, dated 1586, was entirely built of brick. Both church and hall stand together by the side of the little River Croco.

The hall has a symmetrical front with a centre piece between two octagonal towers that flank an entrance. At either side of the front section are two bays, followed by gabled ends, with tilted bay windows two storeys high. The front part has a doorway of about 1830 and a bridge across from tower to tower. The entrance hall is of 1830 and the dining room has a chimneypiece with tapering pilasters above and columns below. The upper section contains a Royal coat of arms. In a first floor room, another chimneypiece has draped female figures and a coat of arms dated 1633. The building was taken over by a girls' school

The **church of St Oswald** is late Perpendicular in style (early part of the 16th century). A chapel existed here in the time of Richard I, then in Astbury parish; it was then made an independent church and parish in the reign of Henry VIII.

The church was built of fair-sized red sandstone blocks during the 15th century. It was probable that before the rebuilding, the church was a wooden structure. The plan is of a nave and aisles, a two-bay chancel and an enclosed battlemented tower. The nave aisles are of five bays including two against the tower. There is a fine perpendicular east window of five lights.

Although the interior was harshly treated by Victorian restorers in the 19th century, the 15th-century roof retains its form and ancient timbers. The main timbers are richly carved. The chancel roof with **beautifully carved bosses**, and set at a lower level, is all original and dates from the late 15th century.

The church contains very fine altar rails of Jacobean carving which were spared during the restoration. The monuments include a tablet to William Brereton, died 1618. His gauntlets, spurs, helmet and surcoat hang above.

BROWN KNOWL [Chester]

SJ4953: 4 miles (6km) S of Tattenhall

The village of Brown Knowl is reached by narrow, hedged lanes. There are cottages in styles of various ages that mix harmoniously with modern designed dwellings. It is good to see one byway quaintly called Reading Room Lane.

Brown Knowl is not mentioned in Domesday. Observant readers of a large-scale map will notice the conventional sign illustrating a church with tower at the south end of the village. Many will assume that this represents an Anglican church – this is not so. Set on rising ground, **Brown Knowl Methodist Church** is a brick construction roofed with blue slate. The tower is enlivened with courses of stone and the castellated upper part is neatly decorated with roundels of stone tracery. A foundation stone is inscribed 'Ebenezer Primitive Methodist Church' and dated 1913. A large east window highlights the well-kept interior. The pulpit and altar are from the first church built on a lower part of the site in 1836 and demolished in 1913.

An interesting architectural point is that on the original plan the drawings for the church included a spire not a tower. John Wedgwood brought Methodism here in 1822 and his grave is in the churchyard. From the village there is access to the **Iron Age fort of Maiden Castle**. The promontory fort of slightly more than half a hectare (1.5 acres) is defended on the south and east by two lines of earth ramparts that still survive to a height of 7ft (2m). Excavation has shown the site to have two structural phases. The earlier consists of the inner rampart 20ft (6m)

thick and probably originally 10ft (3m) or more in height, revetted with stone externally and timber-faced internally. An outer bank was revetted externally with stone and later increased in width.

The confines of the fort and the neighbouring escarpment slopes and edges of the Bickerton Hills lying between the settlements of Brown Knowl and Bickerton are under the guardianship of the National Trust

BROWNLOW HEATH [Congleton]

SJ8358: 3 miles (5km) S of Congleton

Little Moreton Hall is one of the finest black and white half-timbered houses in the land. It has remained largely unchanged since the 16th century. It is remarkable for its carved gables and Elizabethan wood and plasterwork, and is now in the custody of the National Trust.

The Moretons were a family of prosperous gentry who enlarged their home as their lands and wealth increased. Ralph Moreton first began the building of an 'H'-shaped house in about 1480. Its basic plan consisted of a central Great Hall with two wings, one on either side. Further building was carried out by William Moreton and then his son, who constructed the south range which contained the projecting gatehouse and the Long Gallery.

The house is situated in the south-east corner of a square plot enclosed by a moat. From the courtyard there is an excellent view of the impressive two-storey bay windows erected in 1559; these are glazed with intricately patterned leaded lights.

The hall was the location for Granada TV's 1996 adaptation of Daniel Defoe's *Moll Flanders*.

BROXTON [Chester]

SJ4854: 8 miles (13km) N of Whitchurch

The name Broxton is given to the civil parish, but the hamlet of Broxton is basically centred on the crossroads of the A534 and A41. In Domesday the settlement was listed as 'Brosse'. It was held by Roger, Picot, Brictmer and Raven. The latter two free men held it as two manors. Robert, son of Hugh, owned the lands. A league of woodland was recorded. In 1259 its name became 'Broxun' and in 1278 'Brexen'. The name Broxton is a variant of the common name Burwains or Borrans from the Old English 'burgaesn' or 'a burial place'.

BRUERA [Chester]

SJ6043: 4 miles (6km) SSE of Chester

Bruera is a small scatter of cottages and farms in an extensive area of farmland between the Shropshire Union Canal and the River Dee. It lies near to the Buerton Approach Drive leading to the Iron Bridge at Aldford and on to Eaton Hall, home of the Duke of Westminster.

The little **church of St Mary** was in existence in Saxon times, although the settlement is not mentioned in Domesday. Fragments of 10th-century masonry are to be seen near the doorway, together with a few Norman stones.

By the 19th century the church was in a ruinous condition, roofless, and with a deteriorating interior. The ancient building was saved by the generosity of the first **Duke of Westminster** who funded its complete restoration in 1896. However, many of the ancient features were harshly handled and, indeed, lost in the remodelling.

The earliest reference to the church appears to be in 1150 in the Chartulary of St Werburgh's Abbey. The church is small, with the nave some 40ft (12m) in length and the chancel half as long. The walls are of an average thickness of 4ft (1m). The original Norman walls of the 12th century are plainly built with the fine work of this period in the chancel arch.

In the 1896 restoration, the north side of the church, including the piers, was renewed. The south part appears to be original and the three semi-circular columns are capped with splendid carvings of weird faces, eagle beaks and Norman cable decoration. On the south wall is an aumbry in the form of a simply made wall cupboard.

A south chancel was added in the 15th century and joined to the nave. Soon after, hefty buttresses had to be built to support the west end of the nave. The chapel contains the vault to the Cunliffe family. There are standing monuments to Sir Robert Cunliffe, died 1778, and Sir Ellis Cunliffe, died 1769, of Saighton Hall. The sculptured figures are by Joseph Nollekens.

There are two items of interest in the graveyard: a headstone to James Harnett of Huntington; he was the man in charge of the ferry at Ecclestone. Also, there is the tomb to Sibell Mary, Countess Grosvenor, who died in 1929.

BUERTON [Crewe]

SJ6842: 2 miles (3km) E of Audlem

Set amongst a landscape of pastures, hedgerows and copses, this small village lies on the main A525 Woore to Whitchurch road and on the south-east boundary of the county, bordering Shropshire and Staffordshire.

It was recorded in Domesday as 'Burtune', and was described in 1286 as 'Beurton'. Its name is derived from the

Old English 'Byrh-tun' for 'a tun with a byre'. The Domesday scene was one of woodland, enclosures and a hawk's eyrie.

On high ground by Hankelow Lane stands the large brick tower of **Buerton windmill**. When the mill was built the machinery would have been mainly of wooden construction, with compass arm wheels and wooden cogs. It seems likely that a previous windmill of 1653 stood on the site. A date of 1779 is inscribed on the present building. The mill was last used in 1880, and was then virtually intact. The mill is a scheduled building but now stands in a dilapidated condition.

There are two dwellings of note in the village. Buerton Old House, a yeoman's house, is more than 300 years old and now authentically restored. The second building, Buerton House, was originally known as Tythe Barn Farm, and has its medieval identity hidden by Edwardian brickwork.

The village lies at the centre of a network of footpaths leading to Audlem and the surrounding farmsteads.

BUNBURY [Crewe]

SJ5658: 3 miles (5km) S of Tarporley

The charming village of Bunbury is situated in the prominently rural area of south-west Cheshire. The typical scenery comprises gently undulating pastures with tree-dotted hedgerows. The central sandstone ridge is clearly visible to the west.

Twisting roads connect the various parts of this extensive village, now a conservation area, and the buildings display an interesting mixture of styles and periods – everything from timber-frame Tudor to Georgian brick to modern dwellings.

The Domesday Book lists it as 'Boleberie'. Dedol had held Bunbury in 1066, but the landowner was Earl Edwin and Dedol could have been his reeve or factor.

Of the township names of Bunbury parish which occur as Domesday manors, ten were held in 1086 by Robert fitz Hugh, Lord of Malpas. Domesday mentions a priest at 'Boleberie' but not of a church, and also an area of woodland. The imposing medieval sandstone **church of St Boniface** lies in a commanding position above the infant River Gowy. The church is architecturally of great interest with fabric of the Decorated and Perpendicular periods.

The large church consists of a great tower, a spacious nave with aisles, a chancel and a south chapel. Stones from the old Norman church were used in the foundations of the 14th-century building.

Sir Hugh Calveley rebuilt Bunbury church and founded a college and chantry between 1385 and 1386. In origin a minor squire, Sir Hugh won fame and fortune as a companion-in-arms of the Black Prince. He rose to become governor of Brest. Under the Master at Bunbury, Thomas de Thornton, there was a small community of canons and singers. With the exception of the Ridley Chapel, the plan remains of the collegiate church: the tower, south wall to window level, most of the south porch, the chancel arch, the chancel with sedilia and double piscina and the treasury all belong to this period. The west doorway and the upper parts of the tower are of the Perpendicular period.

The fine **monument of Sir Hugh Calveley** is situated in the middle of the chancel. It is the earliest surviving alabaster effigy in the county. An iron grille with spikes encloses the reclining figure on a sarcophagus.

Also in the chancel is the decorated **tomb of Sir George Beeston**. Born in 1499, he fought in France under Henry VIII and in Scotland in the reign of Edward VI. In 1588, when he was 89, he commanded the *Dreadnought* against the Armada. He was knighted for this feat. He died in 1601 at the age of 102.

In 1527 Sir Ralph Egerton of Ridley built a chantry chapel on the south side of the chancel. He was standard-bearer to Henry VIII. The extremely fine stone screen that separates chapel and chancel still has its original green and red decoration. The exterior battlements and pinnacles are typical of a church in the Perpendicular style – but notice how its north and south aisles are different. The aisles are eight bays long, but the windows of four lights are different on the north and south sides.

Due to enemy action on the evening of 24 November 1940, a bomb severely damaged the church. The nave windows were replaced with clear glass, which gives the building a light and airy appearance. Also as a consequence of the explosion, the steeply pitched roof was replaced with an oak ceiling surmounted by another roof of reduced pitch. The ceiling also incorporates the painted bosses from the 1865 roof.

On the south aisle wall are a number of **painted panels** dating from 1450 and depicting the saints. They were restored in 1988 and exhibited in new frames. The tower contains eight bells, which include a 16th-century tenor bell and two 19th-century trebles.

To the east of the village is the restored Bunbury Mill, which was re-opened in 1977. It was built around 1850 to replace an older building, which itself had replaced an even earlier mill.

The **Image House** is situated on the left just past a minor crossroads at Bunbury on the A49. The cottage features in Beatrice Tunstall's *The Shiny Night* and displays faces and images on the front. In reality, a squatter's cottage like this could be built in a day. Then a man could call it his own if smoke was issuing from the chimney within the allotted time.

The Church of St Boniface, Bunbury

Just to the north of the village, Bunbury Locks carry the Shropshire Union Canal from Chester into the Cheshire Plain. At the top of the locks are old stable buildings that housed the teams of horses which pulled the boats.

BURLEYDAM [Crewe]

SJ6040: 4 miles (6km) W of Audlem

This small village is situated on the south-west edge of Cheshire on its border with Shropshire. The settlement lies on the A525, Audlem to Whitchurch road, amid a wide area of excellent agricultural land. Two streams, the Burley and the Walkmill, rise near the village and flow on to join the Weaver.

The **church of St Michael** was built in 1769 at the expense of Sir Lynch Cotton of Combermere Abbey. Until 1869 it was the private chapel of the Cottons. The building is of brick with arched windows and has a wide nave and short transepts. The east end was extended in 1886 and the open timber roof was probably done at the same time.

There is a beautiful stained glass window in the children's corner presented by Lady Crossley. The east window is by Kempe, 1908. There are attractive iron gate piers for the churchyard gates.

The inn, the **Combermere Arms**, is 450 years old. The building is said to be haunted by a ghost, but the story goes on to say that two clergymen persuaded it to enter a bottle and the container was then buried under the entrance step.

Combermere Abbey was a Cistercian house founded by Hugh Malbank in 1133. It was a wealthy establishment and its endowments included substantial salt revenues. However, in the 13th century it developed a reputation for incompetence and maladminstration. At the dissolution the buildings went to Sir George Cotton. He demolished the church and most of the abbey buildings.

Some evidence of the medieval work is in the first floor room, now the library. Concealed behind its plaster ceiling is the hammerbeam roof; this room was probably the abbot's hall. Sir George's son Richard remodelled the house, in 1563. A fireplace was installed in the Great Hall, and the open roof timbers were covered over by a plaster ceiling.

An event of some importance happened in 1690 when William III stayed at Combermere on his way to Ireland and the Battle of the Boyne. In the early part of the 18th century, the house was recorded as having the ground floor partly of stone and the first floor half-timbered.

Sir Robert Cotton did more alterations in 1795. Changes were made again to the house in the Gothic style between 1814 and 1821 by Sir Stapleton Cotton, who had the house castellated and rendered in grey cement. Sir Stapleton Cotton had been raised to the peerage for his military services in 1814; he became Viscount Combermere in 1827 and Field Marshall in 1855. Another famous visitor was the Duke of Wellington in 1820.

There is a beautifully landscaped park and the west front of the house overlooks the lake. The semi-circular-shaped lake of 52 hectares (132 acres) is the largest in any private park in England. It contains Summerhouse Island and Duckbay Island. A smaller lake in the grounds is called Cocked Hat.

At the far end of the park is a tall monument commemorating Lord Combermere, who died in 1865. Later the estate was sold to the Crossleys, in whose family it remains.

BURTON [Chester]

SJ5064: 2 miles (3km) SSE of Tarvin

Burton is an isolated hamlet situated south-east of Tarvin and just south of the A51, Chester to Nantwich road. A wide area of agricultural land surrounds it.

It was mentioned in Domesday as 'Burtone' in Risedon Hundred. The Bishop held Burton himself, as he did before 1066. There is land for seven ploughs; in lordship two ploughs. The settlement has seven villagers, four smallholders, a priest and rider with three ploughs. Domesday records some meadowland. It is interesting to note the listing of a priest. There is no church at Burton, probably because the settlement failed to increase in size.

Burton Hall is a compact, brick manor house, probably built by John Werden, a Chester lawyer, who purchased the estate in 1600. It was designed as a square plan, with tall, symmetrical elevations rising to a single gable. However, one gable appears to have disappeared. The mullioned and transomed windows rise formally, one above the other. Later in the 17th century, the interior of the house was altered to form four rooms of equal size on each floor. The house stands behind a walled forecourt.

BURTON-IN-WIRRAL [Ellesmere Port]

SJ3174: 3 miles (5km) SE of Neston

The village is situated at the south-eastern end of the Wirral peninsula; it is on rising ground between the railway from Chester to Wallasey and the A540. West of the rocky promontory of Burton Point are the dangerous mudbanks and salt-flats of the Dee estuary. The settlement is not mentioned in Domesday.

Burton is an attractive village now declared a conservation area. The main street curves past a delightful variety of small cottages, some built of red sandstone, some of brick, some painted white with contrasting black timbers and some thatched. Many are built on the sandstone bedrock that outcrops at different places.

During the Middle Ages, Burton was an important place on the Wirral, acting as a port for the crossing to Ireland. But the silting up of the Dee estuary finally put paid to that and now there are fields and marshes separating the village from the Dee.

Burton village winds round Burton Hill, a wooded eminence owned by the National Trust.

The **church of St Nicholas** was built in 1721, except for the east end of the north chancel where the window is 1300. The 1721 work includes the west tower, but the chancel was rebuilt in 1870. The interior of the church basically consists of two naves, which are separated by an arcade of five bays. The church contains an 18th-century communion rail and an east window of 1903 by Kempe.

The monuments include a 13th-century coffin lid inscribed with a foliated cross, and one to Richard Congreve who died in 1820.

Burton Manor is a large Edwardian house built for Henry Neville Gladstone, the third son of the Victorian Prime Minister. The house was purchased in 1903 and the earlier building was recased in sandstone. Over the arched entrance is the Gladstone coat of arms which bears the representation of a negro's head; it is a reminder that the family wealth was based on slavery. The centre of the house contains the large music room.

In Victorian times, Burton Manor was the home of the **Congreve family**. General Walter Congreve won the Victoria Cross in the Boer War at Colenso in 1899. His son, William la Touche Congreve, won his Victoria Cross in France seventeen years later.

The Gladstone manor house is now a residential college of adult education where day, weekend or week-long courses are held.

At the other end of the village is the Old School House, a school founded by Bishop Wilson in 1724. He was Bishop of Sodor and Man.

BURTONWOOD [Warrington]

SJ5691: 4 miles (6km) NW of Warrington

Burtonwood is a residential area lying in a northern finger of the county, south of Newton-le-Willows and just west of the Sankey Brook. The village is mainly surrounded by farmland.

At one time the area of Burtonwood was an extensive forest, but by this century most of the woodland had been cleared. Here, in 1938, a site was selected for an airfield because of flat terrain and good drainage.

With the outbreak of the Second World War, the site was developed very quickly and became the **largest United States military base** outside the United States of America. In 1946 the base was handed back to the Royal Air Force, although in 1948 the United States Air Force used Burtonwood to service aircraft for the Berlin Airlift. Nowadays, the M62 runs through the site, which hopes to attract new industry.

The **church of St Michael** Burtonwood was founded in 1606 and rebuilt in 1716. The attractive south aisle with an arcade of Tuscan columns is by E.J. Dod (1939).

The 18th-century building of brick with a south-west tower has stone dressings and arched windows. It has a bench end from a former church with the name of Sir Thomas Bold and the date 1610.

Bradley Old Hall has a ruined gatehouse (c1460-5). It is constructed of yellow stone with buttresses of red stone. The house itself is 18th century and there is a moat on the site.

BURWARDSLEY and HIGHER BURWARDSLEY [Chester]

SJ5156: 9 miles (14km) SE Chester

The scattered rural community of Burwardsley is a charming collection of sandstone cottages, houses and farms nestling on the west side of the Peckforton Hills in south-west Cheshire.

The Domesday Book lists it as 'Burwardeslei'. Aelfric, Colbert and Ravenkel held it as three manors; they were free men. Robert, son of Hugh, owned the lands. In 1110 the settlement's name became 'Berewardesleya' – probably derived from the personal name 'Burgweard's Leah'

The **church of St John** is probably 17th century but much restored in 1795. It has mullioned windows with arched lights and a Victorian bell turret probably erected when a new chancel was built in the late 19th century.

The **Pheasant Inn** at Higher Burwardsley, built in the 17th century, was originally called the Carden Arms. The **craft centre** at Burwardsley known as Cheshire Workshops produces hand-carved candles.

An estate record of 1840 reveals names of local fields. The name 'Riddings' attached to several fields indicates land cleared for farming. An old feature in the village is a pinfold used to hold straying animals.

Many walkers join the **Sandstone Trail** in Upper Burwardsley. This is a 30-mile (48km) walk from Beacon Hill, Frodsham, south to Grindley Brook Locks on the Shropshire border, where it feeds into the Shropshire Way. The trail traverses farmland and parkland, meanders along the sandstone ridges clothed in oak woodland and pine, and continues across sandy heath-clad slopes with heather, silver birch and bracken. The high points such as Raw Head and Maiden Castle afford expansive views across the plain to the Welsh foothills. The trail continues southwards over small ridges of sand and gravel that were deposited at the end of the last Ice Age.

BYLEY [Vale Royal]

SJ7269: 2 miles (3km) NE of Middlewich

Byley is situated in the area of countryside between the M6, the River Dane and the Roman road of King Street. This extensive agricultural area is dotted with the small settlements of Yatehouse, Ravenscroft and Byley. Agriculture remains the chief occupation.

The settlement was mentioned in Domesday as 'Bevelei' in Middlewich Hundred. Godric, Godwin and Arkell held it as three manors, they were free men. There was land for three ploughs. Two riders and two smallholders had one plough. Domesday records meadowland and woodland. The settlement was described as 'Biueleg' in 1260 and its name is derived from 'Beofa's leah'.

After the Dissolution, Sir Geoffrey Shakerley obtained the lands in the area formerly owned by the monks of Birkenhead. In 1846, Sir Walter Shakerley do-

nated a plot of land for a church at Byley. The **church of St John Evangelist** (1846-7), is a Commissioners' church. It is said to have been designed by the Reverend Henry Massey, vicar of Goostry. However, the architect appears to have been John Matthews.

The church is styled in a Norman fashion with few design motifs, but with a wealth of red brick, yellow terracotta and yellow stone. The later south tower has a pyramid roof.

Ravenscroft Hall was built in 1837 for William Buchanan in place of an earlier Jacobean hall and extended in 1877. The main part is a two-storey, five-bay block with tall windows and an Ionic porch. The additions include a belvedere tower. The last family to live there was the Kays. It was sold to become a girls' boarding school.

In the village of Byley, a **blacksmith** still operates: welding, producing wrought-iron work and repairing agricultural machinery.

CAPENHURST [Chester]

SJ3673: 5 miles (8km) NW of Chester

Capenhurst lies on the western fringe of Ellesmere Port. The small village is scattered along the by-roads to Two Mills and Ledsham. Although it adjoins an extensive industrialised area, the neat settlement, a former dairy-farming centre, still has surroundings of farmland.

The settlement was mentioned in Domesday as 'Capeles' in Wilaveston Hundred. David held it from William fitz Nigel. There was land for one plough, with one villager and two smallholders. The settlement was described as 'Capenhurst' in 1278. The name probably derived from the following – the first element 'a look out place' and the second element 'hill'. So its meaning is 'a look out hill' or a 'place to look from'.

From its beginnings as a wartime factory, the site became a branch of the UK Atomic Energy Research Authority. This vast establishment, now **British Nuclear Fuels Limited**, overpowers the village with its many cooling towers.

The **church of Holy Trinity** (1856-9), designed by James Harrison, is built of red sandstone. The building has a **fine west tower** of 1889-90 which was probably designed by John Douglas. It has a **corner stair-turret**, which is not as high as the tower, and supported by broaches at the base of the spire. All the stained glass in the church is by Kempe and dates from 1876 to the end of the century.

The pinfold or pound is situated near to the church. It is a square sandstone enclosure, whose origin goes back to Norman times. In this pinfold, domestic animals were kept, usually for debt, until they were redeemed.

East of the church stood Capenhurst Hall, built in 1792 by Richard Richardson. The family remained lords of the manor until 1945 when the estate was sold. The hall became ruinous and has now been demolished.

CHECKLEY [Crewe]

SJ7346: 2 miles (3km) N of Woore

Checkley is one of a number of scattered, isolated communities lying just north of Woore. They are situated close to the Shropshire border. Not one of these places is a village; all consist of houses sprinkled along country lanes. Around Bridgemere are situated Checkley, Checkley Green and Wheel Green.

The **Bridgemere Garden World** lies on the A51 just north of Woore. The centre has a vast selection of tens of thousands of plants on display. There is a

television setting where 'Gardeners' Diary' is shot. Other attractions include a French rose garden, a woodland setting, a Victorian garden, a cottage garden and a rock and water area. Amongst the $2\frac{1}{2}$ hectares (6 acres) of plants and displays are to be found the Gold Medal winners from the Chelsea Flower Show. There are large glasshouses of houseplants of every description, including uncommon and exceptional varieties. Visitors can enjoy an aquatic house, an extensive bookshop and the restaurant and coffee shop.

Checkley Hall is an attractive brick house of symmetrical design with five bays. It was built in 1694 by the Delves family of Doddington to replace a timber-framed hall. Originally, it had a hipped roof but the attic was rebuilt, leaving the house with two and a half storeys. There is a walled forecourt in front that is entered through stone gate piers.

Checkley was not listed in Domesday. The settlement was described as 'Checkley' in 1130. It may be derived from the personal element 'Ceacca's leah', or 'ceacca' may indicate a hill or knoll.

CHELFORD [Macclesfield]

SJ8174: 6 miles (9km) W of Macclesfield

The village, set amongst farmland, initially grew up around the meeting of two main routes, one north to south, the other east to west. The railway from Stockport to Crewe opened in 1842, and a part of the village moved to the site of the railway station. A cattle market was established as well as an inn and the village hall. Today, this important market attracts farmers and buyers from far and wide.

In 1894, there was a serious railway accident at Chelford when an express train collided with a shunted wagon. Fourteen died and 79 passengers were injured. Nowadays, the rail link to nearby cities provides a vital facility for business commuters.

The quarrying of fine silica sand for the glass making industry takes place in the surrounding areas.

The settlement was recorded in Domesday as 'Celeford' and was described as 'Chelleford' in 1245; its name is derived from 'Ceolla's ford'.

The **church of St John** (1774-6) is situated between the two streams, Snape Brook and Bag Brook, which flow into Astle Pool. The tower, 1840, has a recessed spire and the windows are pointed. The interior contains panelling, box pews, a gallery and a fine Arts and Crafts pulpit. There are also some attractive examples of stained glass.

One of the oldest buildings in Chelford is the Manor House, a black and white timber and plasterwork building. The house is a mixture of Tudor, Stuart, Georgian and Victorian craftsmanship.

CHESTER [Chester]

SJ3966: 25 miles (40km) SW of Warrington

Chester's strategic position was first recognised by the Romans. It is now known that there was a military base here in the late AD50s. This was replaced by a 60-acre earth and timber **legionary fortress** from AD76 to AD78. Its situation on the river gave rise to its Roman name of Castra Deva or Castra Legionum.

The initial garrison, as we know from tombstones, was the 2nd Legion Adiutrix, replaced in about AD87 by the 20th Legion Valeria Victrix. This legion remained at Chester throughout the Roman occupation.

The fort's defences were rebuilt in stone first, followed by the principal internal buildings, at the beginning of the second century. The fort at Chester was established as a secure defensive point against the Welsh; it was also used as a base for controlling the movements of the volatile Brigantes in the Pennines.

The fortress plan is basically the usual Roman 'playing card' rectangular shape. It had four main streets running north-south and east-west, protected by a defensive wall with four main gates. The withdrawal of the Legionary garrison from Chester is now thought to have occurred before the end of the third century. As happened at Caerleon, there is evidence of extensive demolition in the fortress between AD270 and AD290.

The Old English name for Chester was Legacaestir, from the Roman title Castra Legionum. This was supplanted by Ceaster in 1094 and is listed in the Domesday Survey as Cestre. Domesday states that 'in Cheshire the Bishop holds from the King what belongs to his Bishopric. Earl Hugh holds all the rest of the County from the King'.

Duke William granted the title of Earl of Chester to his nephew **Hugh d'Avranches** (Hugh Lupus).

There are many Norman features to be seen in Chester today, both in the Cathedral, which was the Abbey of St Werburgh, and in the parish church of St John the Baptist.

Edward I used the town as a base for his Welsh invasions during the last half of the 13th century. It was during this period and throughout the 14th century that the port of Chester became important, bringing much prosperity to the town.

From 1237, the earldom of Chester passed to the Crown, and Cheshire enjoyed palatinate status until 1536. During the Civil War, Chester supported the

Royalist cause and came under siege between 1644 and 1646. It is recorded that in 1645 Charles I watched the defeat of his army during the Battle of Rowton Moor from the Phoenix Tower at the north-east corner of the walls. The line of the streets within the original Roman fortress has altered little since Tudor times.

The famous **Rows** are a distinctive feature of Chester, where first floor shops can be reached from the street. It appears that between c1485 and c1642, the Rows developed in the form in which we see them today; although the origins of the structures obviously go back before Tudor times.

There are some fine examples of timber-framed buildings to be seen in Chester from the time of the Elizabethan and Jacobean Renaissance (c1530 to c1670). There are also a number of Georgian buildings that are a sure indication of Chester's wealth and burgeoning prosperity.

During the 19th century, there was great expansion due to its position as a county town and as a business centre. Much rebuilding took place at this time, with splendid examples of revivalist black and white Victorian building work.

The **Cathedral church of Christ and St Mary** was originally a Benedictine Abbey founded in 1092 by Hugh Lupus, Earl of Chester. Henry VIII formed the Diocese of Chester in 1541, and the Abbey of St Werburgh became Chester Cathedral. Norman remains can be seen, although much of the existing building dates from the Gothic period of the 14th to 16th centuries. It was substantially damaged during the Civil War.

The south transept is a large area, aisled and as big as the quire. There are four banner-hung aisles, including one that contains the standards captured at Quebec by General Wolfe. Its arcades and aisles are of the late Decorated period, but the tall clerestory is Perpendicu-

By the side of the River Dee, Grosvenor Park, Chester

lar. The nave was begun in about 1360 with the south side replacing the earlier Norman nave. There is a difference of a hundred years between the construction of the south side and the north side.

In the east corner of the window over the pulpit is the **Chester Imp**, a stone carving of a chained devil. The bases of the piers on the north side are perpendicular; those on the south are Decorated.

The Consistory Court Room was the early 16th century beginning of the south-west tower. The furniture is 17th century. The baptistery lies in the west bay of the north aisle and has Norman arches on all sides. The second bay in the north aisle contains the cloister doorway. The Cloister Walls were rebuilt between 1525 and 1537. They were restored between 1911 and 1913 by Sir Giles Gilbert Scott, the English architect (1880-1960) who also designed the nave at Downside Abbey and the new Bodleian Library at Oxford, and was responsible for rebuilding the House of Commons after the Second World War.

The north transept exhibits the most impressive Norman work, probably of around 1100. The upper parts are all Perpendicular, including the roof with big gilded bosses from about 1520. The north door is Early English, as are the three lancet windows in the east wall. The Quire is of the 13th century with well-defined cluster columns. The late 14th-century stalls are richly endowed with pinnacled canopies and poppy heads. There is a marvellously varied display of misericords.

The vaulted Lady Chapel (c1270) contains the 14th-century shrine of St Werburgh, reassembled from small pieces. The crossing part of the Cathedral dates from the early 14th century, with the strengthening transverse arches added in the 15th century. The red and gold ceiling pattern dates from 1969.

The detached belfry, the **Addleshaw Bell Tower,** was designed by George Pace and completed in 1974. It was the first free-standing bell tower to be built for an English Cathedral for 500 years. George Pace was the Consultant Architect of Chester Cathedral, (1962-1975). In 1971 he was awarded the title of 'Commander of the Royal Victorian Order'. He was architect to eight English cathedrals and several hundred churches.

The **church of St John the Baptist** dates back to Saxon times and became a cathedral in 1075. The massive Norman piers date from this time, but building work continued throughout the 12th century. The nave, crossing and first bay of the chancel date from the 11th century. St John's became a parish church in 1541 when the new see of Chester was created.

The **Roman Amphitheatre** was the largest arena of its kind in Britain. Today, only the north half can be seen beyond Newgate. Excavations have shown that the original timber structure was replaced with stone after a few years. The arena wall is well preserved, with entrances on the north and east. In the former, the stone gateposts for the entrance doors are still visible next to the arena wall, as well as one flight of steps leading up to the seating accommodation. The spectators would have sat on wooden seats raised on banks around the arena. The amphitheatre is close to the River Dee and near to St John's Church.

The castle was founded on this site in Saxon times and a Norman building sited here towards the end of the 11th century. Building work continued in the reign of Edward I, but very little of this medieval work can now be seen. The castle was rebuilt as **Civic Buildings** in the Greek Revival style between 1788 and 1822.

The **Shire Hall** is an impressive building of semi-circular design with a ring of ten Ionic columns and ten more against the flat wall. **Agricola's Tower** or Caesar's Tower is the principal medieval survival, being one of the towers of the inner bailey. It contains the beautiful 13th-century chapel of St Mary de Castro.

The **Grosvenor Museum** in Grosvenor Street was built in the Renaissance style between 1885 and 1886. It houses a fascinating collection of Roman military and domestic material, especially the tombstones and inscribed plaques discovered in the environs of the city.

God's Providence House, 9 Watergate Street, dates from 1652, but was rebuilt by one of Chester's notable Victorian architects, James Harrison. It carries the memorable inscription 'God's Providence is Mine Inheritance', said to have been added by the owner in cheating the plague in the late 17th century.

Bishop Lloyd's House, Watergate Street, is a splendid example of an early 17th-century house with crests and carved panels of religious subjects. George Lloyd was Bishop of Chester from 1605 to 1615.

The Falcon in Lower Bridge Street, was originally the town house of the Grosvenors. It was built in 1626 above an earlier foundation that contains a 13th-century crypt. Restoration took place in 1886 and 1982.

Cowper House, 12 Bridge Street, is a genuine timber-framed building dated 1664. Numbers 44 to 46 Bridge Street (Owen Owen) display a very fine Georgian façade. Number 2 Eastgate Street and 1 Bridge Street give access to **the Rows**. Although most of these walkways and most of the nearby buildings are Victorian, the Rows have been part of Chester since the 13th century.

Numbers 9 to 13 Eastgate Street are not genuine timber-framed buildings but late Victorian. The sham black and white façade consists of painted boards fastened to the brickwork. The Pied Bull, Northgate Street, has an 18th-century frontage that covers another building as old as late 16th century. There is a replica of a 1761 **notice board** indicating distances of the various coaches that departed from this spot.

The **Water Tower** in Water Tower Street was built in 1322 to defend the harbour. It is 75ft (22m) high and contains a small museum illustrating Chester's history. It was restored in 1977. **Bonewaldthorne's Tower** in City Walls Road is a medieval tower constructed to guard the river approaches when Chester was a port.

Chester Zoo at Upton-by-Chester is renowned for the spacious enclosures in which animals are kept; it has a marvellous collection of mammals, reptiles, birds and fish from all over the world. There are delightful gardens, and other attractions include the Aquarium, the Tropical House and waterbus trips.

CHILDER THORNTON [Ellesmere Port]

SJ3677: 2 miles (3km) NW of Ellesmere Port

Childer Thornton lies on the main A41 Chester to Birkenhead road. It is a compact residential suburb of Ellesmere Port in the northern part of the borough. Records as long ago as 1220 refer to Childer Thornton. At that time the nearby manor was controlled by Benedictine monks.

Although not mentioned in Domesday, the name is an interesting one. The first element 'Childer' could possibly be derived from a personal name, the Old English 'Cilla'. The second element 'Thornton' is described as a 'tun where thorn bushes grew'. So its full meaning could be 'Cilla's tun where thorn bushes grew'.

The **church of St Paul** (1858-62), was designed by James K. Cooling and built for James K. Naylor, a Liverpool banker from Hooton Hall, at a cost of £5000. The building has been described as 'one of the most spectacular churches in Cheshire'.

The style adopted was partly Norman and partly Italian Romanesque. The church is built of stone, with red and white masonry blocks interacting well together. The nave and aisles are three bays long with transepts and an octagonal crossing tower or lantern. The dome and the crossing are a striking and unusual feature, with light entering from the lantern above. Inside the church the arcades have attractive granite columns of Peterhead stone. There is a splendid square font (1851) of dark green serpentine.

The Roman Catholic church of St Mary of the Angels, 1879, was designed by E.J. Tarver in the 13th-century style. The building has neither aisles nor a tower, but a polygonal apse and a west porch.

CHOLMONDELEY CASTLE [Crewe]

SJ5351: 4 miles (6km) NE of Malpas

Cholmondeley Castle lies south-east of Bickerton. The scattered dwellings and farms of the parish of Cholmondeley, pronounced 'Chumley' are part of the estate owned by the Marquess of Cholmondeley. The name Cholmondeley was listed in Domesday as 'Calmundelei', which became 'Chelmundeleg' in 1287. It is probably derived from a personal name 'Ceolmund's Leah'.

Sir Hugh Cholmondeley built the old hall in 1571, and the building was re-modelled by Sir John Vanbrugh in 1716. The old hall was demolished when the new house was begun in 1801. This was a large castellated building designed by the Marquess. In 1817, Robert Smirke added turrets and towers. The architect, Robert Smirke, was knighted in 1832. Lowther Castle, 1806-1811, in Cumbria, and Eastnor Castle, 1812-1815, in Herefordshire, were the finest examples of Smirke's earlier work. In pseudo-Gothic style, they are not, however, typical of his work as a whole, and he seldom used the style in later life, preferring to use classical forms instead.

The **chapel of St Nicholas**, situated on a rise in the centre of Cholmondeley Park, consists of a 14th-15th-century chancel, which is timber-framed and has a hammerbeam roof. After damage sustained in the Civil War, the building was repaired and enlarged between 1652 and 1655.

In the 1716 restoration, Sir John Vanbrugh encased the chancel with brick and rebuilt the rest of the chapel. The transepts were added in 1829 and the north and south galleries in 1840. The furnishings consist of a screen dated 1655; communion rail of the mid-17th century; box pews and a family pew; an early 18th-century staircase; a lovely east window and small Flemish roundels of stained glass. There are splendid **wrought iron gates** outside the chapel and also west of the castle. These were made, in all probability, by the Davies Brothers of Bersham near Wrexham in the first half of the 18th century. There was a long tradition of ironworking in the Bersham area before the ironmaster Wilkinson arrived. The building Groes Foel was famous as the workshop of the brothers Robert and John Davies. They were renowned as the craftsmen who created the splendid iron gates.

The castle grounds are landscaped down to the lakes and the **outstanding gardens** are full of colour and have all forms of attractions: temples, a waterfall, islands and statues.

CHORLTON LANE [Chester]

SJ4547: 2 miles (3km) W of Malpas

Chorlton Lane consists of a small group of cottages and farmhouses set in secluded open countryside to the west of Malpas. The surrounding landscape is one of lush pastures, rich arable land, hedges and winding lanes.

Chorlton Hall was built in 1666. In 1846, additions were made in the Tudor style, with a central porch and two projecting wings. The dining room has Jacobean-style plasterwork and the drawing room has Gothic-style plasterwork.

The line of the Roman road from Chester to Whitchurch runs a little to the east of Chorlton Lane. In 1870, Roman remains were found at Chorlton Old Hall, suggesting that there may have been a temporary Roman camp here. It is suggested that it may have been an outlying defensive point guarding the route from attacks by the Celts.

Chorlton Lane was not mentioned in Domesday. The settlement was described as 'Cherlton' in 1283, and 'Chorleton' in 1284. The name is derived from 'The tun of Ceolred's people'.

CHRISTLETON [Chester]

SJ4365: 3 miles (5km) E of Chester

Christleton is a large parish east of Chester and south of the line of the Roman road, the A51 towards Nantwich. On the triangular village green stands a sand-stone shelter of 1886 with a wooden-tiled canopy and a water pump and trough.

The village is one of the most pleasant surviving in the neighbourhood of Chester. North of the green is The Square, with a Wesleyan Methodist church of 1888. Beyond that is a large pool faced by a fine range of black and white almshouses with decorative carving. These were built in 1865 to the design of Mr John Scott, father of Sir Gilbert Scott. In the fields behind them is a small tump or windmill site called 'the Mill Mound'. The western boundary of the village is bordered by the Shropshire Union Canal, now busy with leisure craft.

The settlement is recorded in Domesday as 'Cristetone', when a mill was listed. In 1289 it was described as 'Kirkecristelton'. The name is derived from, 'a tun with a cross'.

The fine, interesting **church of St James** stands at the centre of the village and is the fourth building to occupy the present site. The tower is late 15th century, but not its top, with the higher stair turret and the short pyramid roof. This, with the rest of the church, was built in 1875-7. The plan includes a nave with aisles and a chancel, and a continuous roof above a high east window. The interior contains a good deal of chessboard work with red and white sandstone. The screen is made of wrought iron.

Christleton Old Hall is an early 17th-century timber-framed house; it was encased in brick round about 1870. The interior contains good Jacobean plasterwork. Another interesting feature is a set of six early 18th-century bread ovens in the north garden wall.

Christleton Hall is an impressive Georgian brick house built in 1750. It stands in its own grounds and is now a College of Law.

The village featured largely in the

Civil War, when the Parliamentarians occupied it during the siege of Chester. The Old Hall was the Parliamentarian Headquarters. Nearby, the Battle of Rowton Moor, 1645, was watched by King Charles I from the city walls. Later, the Royalist citizens of Chester burned down much of the village in revenge.

A village ceremony, the Beating of the Bounds, takes place every ten years on Rogation Sunday. A procession leaves the village and winds its way over 14 miles through the five townships that make up the parish of Christleton.

The village has won the award for the Best Kept Village Competition a number of times.

CHURCH MINSHULL [Crewe]

SJ6660: 4 miles (6km) NW of Crewe

The village is situated in largely unspoilt rural surroundings on the western bank of the River Weaver. It lies on the B5074, Winsford to Nantwich road. It probably grew up at a suitable crossing point of the river. A three-arched bridge was constructed in 1698 in order to bring stone for the building of the church.

The settlement is mentioned in Domesday as 'Maneshale'. In 1289, it was described as 'Chirchemunshull'. The word 'Minshull' is derived from the Old English 'Monnes scyll' – 'Monn's ledge of land'.

The **church of St Bartholomew** is a brick, oblong building with stone quoins and mouldings. The square tower was built in 1702 and the rest of the building in 1704. This 18th-century church replaced an earlier timber-framed one. It has arched windows, a nave and aisles separated by round piers, and circular windows over the north and south doors. The interior contains a font of 1717.

The houses and cottages in the village are mainly brick with some black and white timbering. The road winds round the church and passes Church Farm, a square-framed black and white dwelling with a projecting upstairs room supported on two columns. It was the home of Elizabeth Minshull before she became the third wife of John Milton, the poet, in 1660.

There are two ancient mill sites in the village. The last one to survive ground corn but closed after the last war. However, the water wheel provided electricity for the whole village until about 1960.

Other buildings of note in the immediate area are Minshull Hall and Wade's Green Hall. The former is a large brick farmhouse on an old moated site. It was the seat of the Minshulls of Vernon, whose crest was two red lion's claws holding a silver crescent moon. The latter house is mainly brick with some black and white timbering showing, and dated about 1620. It has three attractive dormers with decorative timber criss-cross work in the gables.

CHURTON [Chester]

SJ4156: 7 miles (11km) S of Chester

The village is situated on the B5130 road south of Chester and close to the River Dee. Previously Churton was a farming community; now it is a handy base for commuters. The village displays a wide range of architectural styles: from 17th-century black and white cottages to tall Victorian terraced houses and modern bungalows. One old dwelling, dated 1650, has an exposed gable-end cruck frame.

There are two major landowners, one of them being the Grosvenor estates from the Duke of Westminster. In the 19th century, many of the villagers were employed on the restoration of the old Eaton Hall.

There used to be an old cross at the crossroads in the centre of the village. From this point, a trackway called Hof Lane runs westwards down to the River Dee. This used to be a ferry point across the river to Almere. This secluded spot would have made a useful smuggling route across the border.

The village has no church but there is a Methodist chapel that was opened in 1832.

In the village stands **Churton Hall**, a half-timbered house built by the Barnston family. It is an E-shape with projecting gables at both ends and a porch placed to one side. The house carries the date 1569 and the initials W.B.:E.B. It was heavily restored between 1978 and 1980.

Churton was not listed in Domesday. The settlement was described as 'Chirton' in 1260 and as 'Chyrchton' in 1334. The name is derived from the Old English 'Cyric-tun' or 'church tun'. There may have been a church site here in medieval times, but repeated Welsh raids possibly destroyed the early building.

CLOTTON [Chester]

SJ5263: 2 miles (3km) NW of Tarporley

The village is situated on the A51, Chester to Nantwich road; once a busy coaching stop en route from London to Wales. The surroundings are predominantly agricultural and the locality contains a mixture of farmhouses and cottages, with some black and white dwellings in the village. The character of the community has been preserved as it is now a conservation area.

The settlement is recorded in Domesday as 'Clotone', and its name is derived from the Old English 'cloh a ravine'. Hence, 'a tun in a ravine'.

The immediate area contains examples of hedges standing on top of sandstone walls – called cops in these parts.

CLUTTON [Chester]

SJ4654: 4 miles (6km) NW of Malpas

The village lies on the A534, Nantwich to Wrexham road and is situated on higher land above the shallow valley of the Carden Brook. The surroundings consist mainly of agricultural land with hedged pastures and areas of woodland. Just south of the village rise sandstone outcrops above parkland.

The settlement is mentioned in Domesday as 'Clutone'. It was described as 'Clutton' in 1275 and is derived from the Old English 'Clud-tun' – 'a tun by a hill'. Domesday records a picture of ploughland, meadowland and woodland.

Carden Park House was formerly a 16th-century timber-framed mansion. It was rebuilt as an attractive Jacobean house with large and small outer gables and was restored in the early 19th century for John Hurlstone Leche. The building was destroyed by fire in 1912. A round ice house with a saucer dome, stables and two lodges survive. The fine wrought-iron gates to the lodges, attributed to the Davies Brothers of Bersham, are no longer in situ.

Lower Carden Hall is a half-timbered early 17th-century house. It has interesting brick chimneystacks with bricks in zigzag patterns and sets of crow-steps in the form of small gables. The hall was restored in 1899 for Sir John Leche.

CODDINGTON [Chester]

SJ4355: 8 miles (13km) SE of Chester

Coddington is a scattered huddle of houses and farms set in the angle of open

Cheshire countryside between the A41 and A534. In this verdant area of green fields, hedgerows and copses of trees, the narrow lanes twist and turn, glad to be free of the confines of the busy main roads.

It is a typical picture of the English rural scene and delights the countryside explorer. The area is quiet and peaceful and off the beaten track; even the local ducks leave the confines of the village pond to sleep in the middle of the road.

Coddington is listed in Domesday as 'Cotintone'. Ernwy, Ansgot and Dot held the settlement as three manors, and the lands were owned by Earl Hugh. The survey records ploughland, extensive meadowland and a mill. Coddington is recorded as 'Cotintuna' in 1100, which means 'the tun of Cotta people'.

Coddington lies just a short distance from the route of the **Roman road** Watling Street (West). The clear remains of an agger (a raised embankment) can be seen where the Churton to Coddington road, Edgerley Lane, crosses it and makes two sharp turns in doing so. To the south the **agger** lies mainly to the east of a hedge; to the north it can be seen behind the railings at the turn in the road. The **church of St Mary**, 1833, is a type of the Commissioners' churches. There are deep buttresses between the two-light windows. It has a square, stone bell turret.

Nearby, the old school building serves as the **Parish Rooms**. This small, cosy place is used by the community and is the meeting place of the Aldersey and Coddington W.I. group.

Opposite the church lies a meadow with the interesting name of Mud Field. In this field is a tree-covered **mound**, marked on the O.S. map in old printing to indicate some form of antiquity. Some people believe it is a burial place used following a border skirmish between the Mercians and the Welsh. The mill mentioned in Domesday probably lay close on the Coddington Brook. Local sources also state that this little community once had a weekly market and was also allowed a yearly fair in September.

COMBERBACH [Vale Royal]

SJ6377: 3 miles (5km) NNW of Northwich

The village is situated in the parish of Great Budworth and is surrounded by agricultural land with working farms. From a small settlement, Comberbach has grown considerably in size and includes two housing estates. The village is noted for the Spinner and Bergamot Inn, thought to have been named after two famous local racehorses. The ancient tradition of soul-caking has been revived and the villagers have also formed a Morris dance and mummers group.

The settlement was described as 'Comburbach' in 1333, and the name is probably derived from 'the stream valley of Cumbra's people'.

Marbury Hall was the seat of the Merbury family in the Middle Ages, and was acquired in 1684 by Earl Rivers. In 1714, the Marbury estate came to his family, the Barry's.

James Hugh Smith Barry inherited Marbury in 1787, and John, his illegitimate son, succeeded him. The house was enlarged into a vast French château with dormer windows and turrets. A famous collection of paintings and sculptures remained at Marbury until the 1940s. During the Second World War it was an army and prisoner of war camp. The house was demolished in 1968-9, and the grounds are now a country park administered by the Cheshire County Council.

Amongst the interesting legends connected with Marbury Hall are the ghost of a lady and a white horse called "Marbury Dunne".

CONGLETON [Congleton]

SJ8663: 8 miles (12km) S of Macclesfield

The town lies at the point of contrast where high rolling hills meet the pastures and woods of the Cheshire Plain. The sharply pointed crest of The Cloud overlooks Congleton, and at its foot, the lively River Dane emerges from the moors and steep-sided wooded valleys of the south Pennines. It was here in Congleton on the Dane, and in towns like Macclesfield and Bollington, that the early textile mills powered by fast-flowing streams heralded a new industrial world.

In the Domesday Survey Congleton is listed as 'Cogeltone'. The Saxon leader Godwin held the settlement, but the lands were owned by Earl Hugh and administered by Bigot de Loges. The name became 'Congelton' in 1282. The first element of the name is obscure; it may be derived from Old Norse 'kengr' – 'a bend' (Congleton lies on a bend of the Dane). Or, possibly, the word is a combination of a Welsh first element and the Anglo Saxon 'tun'.

Congleton was granted a Charter in 1272 by Henry de Lacy, the lord of the manor. This allowed the town to appoint a mayor, hold a market and use its own corn mill. Floods swept away the town in 1452 and it was then rebuilt on higher ground. In the early 17th century the town was accused of using money meant for a new bible to pay for a bear to be used in bear baiting.

John Bradshaw (1602-59) was an influential 17th-century lawyer who became Chief Justice of Chester. He lived in Congleton from the mid-1630s, and was Mayor of Congleton in 1637. In 1642 he shut up his house and left the town. He sided with Cromwell in the Civil War, and organised the legal case against Charles I. He then supervised the court that found him guilty and condemned him to death. As a reward, he was made president of the Council of State and Chancellor of the duchy of Lancaster. He was buried in Westminster Abbey, but at the Restoration his body was exhumed and he was hanged as a regicide. John Bradshaw's house in Lawton Street was demolished in 1820.

There was silk weaving in Congleton in 1671 if not earlier. John Clayton and Nathaniel Pattison built a large mill on Mill Green in 1752. The machinery was powered by a 19ft (6m) water wheel turned by the River Dane. Trade prospered. By 1773 there were five of these ribbon/silk mills in the town. By 1817, there were seventeen silk mills and five cotton mills in the town.

In 1860, due to the fact that French silk was allowed into the country, trade slumped and by 1910 there were only seven mills left. Today, Berisfords in Congleton manufactures ribbons and bindings from polycotton.

The church of St Peter was rebuilt in brick between 1740 and 1742, and the tower was completed in stone in 1786. The chapel was in use by the early 15th century if not earlier, and thought to have been half-timbered. It soon outgrew its parent church at Astbury.

It is a largish building where the aisles are divided from the nave by seven square pillars on either side. These carry circular Tuscan pillars, which support steeply tiered galleries. The fronts of the galleries are decorated with fine oak panelling.

There are box pews in the nave. The pulpit, standing in the centre of the nave, is Jacobean and came from Astbury. There is also an impressively carved lectern. The Venetian east window is flanked by two mural paintings (1748) of St Peter and St Paul by Edward Penny.

The **church of St James**, West Street, is a Commissioners' Church of 1847-8. It contains a highly decorated pulpit of mid 17th-century Flemish work.

The **Congregational Church**, Antrobus Street, 1876-7, was designed by William Sugden of Leek. The large west window has splendid geometrical tracery. West Street is lined with some good examples of Georgian domestic architecture, including Damion House and Overton House.

The Town Hall, High Street, was designed by E.W. Godwin (1833-86), in a Venetian Gothic style. He was an English architect, and a central figure in the Aesthetic Movement.

There are two 17th-century black and white buildings of note: the White Lion pub in the High Street and the Lion and Swan at the east end of West Street. The White Lion is timber-framed with an irregular front and herringbone bracing.

The **Weavers' Cottages**, Rood Hill, are typical of those used by silk weavers. Handlooms were placed in the top floor garrets, where large windows provided sufficient light.

The **Salford Mill** (Jantex) is a fine example of an 18th-century silk mill with a classical façade. The tall **Brook Mill** was built in 1835, using cast iron columns to support the weight of the silk looms on the upper floors. The handsome **Riverside Mill** was built in the 1870s for cutting thick-twilled cotton cloth (fustian).

The Bridestones is a Neolithic chambered tomb dating back to 2900BC. The monument lies on a low ridge stretching southwards from The Cloud. The county boundary between Cheshire and Staffordshire runs lengthways along the cairn. The tomb, having now lost its covering mound, was thought to have been 295ft (90m) long. Halfway along is a broken porthole of stone, a hole wide enough to allow the passage of a corpse. At the east end of the chamber was a semi-circular forecourt marked by large stones.

The **Macclesfield Canal** lies to the east of Congleton; it was surveyed by Thomas Telford and opened in 1831. It linked the Peak Forest Canal at Marple with the Trent and Mersey near Kidsgrove. There is a spectacular series of twelve locks at Bosley, before crossing the River Dane via Telford's superb iron aqueduct.

The **Clonter Opera Theatre** at Swettenham Heath offers new opera productions in an intimate indoor theatre. The Clonter Opera Prize is the only inter-conservatoire opera prize in the U.K.

Buglawton is the north-eastern suburb of Congleton, centred on the A54 Buxton road and constrained by the River Dane and the Macclesfield Canal. The **church of St John Evangelist**, 1840, was designed by R.B. Rampling. It is in the Norman style with an odd west tower. The square section ends in four gables, but the tower continues in an octagon shape with a recessed spire. The church has no aisles.

Buglawton Hall, now a school, is a house that has been added to haphazardly. It began as a 16th-century brick house with half-timbering but has been extended several times. It was castellated in the 19th century, probably for Samuel Pearson, a silk manufacturer in 1823.

Not mentioned in Domesday, the settlement was described as 'Lauton' in 1278 and 'Buggelauton' in 1287. The name is derived from the Old English 'Hlaw-tun', 'tun by the hill' – a reference to The Cloud. The meaning of the addition 'Bug' is obscure. It may be a family name Bugg, or possibly 'bug' meaning 'a bug-bear, scarecrow'.

COTEBROOK [Vale Royal]

SJ5765: 2 miles (3km) NE of Tarporley

Cotebrook is set in a rolling landscape of low hills, valleys, streams and country lanes. This small linear settlement was formerly part of the royal forest of Mara. The word Delamere means 'de la Mara'.

Severe punishments were inflicted on those people trespassing in the royal preserve; typical crimes were taking game, keeping dogs, taking timber and allowing animals to graze without permission. Regular courts were in session to try offenders and pronounce the fines, and to sentence people on more serious charges.

The Done family in Utkinton Hall were **hereditary foresters of Delamere**. The hall is now a farmhouse and much of the original courtyard house has been demolished. The Done line finished in 1629 with the death of Sir John Done, whose daughter married Sir John Crewe. A chapel was consecrated in 1635, but Royalists plundered the house in 1644.

The front of the house, facing the road, was built around 1700 for Sir John Crewe, but many of the windows are now blocked. Items from inside the house, such as the stained glass and the staircase have been removed. It is interesting that the glass, after its travels, now resides in the famous Burrell Collection in Glasgow.

Cotebrook is not mentioned in Domesday. The Middle English word 'cote' stands for a shelter, probably for animals. So it is possible that the name is derived from the small brook where sheep were 'coted' or penned ready for washing.

The **church of St John** (1874-5), was designed by G.E Street. It has a thin north-east turret with a blunt pyramidal roof. There are a group of three lancet windows at the east end and another group of four at the west end. The chancel is rather short and the east window is by Kempe (1885).

CREWE [Crewe]

SJ7055: 20 miles (32km) SE of Chester

Crewe is listed in Domesday as 'Crev'. Osmer held the settlement and the lands were owned by Richard of Vernon. Some ploughland, meadow and woodland were recorded. In 1288 the settlement's name was 'Cruue'; and in 1346 'Crue'. The word is derived from the Welsh *cryw*, denoting a ford or stepping stones.

In the Middle Ages, Crewe township was part of the parish of Barthomley. The parish of Coppenhall, originally a chapelry of Wybunbury, contained two townships: Church Coppenhall and Monks Coppenhall.

In 1837, the Grand Junction Railway opened the first railway in Cheshire – from Warrington to Birmingham. Crewe Station owes its existence to this early railway company. Crewe then became the focal point for other railways that were speedily laid across the surrounding flat, open farmland. A line from Chester was constructed in 1840, followed by one from Manchester in 1842, from Stoke-on-Trent in 1848 and a route from Shrewsbury in 1858.

The original GJR company did much for the town, building many houses and establishing a locomotive, carriage and wagon works. When amalgamation converted the GJR to the London North Western Railways, the LNWR continued the role of benevolent employer. The town was not only supplied with well-paved streets but was soon provided with gas and piped water. It is interesting to know that houses of different sizes were built for workers, depending on whether they were skilled or unskilled. One row was called 'Gaffers Row' because they were occupied by the foremen.

As the old parish church of Church Coppenhall was outside the town, the LNWR company built the new parish church of Christ Church with a school in 1843. The town's first library was donated by the LNWR in 1846. From 1860 the railway company transferred control of housing, public buildings and other amenities to the new local Board of Health.

Crewe became a borough in 1877. A fascinating point to remember is that in the beginning the GJR company wanted to site its station at nearby Nantwich. However, opposition from the canal companies prevailed on the town's dignitaries to reject the railway proposals.

In 1923, the amalgamation of the various railway companies led to the creation of the 'big four' – London, Midland and Scottish, London North Eastern, Great Western Railway and Southern Railway. Nationalisation followed in 1948, and now rail privatisation has promised an exciting future.

Crewe is no longer a one-company town dependent on railway patronage. Rolls Royce Aero Engines arrived in 1938. After the Second World War, Rolls Royce based its automobile engineering division at Crewe.

Queen's Park, in Victoria Avenue, was given to the town by the railway in celebration of Queen Victoria's Jubilee and the fiftieth anniversary of the Grand Junction Railway. There are 16 hectares (40 acres) of park in an oval plan, with a pool on the stream.

The **Clock Tower** was donated by employees of the LNWR company to commemorate Queen Victoria's Jubilee in 1887, and erected the following year. The heads contained in the finials above the triangular panels of the four-faced clock include Queen Victoria and three members of the board of the LNWR. There is also a memorial to Crewe railwaymen who served in the Boer War, with a model locomotive at its base.

In **The Railway Age Exhibition**, Vernon Way, one can step back in time to the bygone era of steam, with weekend rides on the centre's own running line. There are original signal boxes where visitors can enjoy the hands-on exhibits. There is an indoor children's corner and model railway displays.

The local football club, Crewe Alexandra, was founded in 1876 and is the oldest club in the Football League.

Crewe Hall lies 2 miles (3km) south-east of Crewe centre. In essence, it is a fine example of a Jacobean house, but it was extended in the late 18th century, modernised in 1837 and greatly remodelled after a fire in 1866. Generally, it has been regarded as Victorian.

The house was built for Sir Randulph Crewe between 1615 and 1639, with the estate being in the de Crewe family since the 13th century. Sir Randulph became Lord Chief Justice in 1625, but his appointment was short-lived. After the death of James I, the new sovereign dismissed him because he declined to confirm the legality of a certain loan.

The house underwent major changes in the 18th and 19th centuries with additions and improvements. The architects used were the local Nantwich men, George Latham and Edward Blore.

After the destruction by fire in 1866, the job of rebuilding (1866-70), was given to **E.M. Barry**, son of Sir Charles Barry, designer of the Houses of Parliament. The exterior of the main Jacobean block survives in its original state. A tower was added, and a central court was created with a **hammerbeam roof** lit from brightly coloured, stained-glass panels.

The original plain chapel, was decorated with stained glass, murals, bronze medallions of biblical characters, painting and stencilling – all splendidly Victorian. The Jacobean staircase was magnificently rebuilt by Barry and the supporting central posts carry heraldic beasts.

On the death of the 3rd Baron in 1894, the estate passed to his nephew, Lord Houghton, who, in 1931, offered the hall to Cheshire County Council. This offer was not accepted and the major part of the estate was sold to the Duchy of Lancaster. Since the end of the Second World War, the hall has been used for offices and from 1966 has been the headquarters of the Wellcome Foundation.

CROFT [Warrington]

SJ6493: 4 miles (6km) NNE of Warrington

Croft village, originally in Lancashire, is situated north of Warrington and close to junction 21 of the M6 and M62.

The settlement was not mentioned in Domesday. The name was 'Croft' in 1212, meaning 'the enclosure'. The Old English word 'croft' means a piece of enclosed land used for tillage or pasture.

In 1212 the lord of the manor was Gilbert de Croft. The present hall, which is situated on the road to Winwick, replaced the original building destroyed by fire in the 1930s.

Christ Church, in Lady Lane, is a Commissioners' church designed by Edward Blore. It was built in 1832-3 in red sandstone and cost £1457. The church has a south-west steeple and an imaginative spire. The building has lancet windows and a short chancel.

The Roman Catholic **church of St Lewis**, Little Town, was built in brick in 1826-7. The building has arched windows and a pedimented west porch. Inside the church, shallow piers or pilasters, are attached to the east wall.

CROWTON [Vale Royal]

SJ5874: 5 miles (8km) W of Northwich

Crowton is a scattered farming community south of the River Weaver; it lies on the B5153 Northwich to Kingsley road, which then continues on to Frodsham. The first settlement site was probably established in a forest clearing. Then as the boundaries of the forest were pushed back so the settlement pattern became more scattered.

Crowton is not listed in Domesday. The name was described as 'Crouton' in 1260. The first element suggests that it is Celtic in origin: the Welsh word 'cryw' meaning 'a ford'.

In the centre of the village are old stone houses dating from 1686, which later became almshouses. To the north, the **Dutton railway viaduct** crosses the Weaver Navigation. Irish labourers were brought to help in the construction and a number of white, terraced cottages were built to house them. The project was engineered by **George Stephenson** and supervised by **Joseph Locke**. The railway bridge was built in stone with twenty arches; it was 1400ft (427m) in length. The opening of the viaduct for the Grand Junction Railway took place on 4 July 1837.

Christ Church, designed by J.L. Pearson in late 13th-century style, was built in 1871. The building has no aisles but there is a north transept. A pleasing feature is the two-tier bellcot. The former vicarage is partly brick built and partly half-timbered. It is said that it was also designed by Pearson.

A fascinating local by-law still exists to prohibit people swimming in the River Weaver on a Sunday; it is an offence punishable by deportation to the Colonies!

CUDDINGTON and SANDIWAY [Vale Royal]

SJ5970: 4 miles (6km) W of Northwich

Cuddington and Sandiway once existed as separate villages and did not officially come together until 1935. Both settlements lie to the west of Northwich on the fringes of Delamere Forest and close to two important trunk roads, the A49 and the A556.

In Norman times, this area was part of the ancient forest of Mara and the rigid forest laws were particularly severe on inhabitants who transgressed.

During the time of Edward I, Sandiway was included in the lands he endowed to the Abbey of Vale Royal. He built this religious establishment in gratitude for his survival from shipwreck.

Cuddington was described as 'Cudinton' in 1278 and the name is derived from 'the tun of Cuda's people'.

There is a station serving the community on the Manchester to Chester railway line, which was opened in 1870. The old branch line to Winsford now forms a walking route through the countryside known as the Whitegate Way. The line, also opened in 1870, was built to serve the salt mining industry. It ran from Winsford to Cuddington, a distance of almost six miles. The passenger service closed in 1930, and all goods traffic ceased in 1963.

In 1970, the Cheshire County Council bought the trackbed and turned it into a footpath-cum-bridleway. There are toilet facilities, a car park and a picnic site by the former station at Whitegate.

Just north of Cuddington lies Delamere Park, the former site of Delamere House, the home of the Wilbrahams. The house was demolished in 1939 and the area used by the United States Army during the Second World War. The site is now a residential area with its own leisure facilities.

John Douglas, the well-known architect for the Grosvenor estates, was born in Sandiway. He became lord of the manor and paid for the site of the church, as well as contributing to the cost of the building.

The **church of St John the Evangelist** was designed by John Douglas and built between 1902 and 1903. The building has a west tower and has no aisles. The interior is in the Perpendicular style with an east window in the Decorated style. The chancel is higher than the nave. John Douglas also designed the cottages by the church.

Oakmere Hall was designed by Douglas and built for John Higson, a Liverpool merchant. This was at an earlier time in Douglas's career. The building has a date of 1867 inscribed in the massive tower, which lies on the east side of the house. On the south side of the building are two round angle turrets. The interior contains a great hall that rises up to a pitched roof. This is a dramatic space with a gallery.

CUERDLEY CROSS [Warrington]

SJ5486: 1 mile (1.6km) E of Widnes

Cuerdley Cross is a very small residential development between the eastern outskirts of Widnes and the western suburbs of Warrington.

Between the A562 and the River Mersey, immediately adjoining Cuerdley

Cross, is an extensive area of industrialisation. Here, a chemical works and the giant towers and buildings of the Fiddler's Ferry Power Station occupy the land.

CULCHETH [Warrington]

SJ6595: 5 miles (8km) NE of Warrington centre

Culcheth lies to the north-east of Warrington, astride the A574 road to Leigh. The settlement is still a village surrounded by farmland and working farms. In 1974, it finally became an integral part of Warrington, after periods of time with Leigh and then Golborne.

Just south of Culcheth lies the extensive site of the Risley Remand Centre. A little further south and to the east of Warrington is **Risley Moss**. Here is one of the last remaining areas of post-glacial mossland in the country. The Moss itself is all that remains of the raised bogs that once covered much of the Mersey Valley.

Newchurch parish church, which gave its name to part of Culcheth, began as a Tudor chapel of ease for Winwick church. A fire destroyed the old church in 1903.

The **church of Holy Trinity**, Newchurch was designed by Travers and Ramsden and built between 1904 and 5 in the neo-Norman style. The church contains a brass inscription to Elizabeth Egerton, died 1646.

DARESBURY [Hatton]

SJ5782: 4 miles (6km) SW of Warrington

The village of Daresbury lies between Warrington and Runcorn, just east of the Bridgewater Canal and south of the River Mersey. The village has now been by-passed and the old main road has become a quiet haven. A sprinkling of houses, some brick and some sandstone, make up the settlement, amidst surroundings of lush farmland.

Daresbury was the village where Charles Lutwidge Dodgson, alias Lewis Carroll, spent his childhood.

The **church of All Saints** was entirely rebuilt in the modern Perpendicular style in 1872, with the exception of the tower which dates from 1550. The sturdy tower has corner buttresses rising to battlements surmounted by a weathervane in the shape of a fish.

A rhyming set of rules for the bell ringers is common in most belfries but at Frodsham and Daresbury the lines form an acrostic of the place name.

Dare not to come into this Sacred Place
All you good Ringers, but in Awfull Grace
Ring not with Hatt nor Spurs nor Insolence
Each one that does, for every such offence
Shall forfeit Hatt or Spurs or Twelve Pence
But who disturbs a peal, the same offender
Unto the Box his Sixpence shall down Tender
Rules such no doubt in every church are Used
You and your Bells that may not be Abused

The church contains the under surface of the original screen and a beautifully carved Jacobean pulpit. Here the features include arches formed by angels between pillars carrying grotesque shapes. Some people believe this was the inspiration for Lewis Carroll's weird creatures.

A large octagonal font now stands outside the south door, and it was in this bowl that the infant son of the incumbent was baptised Charles Lutwidge Dodgson on 11 July 1832. His family left when he was eleven. The east window is his memorial and was erected for the centenary of his birth. At the foot of the window, displayed in five panes, are his characters, including the March Hare, the Dodo, the Knave of Hearts, the Cheshire Cat and the Queen of Hearts.

Lewis Carroll (1832-98), was the pseudonym of Charles Lutwidge

Dodgson. He was the author of the children's classics *Alice's Adventures in Wonderland* (1865) and its sequel, *Through the Looking Glass* (1872). In 1876 he wrote the mock-heroic narrative poem *The Hunting of the Snark*.

Dodgson lectured in mathematics at Oxford University from 1855 to 1881. Whilst he was there he told fantasy stories to Alice Liddle and her sisters, daughters of the Dean of Christ Church. He published a number of mathematical games and problems that required the use of logic. He also wrote mathematical textbooks for the general syllabus and several works on mathematical puzzles. Dodgson was one of the pioneers of portrait photography, which included many charming studies of young girls.

The **Ring o' Bells** was once a coaching inn and adjoining the building is the courtroom where the local sessions were formerly heard. This building and the adjacent barn have been converted into an exhibition centre illustrating the life and works of Lewis Carroll.

DARNHALL [Vale Royal]

SJ6363: 3 miles (5km) S of Winsford

The hamlet of Darnhall lies at the heart of pastoral Cheshire. It is a sequestered spot on the woodland banks of the Ash Brook and is approached by a byroad just south-west of Winsford. The community is situated close to the M6 motorway and is convenient for Manchester Airport, Warrington, Shropshire and North Wales.

The surrounding fields and pastures contain numerous ponds. A larger stretch of water, called The Lake, lies between Hall Wood and Mill Wood. Here the Ash Brook flows down to Darnhall Bridge and continues past larger tracts of woodland before joining the River Weaver.

Darnhall boasted a mill, dating back to 1829, which with its twin waterwheels was fully operational until 1970.

The settlement was described as 'Dernhal' in 1240 and 'Darnhale' in 1275. Its name means 'hidden halh', 'halh' being a quiet nook.

Darnhall was considered as the site for a Cistercian settlement but this proved unsuitable and an alternative was found four miles away. King Edward named this other location Vale Royal.

From the end of the 19th century, the final occupants of the hall were the Verdin family, owners of the largest salt mine in the area. The last occupant, Sir Richard Verdin, died in the 1970s.

DAVENHAM [Vale Royal]

SJ6571: 2 miles (3km) S of Northwich

Davenham is mentioned in the Domesday Survey as 'Deveneham' in Middlewich Hundred. Osmer, a free man, held it. There was land for two ploughs, in lordship one plough. There were two slaves, a priest with a church, one villager and one smallholder with half plough.

The settlement was described as 'Davenham' in 1278 and the name is derived from 'Ham and town on River Dane'.

Davenham is a large residential suburb of Northwich. It lies just south of the town, between the River Dane and the Weaver Navigation. The village is bisected by the A533 from Northwich to Middlewich.

Tradition tells that pagan Celts practised their rites here, and that later St Wilfred established a church at

Davenham during his journeys through Cheshire.

The **church of St Wilfred** is a large Victorian church, mainly as the result of gradual rebuilding between 1844 and 1870. The latter date refers to the chancel and transepts. The west tower with a recessed spire was built in 1850. In the 1841 reconstruction, the church was lengthened and the nave and aisles widened. The stained glass in the aisle west windows consists of large figures in bright colours.

Davenham Hall is a neoclassical late Georgian house built for Thomas Ravenscroft to replace the half-timbered Davenham Lodge. The entrance front is symmetrical with a wide porch of six Tuscan columns. The interiors contain fine plasterwork in the Wyatt style but the main feature is the central staircase hall lit from a dome. The staircase with a wrought-iron balustrade rises to the first floor landing. In 1980, the house was restored for use as a nursing home

DEAN ROW [Macclesfield]

SJ8781: 2 miles (3km) E of Wilmslow

Dean Row lies to the east of Wilmslow between the River Bollin and the River Dean, and straddles the main road to Poynton.

The first element, 'dean', is derived from the Old English 'denu' meaning 'valley', and the second element, means 'rough ground'

Various industries were established in this small community, including Dean Row smithy built in 1840. Local clay was dug for brick making and oak bark obtained from nearby estates was used in the tanning process. Raw material for handloom silk weaving was collected by women who walked to Macclesfield, and

then returned there with the finished articles!

Dean Row Chapel, 1693, was originally Presbyterian and later became Unitarian. It is said to be the oldest Nonconformist place of worship in Cheshire. It is a rectangular building with two tiers of mullioned windows. The two end bays have ground-level entrances, as well as stairs rising across the front to the upper galleries. The old chapel is now scheduled as a listed building.

DELAMERE [Vale Royal]

SJ5569: 10 miles (16km) E of Chester

Delamere is a scattered community on the edge of the Delamere Forest and a small huddle of houses constitutes the village. It lies on the B5152, Frodsham to Four-Lane Ends road at the foot of Eddisbury Hill. A station on the Chester to Northwich railway line serves the community.

The name of the settlement was described as 'Foresta de Mara' in 1248, and 'de la Mare' in 1249. The Old English word 'mere' means 'a lake'. 'Dela' is the French *de la*.

Eddisbury Hill is crowned with a large Iron Age hill fort, with well-preserved defences of ditches and banks on the east. Initially, the south-eastern section of the hill was defended with a single earthwork. Later, more substantial double ramparts were constructed and a new entrance was created at the far end of the camp. Eventually, the fort was destroyed, perhaps by the Romans, and the defences largely demolished. However, according to the Anglo-Saxon Chronicle, the fort was rebuilt in AD 914.

The Roman road from Chester to Northwich ran just below the hill fort, and its line is clearly visible across the fields to the west.

Delamere Forest was one of the three great medieval forests of Cheshire; it was, in the first instance, the twin forests of Mara and Mondrem. Although Saxon kings and earls had their hunting grounds, the reservation of great tracts of countryside for hunting game was a policy formulated by the Norman monarchs.

Archaeological investigations on a spur of Eddisbury Hill discovered the remains of drainage and buildings dating from the late Middle Ages. This evidence confirms it as the site for the Chamber of the Forest – a form of medieval headquarters for the administration of the forest.

The present area of Delamere Forest stretches north-westwards from Delamere Station, but considerable tracts of ground have been planted largely with conifers by the Forestry Commission. Nevertheless, those parts of the forest that have native oak and beech are particularly charming. For example, Hunger Hill, which is popular with visitors.

Of the forest meres, Hatchmere remains beside the B5152. Linmere has been drained, but a stretch of land alongside the railway line has been converted into the Linmere Picnic Area. Beyond this is the Forest Administration Centre and the **Forest Museum**. Near the A49 lies another forest pool, Oak Mere. There are the earthworks of an ancient settlement on its eastern side and a dug-out canoe has been recovered from the lake.

The **church of St Peter**, 1816-17, was designed by J. Gunnery and much altered in 1878. It has a west tower, transepts and stained glass in the east window by Kempe and Tower, 1906. Money was given by the Government for church building to celebrate the Battle of Waterloo. St Peter's Church was built on Crown land in a clearing in the forest.

The **Sandstone Trail**, a 30-mile (48km) walking route from Beacon Hill, Frodsham to Grindley Brook on the Shropshire border, passes through the forest just west of the Linmere Picnic Area.

DISLEY [Macclesfield]

SJ9784: 6 miles (10km) SE of Stockport

Disley is a residential area situated in the narrows of the Goyt Valley, between Black Hill and Lyme Park to the south and Mellor Moor to the north. It is a gateway to the High Peak of Derbyshire. Disley has a handsome little town centre with a classical fountain in Fountain Square. Richard Thomas Orford erected it in 1834, and the attractive work is protected by iron railings. The Hungry Horse Inn, formerly the Ram's Head, is an early Victorian Tudor hostelry with gables.

Disley is not mentioned in Domesday. The name of the settlement was described as 'Distislegh' in 1285 and 'Distelee' in 1288. Although the first element suggests a personal name, it may well be the Old English 'dystig' or 'dusty'.

Disley's growth and rebuilding began before the railway came, partly because of the Leghs of Lyme at whose park gates it stands. The first turnpiked route between Manchester and London passed through Disley from 1724. Before the 19th century, this part of the township was larger and faster growing than the original settlement of High Disley. The establishment of cotton spinning, weaving and printing stimulated house building and the opening of the village to commuters from Stockport and Manchester. The railway was opened from those large conurbations in 1857 and the other line on the north side of the valley from Marple to New Mills in 1865.

The **church of St Mary**, with a Perpendicular west tower, was built by Sir Piers Legh who died in 1527, before the building was completed. The present church is a rebuilding of 1824-35. It has windows of three lights with tracery, a low chancel, tall octagonal piers and three galleries. The fine 16th-century timber roof with its many bosses was preserved.

The stained glass in the east window is probably Dutch or mid-European. It represents scenes of the Passion and under one tableau is the name 'Steynfrit 1535'. In the other windows of the church are fragments of medieval glass.

The monuments in the church include one to George Barbor (died 1779) – a kneeling figure by an altar, and one to Thomas Legh (died 1857) by A. Gatley 'Rome 1858' – an angel with a trumpet on a sarcophagus.

In 1794 an Act was passed to authorise the construction of the **Peak Forest Canal** to link up the quarries at Doveholes with the Ashton-under-Lyme Canal into Manchester. Benjamin Outram was the engineer. By 1804, the upper and lower levels of the canal to Bugsworth and the tramway to Dove Holes were in use. A further branch was made to Whaley Bridge to link up with the Cromford and High Peak Railway in 1835.

Samuel Oldknow, a muslin manufacturer of Stockport, played an important part in promoting the Peak Forest Canal. The canal closely follows the River Goyt along the valley at Disley towards Marple. Here there is a wonderful series of sixteen locks and a superb aqueduct.

The northern tip of **Lyme Park** estate comes down to the valley at Disley. Sir Piers Legh, who married the daughter of Sir Thomas Danyers, came here in 1388. In the early 18th century, Peter Legh re-

built Lyme Park and an Italianate palace replaced the Elizabethan house. The architect was the famous Venetian **Leoni**. He completely rebuilt the south front with fifteen bays adorned with giant pilasters. He left the Elizabethan porch of four tiers and some of the **Elizabethan interiors**, even the long gallery. There are Elizabethan and Jacobean fireplaces with elaborate overmantles.

Some of the staterooms are adorned by **Mortlake tapestries, Grinling Gibbons woodcarvings** and an important collection of English clocks. In 1946, the third baron Newton gave the hall and park to the National Trust.

The Victorian garden contains Wyatt's famous conservatory and the great house is surrounded by a medieval **deer park** complete with hunting tower. Red and fallow deer can still be seen in the park.

Lyme Park appeared as **Pemberley** in the BBC's adaptation of the Jane Austen novel *Pride and Prejudice*.

On the eastern edge of Park Moor, south-east of Lyme Hall, are the **Bow Stones**. These two stone pillars, 3ft (0.9m) high, are possibly the remains of Anglo-Saxon crosses. This area was part of the royal forest and so it has been suggested that they were used for bending long bows in order to string them.

The **Gritstone Trail** is an 18-mile (29km) walk from Lyme Park to Rushton Spencer in Staffordshire. It is waymarked with a yellow footprint engraved with a letter 'G'. From Lyme Park the route climbs to the moors above Kettleshulme and climbs shapely Kerridge Hill. It passes through Tegg's Nose Country Park and across Croker Hill then makes a long descent into the Dane Valley to meet the 95-mile (152km) Staffordshire Way.

DITTON [Halton]

SJ4986: 1½ miles (2km) W of Widnes

Ditton is that part of Widnes that has spread westwards with residential and industrial development. West of the county boundary, there is a moderate area of farmland, before the dense conurbation appears that marks the eastern fringe of Liverpool.

The settlement, which was described as 'Ditton' in 1194, is derived from the Old English 'Dictun' meaning 'a tun by a dike or ditch'.

The railway bridge crossing the Runcorn Gap was officially opened on May 21 1868. Its foundations had to be rooted in solid rock some 45ft (13m) below the water level. The **viaduct** of 49 arches over Ditton Marsh was also opened in 1868.

The Roman Catrholic **church of St Michael**, was designed by Henry Clutton and built between 1876 and 9. This is a large church built in connection with the arrival in the area of a community of Jesuits expelled from Germany. The church is built of red brick, with a strong-looking west tower and a steep saddleback roof. There is a bell-stage of three lancets framed by shafts. There are lancet windows and several of the rose windows favoured by Clutton. There are slender columns and an arcade running from west to east with eight bays. The interior of the church is spacious and airy.

DODLESTON [Chester]

SJ3561: 4 miles (6km) SW of Chester

Dodleston, which looks across to the Welsh hills, lies to the west of the River Dee, and the parish protrudes right into the Principality. Evidence of the history of this border settlement is seen in the motte and bailey castle mound and the well-preserved defence earthworks. Within these defences stood Dodleston Old Hall, which was Colonel Brereton's headquarters during the siege of Chester.

The settlement is mentioned in Domesday as 'Dodestune', and woodland is recorded. It was described as 'Dodeliston' in 1205, and the name is derived from 'Duddel's tun'.

The sandstone **church of St Mary**, 1870, was rebuilt by the Grosvenor estate to the design of John Douglas. The base of the square tower remains from an earlier building and the tower carries a short spire. The church has a nave, chancel, a north aisle and a five-light east window. The interior contains several tablets and monuments and an octagonal stone font. Some of the stone from the old church was re-used in the new building.

The new Dodleston Hall lies to the north, a three-storey brick house and also a moated site. The hall was the residence of Thomas Egerton who became Lord Chancellor and was buried at Dodleston in 1599. His monument may be found in the church.

Dodleston is an Eaton estate village and there are many dwellings typical of those dating from the time of the first Duke of Westminster. In fact, many of the cottages have the date and a 'W' in the brickwork

DUDDON [Chester]

SJ5165: 2 miles (3km) SE of Tarvin

Duddon once stood on the boundary of Delamere Forest. It is a compact little village situated on the A51, with views north to the Willington Hills and south to Beeston and Peckforton Hills. The surroundings are mainly agricultural with farms and cottages, although two small housing estates have been established. The settlement was described as Duddon in 1288, and the name is derived from 'Dudda's dun'.

The **church of St Peter**, 1835, is a box-like building of brick construction, with a bellcot, lancet windows and no chapel.

Various cottages in the village have been modernised and extended and the dwelling next to the school was the community's first inn. The present hostelry, the Headless Woman, is said to be haunted. It derives its name from the legend of a servant beheaded by Parliamentarian troopers for refusing to reveal the hiding place of her mistress's jewellery.

Duddon Old Hall is a black and white building. A fine gable projection has splendid black and white decoration with concave-sided lozenges.

The site of Duddon Mill is at the farm along Mill Lane.

DUNHAM-ON-THE-HILL [Chester]

SJ4673: 6 miles (9km) NE of Chester

Dunham is mentioned in Domesday as 'Doneham' in Roelau Hundred. Aescwulf held it, jointly, as a free man. There is land for nine ploughs, seven villagers, a smith and three smallholders. Domesday records meadowland and woodland.

The settlement is described as 'Dunham' in 1302 and the name is derived from 'ham on a dun or hill'. Early landowners were the fitz Allans, who later became the Earls of Arundel.

Dunham is a small linear village just off the A56, south-west of Helsby and surrounded by extensive farmland. The main street cuts through the sandstone rock and

many of the older houses contain cellars hewn out of the same bedrock.

The **church of St Luke** was designed by James Harrison and built in 1860-1 in the early 14th-century style. The building consists of a nave and chancel. It is rock-faced and has a bellcot. The church possesses the fine cross from over the choir screen of Chester Cathedral. This is Victorian in its detail and thick relief and was transferred from the cathedral in 1921.

DUTTON [Vale Royal]

SJ5779: 3 miles (5km) SE of Runcorn

Dutton was mentioned in Domesday as 'Duntune' in Tunendune Hundred. Odard held Dutton from the Earl. There was land for one plough, with one rider and one slave. Domesday records a large tract of woodland and a hawk's eyrie. The settlement is described as 'Dutton' in 1288, which is derived from 'Dudda's tun'.

Dutton is a tiny hamlet with scattered dwellings on the south-eastern outskirts of Runcorn. The settlement lies close to the main West Coast railway line and the Trent and Mersey Canal. The surroundings consist of farmland.

The Dutton Viaduct was engineered by George Stephenson and supervised by Joseph Locke. It was built in stone with twenty arches and opened in 1837 for the Grand Junction Railway.

EATON [Congleton]

SJ8765: 2 miles (3km) N of Congleton

The village contains a mixture of modern dwellings and older cottages and houses. It is situated just north of Congleton on the A536 Macclesfield road. The immediate surroundings consist of good agricultural land dotted with copses of woodland. The village adjoins the valley of the River Dane.

Christ Church was designed by Raffles Brown and built between 1856 and 8. The building has a west tower, nave and chancel. There is some attempt at Decorated tracery.

A Quaker burial ground remains, but there is no meeting house.

Eaton Hall was designed by Lewis Wyatt. It is a very large building in brick in the Jacobean style with decorated gables. The stables are dated 1831.

EATON-BY-TARPORLEY [Vale Royal]

SJ5763: 2 miles (3km) NE of Tarporley

This small village is situated in central Cheshire. It occupies a sheltered position on a spur of the sandstone ridge that runs through the county from north to south. In geological terms, Keuper sandstone underlies the area and the rocks associated with the Permo-Triassic period yield abundant flows of water. Lanes and roads lead out of Eaton like the spokes of a wheel. Lightfoot Lane is one of the oldest routes, an ancient track leading from the village to the fields and higher pastures.

Steeper Lane, from the Old English 'steap' meaning a steep place, heads northwards to the supposed site of a windmill on Luddington Hill. From here there are wide-reaching views to the south Pennines and Mow Cop; across the Cheshire Plain to Beeston Castle, Peckforton and Bickerton; to Delamere Forest and Vale Royal country and to the recognisable landmarks of the spire of Over Church and the Jodrell Bank telescopes.

Eaton-by-Tarporley is a small village where traditional black and white,

thatched cottages nestle side by side with modern dwellings. Until about 1950, Eaton had 20 thatched buildings and today about a third of that number remain. The older houses, whether black and white, stone or brick-built, have sandstone foundation courses. The timber-framed black and white dwellings are Oak Tree Farm, Well House Farm, Church Cottage and Hunters Close. Bay Tree Cottage is the only surviving 'long house'. This type of dwelling, often found in the Pennine dales, housed humans and animals under one roof, with a cross passage division running the width of the house.

Eaton is not mentioned in Domesday but the village lies in the civil parish of Rushton, which is recorded as 'Rusitone'. Chipping held it and the lands were owned by Earl Hugh Lupus. Some ploughland is listed. Eaton was described as 'Ayton' and 'Eyton' in 1304, and its name means 'a tun or homestead by a spring or stream'.

In the summer of 1980 a dig was carried out on Eaton Cottage land. The excavations resulted in the uncovering of a section of Roman wall and part of a hypocaust. Another interesting discovery was a medieval kiln built with stones taken from the Roman wall. Evidence from a further excavation in 1981 suggested the presence of a Roman villa here.

Delamere Forest formerly consisted of two forests: Mara and Mondrum. Mara stretched from the Mersey to the south end of what is now Delamere parish, while Mondrum extended practically to Nantwich. In Norman times it was a royal hunting ground for the Earls of Chester, who pursued wild game across an extensive area of native woodland, heath and rough pasture.

Since Eaton was within the forest

boundary, the villagers would have been very familiar with the harsh forest laws. The forest dwellers had their rights, for example the right of pannage (food for swine, acorns, beech mast). The right of pannage was subject to a payment in kind. Seventeen pigs were claimed annually by the Earl from the villages on the forest confines.

There is an interesting local story of the Civil War. According to an account by Nathaniel Lancaster, rector of Tarporley 1638-1661, 'The Royalist forces made a sortie from Chester, capturing Captain Glegg and his troops and were marching towards Beeston when the Tarvin garrison attacked, rescued the prisoners and chased the Royalists in Eaton, Rushton and about the Forest.'

The **church of St Thomas** is built of brick with stone facings and comprises a nave and chancel, a small vestry and a porch. A foundation stone containing a parish magazine, coins and a newspaper of the day was laid on 18 December 1895. The opening and dedication of the church by the Bishop of Chester took place on 26 May 1896.

A baptistry was built and the vestry enlarged in 1936 by the Honourable Marshall Brooks of Portal, who also gave the font cover, the pulpit, new choir stalls and the finely carved and richly coloured reredos in memory of his wife, Florence Brooks. The lectern came from Tarporley church and the bell turret was erected in 1930.

The Wesleyan Chapel was erected in 1840. It closed in the mid-1960s and was converted to residential use in 1977, retaining some of the original external features.

Arderne Hall was erected in 1867 in the Neo-Gothic style. It was a handsome mansion of brick with stone dressings and became the Cheshire home of the Earl and Countess of Haddington. The house was demolished in 1959 and a modern hall built in the late 1960s and early 1970s. The North Lodge and Royal Lodge are still in existence.

ECCLESTON [Chester]

SJ4062: 2 miles (3km) S of Chester

Eccleston is a notable and attractive Eaton estate village situated on the west bank of the River Dee. It stands on the line of the Roman road, Watling Street (West) from Chester to Wroxeter. The houses of brick and stone blend well with the village's Tudor-type cottages. There is an imposing château-like building called The Paddocks, 1883, which was designed by John Douglas and built for the estate agent. In the middle of the village stands a stone shelter, the 1874 pumphouse, with a tiled roof, which was also designed by John Douglas.

This section of the River Dee was once a favourite excursion for Edwardian boating parties. An attractively sited ferry cottage on the opposite side of the river is a reminder of the time when a ferry crossed the river at this point.

The settlement was mentioned in Domesday as 'Eclestone', and ploughland, a meadow, and a boat and net are recorded. It was described as 'Eccleston' in 1285. The first element of the name is probably derived from 'ecles' or 'church'. In Old Welsh the element is 'eccluys', in Welsh 'eglwys'.

A broad avenue of lime trees leads one through a spacious churchyard to the **church of St Mary**. The fine set of early 18th-century wrought-iron gates by the Davies Brothers of Bersham, originally stood at Emral Hall, Flintshire. At the south-west corner of the churchyard is a brick and stone cottage, 1870, by John

Douglas. In the north-east part of the churchyard is a fragment of the former church, which was rebuilt in 1809-13.

The present church, designed by G.F. Bodley, was rebuilt in 1899 at the expense of the 1st Duke of Westminster. The Duke died in the year that the church was built. This fine building is in the 14th-century style with Decorated tracery. The large, square, battlemented tower has two bell openings, and an irregular arrangement of buttresses. The north and south walls of the church rise to a level with the high clerestory. The splendid, unified interior has black and white marble paving, rib vaulting and abundant furnishings – screens, reredoses, carved bench ends and stained glass.

The approach to Eaton Hall from the north begins just south of the Dee in Chester, and crosses the byroad to Eccleston village by means of a narrow stone bridge.

ELLESMERE PORT [Ellesmere Port]

SJ4076: 6 miles (10km) N of Chester

The Ellesmere Canal Company were authorised by an Act of Parliament of 1793 to build a canal from the Mersey to the Severn. The canal started at Netherpool (subsequently called Ellesmere Port) and crossed the Wirral peninsula to join the Chester Canal at Northgate Locks. The date of the birth of Ellesmere Port is known exactly as the 1 July 1795, when the **Ellesmere Canal** opened for business.

The locks at Ellesmere Port did not come into use until 1796. William Jessop was the engineer, assisted by Thomas Telford. A tidal basin was created at the Mersey end by Telford and completed in 1801.

A popular passenger packet service was established between Liverpool and Chester. There were taverns along the route for accommodation and food, stables for horses and refreshments such as wine, ale, porter and cider.

By 1815, the first steam packet was seen on the Mersey. In 1816 Telford was instructed by the Canal Company to purchase a **steam packet boat** for the Mersey crossing in order to compete with the other Mersey ferries. The boat was 90ft (27m) long, 31ft (9m) wide and had a 32 horse-power engine. It was furnished with a principal cabin and a private apartment for ladies.

Telford laid out an estate in 1830 and began to build warehouses. A great increase in the trade of Ellesmere Port came with the Birmingham and Liverpool junction canal in 1835. After Telford's death on 2 September 1834, William Cubbit built the sea lock and a new dock (1839-40). The place was turned from a simple canal terminus into a port. The coming of the railway in 1863 had little effect on the volume of trade handled by the port. However, what did affect the port was the cutting of the **Manchester Ship Canal**.

After two unsuccessful attempts, the bill authorising the canal was passed in 1885. Construction of the canal began in November 1887. In July 1891, the really big job was to close the river channel to Ellesmere Port and remove the dam. Until these works were completed, the section to Ince could not be opened, nor could vessels use the ship canal to Ellesmere Port. Over a weekend the gap was filled in but the material was washed away by the tide. Using heavy boulders, clay and piling, the gap was once more filled in and again the tide washed the bank away. A third attempt was made and this time succeeded after thirty hours of non-stop effort. The embankment held and has done ever since.

Nearby **Stanlow** is the heart of the petro-chemical refinery. Stanlow itself is an island in the Mersey cut off from the mainland by the ship canal. Before oil came this was a bleak place surrounded by barren marsh. Small wonder that the Cistercian monks founded an abbey here in 1178. However, floods and gales made life impossible for the monks as the abbey was almost destroyed in 1279. The great tower fell in 1287 and in 1289 a fire destroyed most of the buildings. After these catastrophes, all but four of the monks moved to Whalley Abbey in Lancashire. Today, only a few stones and foundations remain.

The decline in the Ellesmere canal's trade coincided with the coming of oil refining and this has developed eastwards along the banks of the Mersey. The oil docks handle millions of tons of oil products each year. Miles of pipeline connect oil tankers to the refinery complex. There are no cars and smoking is forbidden. The refinery has its own ferry service, fire brigade and police force. Nevertheless, this seemingly sterile environment is a sanctuary for wildlife – a favourite resting place for a great variety of birds.

The British Petroleum Company and the Shell-Mex company first established ocean terminals at Stanlow in 1922, after the Manchester Ship Canal had excavated the first oil dock at Stanlow Point. Initially, there was only the blending of products, but in 1924 Shell-Mex (the name came from the original Shell oilfields in Mexico) began to refine oil at Stanlow and added plant for the manufacture of bitumen.

There was expansion of the Shell refineries with the advent of the Second World War. More storage tanks were built and the Gowy marshes were drained for new

construction work. In 1946 a chemical plant was built to produce solvents, which are by-products of the refining process.

In 1960 Shell's interests covered 720 hectares (1800 acres, 7.2 sq km) and were 2.5 miles (4km) long from end to end. There were hundreds of storage tanks capable of holding more than one million tons of oil at any one time.

Vauxhall Motors opened in 1961. The factory was extended after 1963. It produced the small car, the Viva almost in its entirety (body, engine, transmission and paintwork). Bowaters Pulp and Paper Mills (1930) were built on the site and on land of Poole Hall, a former 16th-century manor house which was demolished. Other industries associated with the borough are galvanising, creosoting, propane gas manufacture and dyestuffs.

The town's **modern centre** is the former hamlet of Whitby, where there is a 20th-century range of buildings. These include the Civic Hall (1954), shopping precinct (1958), central library (1962) and the Municipal Offices (1968-9).

The original port site has been turned into a fascinating boat museum. From here there are fine views of the Manchester Ship Canal and the Mersey, as it sweeps round to Runcorn. In the distance the huge, arched road bridge is clearly visible as well as the higher land behind Helsby and Frodsham.

There was a royal day in the history of the town on 7 May 1955 when HRH the Duchess of Kent opened the Civic Hall and presented to Ellesmere Port the Royal Charter of Incorporation as a Municipal Borough.

Christ Church was built when the original became too small. In 1867 the vicar began to raise funds for the project. The Marquess of Westminster promised a thousand pounds if the parishioners could raise a similar sum. The Canal Company gave one hundred pounds, and eventually enough money was raised and the building was completed in 1869 at a cost of £2900. The church is described as being after the Early Decorated style of architecture. It has a nave and chancel, and a striking arrangement of the south tower with a gabled transept and gabled vestry. The nave was later extended to the west.

Whitby Primitive Methodist Chapel and schoolrooms were built in Whitby Road in 1873, the Canal Company giving twenty five pounds towards the cost.

The **Boat Museum** at Ellesmere Port portrays the life of the boatmen and women that lived and worked on the canal boats. The exhibits show aspects of canal and river activities earlier this century when Ellesmere Port was a great dock complex bustling with activity. One is able to appreciate the great variety of cargoes that were transferred to and from coastal craft and boats of the inland waterways. Some of the former buildings have gone, such as the famous Winged Warehouse (1835) designed by Thomas Telford, which was destroyed by fire in 1970. However, many of the buildings from that time have been preserved; such as the Island Warehouse, Pump House and Power Hall, Georgian Houses, Lighthouse, Iron Shed, Toll House and Pattern Shop. The site now houses an Archive and Resource Centre and a Conference Centre.

The museum has a unique floating collection of traditional canal craft. The collection ranges from small coracles through pleasure, maintenance and narrow boats; to mine boats, barges, tugs, ice-breakers and larger craft such as the Daniel Adamson and the Basuto, a Clyde Puffer built in 1902. The museum is situated adjacent to junction 9 of the M53.

The **Blue Planet Aquarium** offers a wonderful range of aquatic environments under one roof. There are a number of themed areas and displays of interactive exhibits. One is able to take an exhilarating journey on an aquatic safari by travelling on a moving walkway through a long underwater tunnel. The Blue Planet Aquarium is accessible from junction 10 of the M53 and then by following the signs.

ELTON [Chester]
SJ4575: 3 miles (5km) E of Ellesmere Port

Elton is situated between Ince and Thornton-le-Moors and just south of the Mersey estuary and the Manchester Ship Canal. The settlement is recorded in Domesday as 'Eltone', and was described as 'Elton' in 1281. Its name is probably derived from 'Ella's tun'.

This small isolated community grew rapidly with the coming of the giant Shell complex and power station. This attracted people, houses and shops to become a sizeable community. In time, money was raised to build a community centre.

The surrounding view presents an impressive skyline of the huge cooling towers of the electricity generating station, and the tall chimneys of the oil refinery illuminated by a constantly flaring flame. But, despite this industrial background, one may still notice a village house inscribed 'JWM 1705'.

ELWORTH [Congleton]
SJ7461: 1½ miles (2km) WNW of Sandbach

Elworth is a large residential area on the western outskirts of Sandbach. It lies on the A533 road to Middlewich, and is also connected by rail, being on the main line from Crewe to Manchester. The station is referred to as Sandbach station. The Trent and Mersey Canal passes close to the western fringe of Elworth. Also in the same area are the flashes, which formed because of subsidence due to wild brine pumping.

Elworth grew in size when George Hancock began to manufacture agricultural machinery. Edwin Foden joined the firm and ultimately gained control to give it the name of Foden's Motor Works.

The Elworth Silver Band was reformed and became the famous **Foden Motor Works Band**. Their conductors, Fred, Harry and Rex Mortimer became household names. After the collapse of Foden's the sponsorship of the band passed to the Britannia Building Society. The motor works was taken over by an American company who streamlined production, buildings and the workforce.

The **church of St Peter** was designed by John Matthews and built between 1845 and 6. This is a Commissioners' church. It is rock-faced and has a nave, chancel and a bellcot, together with lancet windows.

The small settlement of Ettiley Heath is situated on the southern outskirts of Elworth, close to the Trent and Mersey Canal. Nearby is Elton Flash, a nature reserve. Another nature reserve may be found adjoining the River Wheelock to the south-west of Ettiley Heath.

FARNDON [Chester]

SJ4154: 5 miles (8km) NE of Wrexham

Farndon is mentioned in Domesday as 'Ferentone'. Earl Edwin held the settlement and lands were owned by Bigot de Loges. The survey records ploughland, a

mill, meadowland and a fishery. The name was recorded as 'Farendun' in 1195 and is derived from the Old English 'fearn-dun' or a 'fern-clad dun'. A dun is a fortified hill.

Farndon is an important crossing point of the River Dee; it stands in an elevated position and looks westwards across the river to the Welsh village of Holt. The old sandstone bridge of 1345 is now relieved of much of its heavy traffic by the modern bridge over the river south of Farndon. The **medieval bridge**, which originally had a gatehouse on the Welsh end, has nine segmented arches, five over the water. It also has angular projections on both sides.

A **legend** has grown up of two young Welsh princes who were thrown over the bridge and drowned. It is said that their ghosts can be seen and their screams heard on certain occasions. From the river, Farndon and Holt are splendid sights, each with a medieval church taking the skyline.

During the **Civil War**, a battle broke out here on 9 November 1643 when Sir William Brereton appeared with two thousand Parliamentarian soldiers. The Welsh defenders in the gatehouse were outflanked by sections of Brereton's troops who crossed the river lower down. The bridge was taken and within days the towns of Wrexham and Hawarden were captured.

The **church of St Chad** was occupied for a considerable time by Parliamentarian troops. Whoever were the despoilers, Welsh or English, the church was so badly damaged that almost all of it had to be rebuilt.

The lower sections of the tower were medieval. The round piers and the clerestory mullioned windows are of 1658, and the aisle windows are most probably Victorian. There is a fascinating **window**

The medieval bridge at Farndon

of historical interest in the Barnston Chapel. It depicts a number of Royalist Cheshire gentry, including Sir Richard Grosvenor, Sir William Mainwaring, Sir Francis Gamull, Thomas Berrington and William Barnston. They are placed round a central panel that illustrates a **collection of weapons**, equipment and clothing at the time of the Civil War.

In the nave there is a recumbent sandstone **effigy** of a knight, not cross-legged, c1340 to 1350. Farndon is another church where **rush-bearing** is observed, this time on the first Sunday after the 12 July. The whole weekend is one of celebrations and special events.

The **Barnston Monument** is an obelisk that stands on the edge of the village on the Chester road. It commemorates Major Roger Barnston who fought in the Crimea War and lost his life during the Indian Mutiny. He had previously led his regiment to the relief of Lucknow. The monument was erected in 1858; it is of a rather slim design and stands on four lions.

John Speed, one of England's greatest mapmakers, was born in Farndon in 1552. He became a tailor and was admitted to the Freedom of the Merchant Taylor's Company in 1580. He prospered and in his leisure took a keen interest in antiquities and historical research. He produced the best known, the most appealing and most popular of all the **early maps**.

He introduced entirely new features into his cartography, including plans of principal towns and views of important buildings. He also inserted into the corners of each map, coats-of-arms of the leading families and college arms. He included illustrations of the inhabitants in contemporary costumes in the borders of the general maps of the kingdom.

He worked in London, was father of 18 children and died in 1629. He is buried in St Giles, Cripplegate, London.

FRODSHAM [Vale Royal]

SJ5177: 8 miles (12km) NE of Chester

Frodsham nestles under the bluff of
Overton Hill, which is an outstanding
sandstone hill rising to 365ft (111m).
From the summit there are panoramic
views overlooking the town, across the
Mersey estuary and sweeping round to
the Welsh hills. Frodsham lies a short distance to the south of Runcorn, just above
the west bank of the River Weaver and its
confluence with the Mersey.

Below Frodsham there is a stretch of
land, built up on river gravels and alluvial
sands, across Frodsham marshes to the
line of the Ship Canal. This is separated
from the mudbanks of the Mersey estuary
by a finger of marshy land called
Frodsham Score.

In medieval times Frodsham was a
busy port collecting salt from the
Cheshire wickes and exporting it by river
to Liverpool and beyond. Cheese was
stored in a warehouse on the riverbank
before being loaded on boats. Most of the
vessels were sailing flats and barges that
were used on the River Weaver. In the
early 1700s a small shipbuilding and repair yard was established on the riverbank.

In the course of time the nearby
marshes were reclaimed, the River
Weaver was canalised becoming navigable for some distance inland, and the
Manchester Ship Canal was constructed.
The River Weaver at Frodsham is a major
river with fairly large locks and sluices,
and connects directly with the Ship Canal.

The settlement was listed in Domesday
as 'Frotesham' in Roelau Hundred. The
lands were owned by Earl Hugh but formerly by Earl Edwin. Frodsham was one
of the principal manors of Edwin, the last
Saxon Earl of Mercia. Domesday records

land for nine ploughs, with eight villagers and three smallholders with two
ploughs. A priest and a church are mentioned, together with a winter mill, two
and a half fisheries, meadowland, woodland and enclosures. Half a salthouse in
Wich serves the manor.

The village was described as
'Frodesham' in 1100, which derived
from the personal name 'Frod's ham' or
the settlement of Frod. In later times the
inhabitants of Frodsham strove to drain
part of the marshes and keep them from
flooding by means of dykes and a sluice.

Coming from an easterly direction, the
A56 crosses the River Weaver by a
three-arch brick bridge. This present
structure is one of many crossings going
back to a wooden bridge in the Middle
Ages. Below the road bridge, the
Warrington to Chester railway line,
opened in 1850, crosses the Weaver valley by a long **viaduct** of twenty-one
stone arches. Two large iron bridges
span the river itself.

Within the last few years, a third important route has had to cross the river
further downstream. The M56, supported on concrete stilts, strides over the
river and travels through the area of the
Frodsham and Helsby marshes on lands
only drained in comparatively recent
times.

In Frodsham the chief thoroughfare,
Main Street, runs north of the railway. It
is a wide street with tree-lined pavements, from which small lanes ascend
the sandstone hillside. One notable
building in Main Street is the old sandstone inn, the Bear's Paw (1632), with
mullioned and transomed windows. Although restored between 1903 and 4, the
hostelry, with its gables, archway and
courtyard, still gives a very good impression of an old coaching inn. The inn sign,
a bear's paw, was the crest of Earl Rivers

of the Savage family, who were the lords of the manor of Frodsham.

Also in Main Street there are a number of 17th-century timber-framed cottages. The oldest surviving cottages stand on The Rock, on the original route through the village. A number of Georgian houses remain unaltered and in fine condition. Each Thursday a market is held in Main Street, with its charter dating back to the beginning of the 12th century.

A little above the village is **Castle Park**, which is now a large park and attractive gardens. This is the site of the Norman castle, which from the 14th century was used as the local gaol. The castle was burnt down in 1654 and the present house, Park Place, built on the site. This large Georgian house contains the offices of the Vale Royal District Council.

The ancient parish **church of St Lawrence** stands on high ground overlooking the town and is built of local red sandstone. A church was recorded here in Domesday before 1086, and in 1093 Earl Hugh Lupus gave the tithes to the abbot of St Werburgh's, Chester.

The original plan of the Norman church consisted of nave, chancel and side aisles. Portions remain of the late 12th-century church, particularly in the nave. The nave is divided from the side aisles by arcades of three arches, of which two on each side are Norman.

In the 14th century the aisles were rebuilt, the tower with fine gargoyles was built, and the chancel was lengthened. The fine **Norman columns** rise from good square bases and the clerestory is also 12th century. The chancel arch is 14th century and on either side of the chancel are two broad 14th-century arches rising from octagonal piers, largely rebuilt in 1880.

The south aisle was rebuilt at the beginning of the 18th century and also towards the end of the 19th century. In the interior of the south wall of the tower are preserved a fine fragment of a **Saxon carving** and other carved stones of a later date. At the time of the 1880 restoration, the whole church, except the north chapel, had plaster ceilings. The plaster was removed and it was found necessary to replace all the wood underneath. At the same time the pitch of the nave roof was heightened.

In the north chapel is a good late **17th-century reredos**; it consists of five panels divided by Corinthian columns surmounted by a carved frieze. The communion rail in the chancel is from around 1700 and has twisted balusters. There is also a fine **three-tier brass chandelier** (1805). The well-preserved Georgian Royal coat of arms is mounted in a gilt frame.

A curious memorial tablet in the south aisle states: 'Near this place lies the body of Peter Banner, carpenter, of Frodsham, who died of dropsy, October 21st 1749, aged 50. In 33 weeks he was tapped 58 times and had 1032 quarts of water taken from him.'

Another oddity is a rhyming set of rules for the bell ringers. As at Daresbury, the lines form an acrostic of the place name:

'From faults observe you ringers well,
Ring true and don't o'erturn your bell;
On each default by him that's made,
Down sixpence surely shall be paid;
Swear not in this most sacred place,
Here come not but with aweful grace.
And who e'er rings with spur or hat,
Must sixpence pay or forfiet that.
Edward Moss,
Samuel Bircwood, Wardens, 1776'

Frodsham has had its fair share of characterful incumbents, such as **William Cotton**, vicar of St Lawrence from 1857-79. He was an authority on honey bees, having introduced them to New

Zealand while serving there as a chaplain. His constant travelling companion was a parrot called Papagay. He also had a Maori welcome inscribed on his vicarage doorstep. In his memory there is a carving of a bee in the church.

There are two **Iron Age hill forts** situated just over a mile south of Frodsham. South-south-west is a roughly rectangular hill fort enclosing an area of approximately 1.5 hectares (3¾ acres). A single earthen bank is best preserved on the east side, where it is 5ft (1.5m) high and 35ft (10.5m) wide. On the west side the defences seem to consist of disjointed lengths of low bank and it appears that the fort was never finished.

To the south-east lies a small univallate hill fort (single earthwork and external ditch), enclosing an area of half a hectare (1¼ acres). The defences are best preserved on the south and east. The northern flank appears to have been protected by the steeply sloping bank of a stream.

The **Sandstone Trail** follows the backbone of a range of meandering sandstone hills, the mid-Cheshire Ridge, for a distance of 30 miles (48km) from Beacon Hill, Frodsham, south to Grindley Brook locks on the Shropshire border.

As the route descends from the Beacon Hill car park, a panoramic view unfolds showing contrasting views of the county. Ahead lies the sharp profile of Helsby Hill; to the south is rich, wooded countryside; and north along the Mersey are the domes and cylinders of the Stanlow petro-chemical complex alongside the Manchester Ship Canal.

GAWSWORTH [Macclesfield]

SJ8869: 3 miles (5km) SW of Macclesfield

The village is situated on the eastern edge of the Cheshire Plain, with views to the hills of the south Pennines. It is a peaceful and beautiful place and regarded as one of the loveliest sights in Cheshire. The scattered cottages and farms merge with the grandeur of the halls, church, pools and leafy lanes.

The settlement was listed in Domesday as 'Govesurde'. Bernwulf held it and the lands were owned by Earl Hugh. The survey records extensive woodland and two enclosures for oxen. In 1276 the name was 'Gousewrdth' and 'Gowesworth' in 1287. The first element could well be Welsh from the word 'gof' – 'a smith'. This Welsh word is the source of the family name Gough.

Gawsworth Old Hall is a classic black and white timber-framed house and has been the seat of the lords of the manor since Norman times. Largely of the 15th century, it is a wonderful sight when seen across the pool. Inside it is beautifully furnished, and still very much a family home. At one time the building consisted of three to four ranges but now there are two and a small section.

The east range has diagonal bracing and clover-leaf decorations, and the south range has a frieze of patterned timber work. On the north front is the Fitton coat of arms, carved in 1570, including the carver's name. The Fyttons or Fittons were the ancient lords of the manor of Gawsworth. They became nationally important through the services they rendered and the lands they acquired in Ireland.

During the summer months, there is a programme of music and drama, with the old house providing a splendid backcloth to these events.

The Old Rectory is also an impressive timber-framed house of the late 15th century and retains a timbered hall that is still open to the roof.

Gawsworth New Hall is a large and stately Georgian residence that looks out across the pool towards the Old Hall. It was built by Lord Mohun, who fought a famous duel with the Duke of Hamilton over a dispute about the property. This took place in 1712 and both men were killed.

The **church of St James** , built of red and yellow sandstone, dates from the 15th and 16th centuries. The building is unusual in that it has no aisles and a very wide nave, which is not separated from the chancel. The furniture includes a large octagonal font and the stained glass contains many 15th-century fragments. The church suffered heavily from severe restoration in 1851.

There are four monuments to the Fitton family, including one of Dame Alice Fitton (1627) as a seated figure with her children kneeling in front and behind her. Her daughter, Mary Fitton, is famed in history as the Maid of Honour to Queen Elizabeth, and possibly the Dark Lady of Shakespeare's sonnets. There is no evidence that the bard ever met Mary, and historical evidence only records her affair with the Earl of Pembroke.

The tomb of Maggoty Johnson or 'Lord Flame', 1773, lies in a small wood north of the church. He was one of the last paid court jesters in England and lived at the Old Hall until his death.

GINCLOUGH [Macclesfield]

SJ9576: 3 miles (5km) NE of Macclesfield

Ginclough is situated on the A5002, Macclesfield to Whaley Bridge road. It is set in fine scenery amongst the rolling hill country of east Cheshire and on the edge of the Peak District National Park.

It is not mentioned in Domesday. Ginclough is supposed to get its name from the time when all the surrounding area was called the Forest of Macclesfield. Wild animals were driven into the narrow valleys called cloughs where they could be easily trapped. They included animals such as deer, foxes, badgers and polecats.

The hamlet of Ginclough and the neighbouring village of Rainow, strung out along the turnpike road, were largely built during the 17th, 18th and early 19th centuries. During this period of industrialisation, when local coal, wood and stone were much in demand, many water-powered cotton mills were built on the River Dean and its tributaries within the township. There is much evidence of old roads, bridleways and stone-flagged causeways in the area today.

Ginclough Mill still stands across the clough, below the sharp bend on the road beyond Washpool Cottages. The factory must have been one of the smallest cotton mills in the vicinity when it was originally built in 1794. It measured only 30ft (9m) long and 23ft (7m) wide. A change in the stonework indicates an extension built around 1824, when the mill was converted to silk throwing. James Sharpley worked the mill, and it is said that the silk was carried to and from Macclesfield by means of a donkey with panniers on each side. The waterwheel originally stood at the north end of the building. The boilerhouse and chimney, which were situated at the road end of the mill, were added in the 1850s or 1860s.

Ginclough was a busy place in the 19th century. There were cottages, stables, a smithy and, before 1822, an inn. Old maps of the area show quarries, coal pits, moorland and mills. Industrial activity diminished later in the 19th century, although stone is still quarried. The Ginclough Mill became a sawmill and is now a private residence.

A little way to the south-east, lying in a sequestered hollow in the upper reaches of the River Dean, is the **Lamaload Reservoir**. A network of footpaths in the locality makes this a fine walking area. A narrow, hilly road leaves the A5470 just above Ginclough and swings south to reach the **memorial stone** of John Turner of nearby Saltersford Hall. He ran a team of packhorses and on Christmas Eve 1735 was returning home from Bollington when he was caught in a snowstorm.

The stone is inscribed on both sides and the south-facing side reads:

'Here John Tur
ner was cast
away in a heavy
snowstorm in
the night in or
about the year
1755'

The discrepancy in the date is accounted for by the fact that the stone is said to be the third one marking the spot. James Mellor of Hough Hole House, Rainow erected the original. It would seem that the inscription must have been incorrectly copied when a replacement was carved. The difference in the date and the inscription carved on the north-facing side of the stone make one wonder about an unsolved mystery.

'The print of a
woman's shoe was
found by his side
in the snow were
he lay dead
H'

The road continues to Lamaload Reservoir. Here, facilities for visitors include a car park, toilets and a picnic site.

GLAZEBURY [Warrington]

SJ6797: 6 miles (10km) NE of Warrington

Glazebury is a mainly residential development situated on the western bank of the Glaze Brook. It lies between Culcheth and Leigh in Greater Manchester and is a 19th-century linear settlement sandwiched between the A574 and the county boundary of the Glaze Brook. It was originally known as Bury Lane.

The settlement is not mentioned in Domesday. The stream Glaze Brook was described as 'Glasebroc' in 1230. 'Glas' is a British river-name derived from the Welsh 'glas' for 'blue, green, grey'. Glazebury is a late name formed from 'glaze' in Glazebrook.

The Manchester to Liverpool railway passes through the village but there is no station, although it did have one called Glazebury and Bury Lane. The engineers of the day encountered a tremendous problem when they attempted to lay a trackbed across **Chat Moss**. They were unable to establish a firm foundation due to the marshy and boggy nature of the ground. After much time and considerable expense, **George Stephenson** decided to use hurdles made from birch trees. These were laid, together with layers of cotton waste, until a solid base was formed.

Eventually, all the surroundings were tamed and the moss and peat turned into an area of fertile ground. Today, the area supports a market garden industry that is famous for the production of potatoes and lettuce.

Hurst Hall stands alone on the western side of Glazebury. The barn seems to have been the hall of the original house and dates from the 15th century. Heavy timbers were used in its construction with supporting tie-beams on arched braces.

Light Oaks Hall is noted for its splendid east side, which points to the fact that the original house was a larger building. There is a large transomed window on the ground floor next to a doorway.

There are further similar windows and a date of 1657.

The **church of All Saints** was designed by E.H. Shellard and built in 1851.

GOOSTREY [Congleton]

SJ7771: 2 miles (3km) NE of Holmes Chapel

Goostrey is a large village set amongst surrounding farmland. It lies between the A50 and the A535, and has become an ideal base for commuters. Private building estates are an integral part of recent housing developments. Goostrey Station lies on the Crewe to Manchester railway line and there is easy access to the M6 motorway.

Looking at the 1975 edition of the Ordnance Survey 1:50 000 map, there appears to have been a mineral line leaving the main line at Goostrey Station and following the lane towards the village.

The settlement was mentioned in Domesday as 'Gostrel' in Middlewich Hundred. Godric held it, he was a free man. The lands were owned by Hugh fitz Norman for the Earl. There was enough land for one and a half ploughs.

The settlement was described as 'Gosetre' in 1119 and 'Gorstre' in 1267. It may be that the name is derived from 'Godhere's tree'. In 1799, it was known as Goostrey-cum-Barnshaw; the Bartholomew's half inch map of 1946 also indicates the same title.

The **church of St Luke** (1792-6) is a brick building with a west tower and arched windows. The nave side has a doorway and three windows. Inside there is an octagonal **decorated font** with a panelled stem and a monument to W. Booth (died 1810) by Michael Crake of London. It has a naval design at the top. Local legend states that the ancient yew

tree outside the church door provided arrows for local bowmen.

There is a caravan site in the village near to the quaintly named Dromedary Lodge. One famous custom in the area is the annual **Gooseberry Show**.

Crook Hall, 1½ miles (2km) to the north-east is a late 16th-century, red-brick house with three gables. Although the arrangement of the windows has been altered, the interior contains an unusual staircase with twisted balusters.

GRAPPENHALL [Warrington]

SJ6386: 3 miles (5km) SE of Warrington

The suburbs of Warrington have now spread across the Ship Canal to reach the village of Grappenhall. When the Bridgewater Canal was constructed, it was routed through the settlement, winding its way round the church. The housing developments on the north bank are a contrast to the green fields, grazing cows, farms and woodlands beyond the south bank of the Bridgewater Canal. During the summer months a great variety of leisure craft passes through the village.

Evidence of Bronze Age people has been found in the district, with a circle of large stones indicating the site of a cairn or burial ground. Dug-out canoes were unearthed when the Ship Canal was being constructed.

The settlement is recorded in Domesday as 'Gropenhale'. It was described as 'Gropenhal' in 1291. The first element may be derived from the Old English 'grope' for 'a ditch or drain'. The second element 'halh' has meant in the North of England 'a piece of flat land by the side of a river'.

The sandstone built **church of St Wilfred** is an interesting building with

Norman fragments included in the south wall of the nave. The south chapel has Decorated windows, and a chantry was founded in 1334 by the Boydell family, which is now incorporated in the south aisle. Fragments of medieval glass, with outstanding colours of rich greens and yellows, have been preserved from this early chapel. It is the most extensive medieval stained glass in Cheshire.

The church was rebuilt about 1525-39, and the tower and nave with aisles are of this period. There are seven bays with octagonal piers. Paley and Austin restored the building in 1874. There is a **'Scratch' dial** on the tower; it is a simple sundial without its gnomon and is marked with grooves indicating the times of services. On the outside of the church tower is the figure of a cat, possibly the typical Cheshire cat renowned for its grin.

By the churchyard gate is a small, railed enclosure containing the two stone uprights of the village stocks.

The old, attractive part of the village is entered by two humpbacked bridges over the canal. The various styles of buildings blend in with one another. There is a cobbled area in front of the church, and the sandstone built Ram's Head Inn has its porch supported by two large round pillars – the ram's head was the crest of the Leghs of Lyme. There is the Parr Arms and, south of the church, is the early 19th-century rectory.

Fustian production took place on the banks of the Bridgewater Canal until about 1925. This process turned plain cotton material into velvet or velveteen. The raw material came by barge and the finished product was returned to Manchester to be dyed and sold.

GREAT BARROW [Chester]

SJ4768: 4 miles (6km) E of Chester

This farming village adjoins the River Gowy just a few miles beyond the eastern edge of Chester. The number of farms in the centre of the settlement is probably the result of the need for communal protection. In past times, the local communities were fearful of Welsh attacks.

Farming has been the main pre-occupation as from the 14th century until the 1920s the village was owned by successive estates; at first the Savages then the Rock Savages and ultimately the Cholmondeleys.

The settlement was mentioned in Domesday as 'Bero' in Risedon Hundred. Thored held it as a free man, and the lands were owned by William fitz Nigel for the Earl. There was land for eight ploughs and the settlement contained two villagers, four smallholders and two Frenchmen. Domesday records two mills, meadowland and woodland. The settlement was described as 'Barue' in 958. It may be derived from the Old English 'beorg', indicating a 'hill' or 'mound'

Some of the cottages and farmhouses date back to the 17th century, one of strong, well-weathered brick construction. The centre of the village contains an attractive **water pump** that was rightly restored to mark the Queen's Silver Jubilee.

The **church of St Bartholomew** is hidden behind the houses, with its fine west tower of red sandstone (1744) overlooking open countryside. John Douglas carefully restored the nave in 1883. The chancel of 1671 has fine mullioned windows with arched lights and a hammerbeam truss is splendidly decorated with some shields. The chancel was built by the generosity of a Dean of Chester Cathedral. There is an octagonal plain font of 1713 and some stained glass by Kempe (1884 and 1894). The monument to Mrs Wallis (died 1848) is by T. and E. Gaffin.

On the western side of Great Barrow is a right of way to Barrow Hill. From this point there are splendid views of Plemstall Church in the valley of the River Gowy and Helsby Hill and the Merseyside skyline of Stanlow and Ellesmere Port further away.

Greysfield is a large half-timbered house built in 1878. It was then greatly enlarged for Edward Paul, a Liverpool grain merchant.

GREAT BOUGHTON [Chester]

SJ4265: 1 mile (1.6km) E of Chester

The settlement of Boughton was recorded in Domesday as 'Bocstone'. In 1100 it was described as 'Bocthona' and the name is derived from the Old English 'Boc-tun' – 'a tun where beeches grew'.

Great Boughton and Boughton Heath today are popular residential areas to the east and south-east respectively of Chester, and lying adjacent to the River Dee.

The River Dee marked the Welsh border and the area became accustomed to cattle rustling and frequent skirmishes. The Benedictine abbey of St Werbergh owned the land and it administered the leper hospital known as Spital Boughton or Hospital Boughton.

Gallows Hill, situated on a steep bank of the Dee, was a place of public execution until 1801. A memorial erected in 1898 commemorates the martyrdom of Protestant George Marsh and Catholic John Plessington, in 1555 and 1679 respectively. There are also reported tales of witches being put into barrels and rolled down Gallows Hill into the Dee. If the poor unfortunates drowned they were deemed innocent; if they survived the ordeal they were proved guilty – later to be executed.

Boughton suffered during the Civil War. In 1643 the defending Royalists demolished all buildings in order to deny cover or shelter to any attacking Parliamentarians.

The advent of the Shropshire Union Canal through the northern part of the district brought increased trade and prosperity. This led to the need for larger, desirable properties in attractive locations, and many of these new houses were built on levelled sites along the high riverbank.

Built on steeply falling ground, the impressive-looking **church of St Paul**, Boughton, 1876, was designed by John Douglas. The interior contains fine timberwork with large roof timbers and lancet windows. The nave and original aisles are to be found under the main roof. There is an attractive wrought-iron screen and an interesting, painted, Arts and Crafts wall decoration of around 1902. There are some fine examples of stained glass, particularly the apse east window.

Some notable houses in the area include a group of late Georgian residences near St Paul's Church and a terrace of large Italianate-style houses with a river frontage from the early 1850s. In Dee Banks stands the fine stone house of Walmoor Hill, 1896, which was designed by John Douglas as his own residence. Its mullioned and transomed windows look out from its steep riverbank site.

GREAT BUDWORTH [Vale Royal]

SJ6577: 2 miles (3km) N of Northwich

Great Budworth is a picturesque village of great appeal set in attractive undulating countryside. It contains all the elements of a complete settlement, with the ancient church dominating the scene. The village is notable for its narrow main street with cobbled pavements and lined with dwellings of different architectural styles – 17th century, Georgian and Victorian. There are cottages built of local red brick with steep roofs and tall chimneys, plus timber-framed and sandstone houses.

There are delightful views of the placid Budworth Mere and across the Cheshire Plain. At the time of the Norman Conquest this was one of the largest parishes in England. In the Domesday Survey the settlement was listed as 'Budewrde'. It was held by Edward and administered by Payne. The lands were owned by Earl Hugh. The name of the settlement became 'Buddewrtha' and is derived from 'Bud(d)a's worp'. Domesday records that the place had a priest, so there could have been a wooden church. It had a mill that served the manor, a meadow and one of the inhabitants was a slave.

The imposing and handsome **church of St Mary and All Saints** is one of the finest examples of ecclesiastical architecture in Cheshire. William, Constable of Chester and baron of Halton gave the church to the Priory of Norton towards the end of the reign of Henry I, about 1130.

The present church was planned in the 14th century and the design included a broad nave with wide aisles, a three-bay chancel, a western tower and a Lady Chapel. It is possible that the remodelling of the church took place in the late 15th century. The remains of the 14th-century building include the north nave arcade, the east wall of the tower, the east wall of the nave, chancel walls and the whole of the Lady Chapel.

The magnificent nave roof, impressive in appearance, dates from the first part of the 16th century. The great main timbers divide the roof into six bays that, in turn, are sub-divided into numerous panels. The monuments include a damaged alabaster effigy of Sir John Warburton, died 1575, and one to Sir Peter Warburton, died 1813. The **Arley Chapel** was appropriated exclusively for the Warburtons who had moved to Arley Hall in 1469.

Sir Peter Warburton was the 5th and last baronet and died without issue. Arley Hall was left to his great-nephew Rowland Egerton.

There are two fine old chests of note in the church: a medieval iron-bound one with four locks and five staples and another inscribed NC1680 with carved panels with two bottom drawers. There is a 15th-century octagonal font. By the south-west porch is a fine sundial comprising a stone column set on a circular stone step.

GREAT SUTTON [Ellesmere Port]

SJ3775: 1 mile (1.6km) W of Ellesmere Port

Today the village of Great Sutton is very much a part of its giant neighbour Ellesmere Port. For many centuries it was a quiet agricultural community. Today, the original farmland is covered with extensive council estates built in the 1950s and 1960s and also modern private housing development.

The settlement was mentioned in Domesday as 'Sudtone' in Wilaveston Hundred. The church holds Sutton and also held it before 1066. There was land for five ploughs, and there were five villagers and nine smallholders. The settlement's name is a very common name and is derived from Sup-tun or 'southern homestead'.

The **church of St John Evangelist**, designed by David Walker, was built between 1879 and 1880. It has an attractive-looking south-west turret with a conical spire.

GUILDEN SUTTON [Chester]

SJ4367: 3 miles (5km) E of Chester

Guilden Sutton is a fairly compact community. It is almost a suburb of Chester but it is also on the edge of farmland. It is accessible to the Chester ring road, the A56 and A51 and the M53. The nearest station is Chester city.

The settlement was mentioned in Domesday as 'Sudtone' in Wilaveston Hundred. Toki held it as a free man, and the lands were owned by Robert fitz Hugh. There was land for three ploughs and three smallholders. The Domesday Survey lists meadowland.

The settlement was described as 'Guldenesutton' in 1209. The first element may relate to the yellow flower, the marsh marigold, which grew along the banks of the River Gowy. Hence the name – 'southern homestead where golden flowers grew'.

The **church of St John Baptist** (1815) is a small brick building with four bays and round-arched windows. It has a Victorian bellcot. The church contains an almost plain round font of 1635, decorated with a single flower.

HACK GREEN [Crewe]

SJ6548: 3 miles (5km) S of Nantwich

This community of scattered dwellings is surrounded by farmland and is situated between the Shropshire Union Canal and the River Weaver.

The Hack Green **secret nuclear bunker** has been declassified. It was first built as a Second World War operational radar station, and this amazing building became a secret Regional Government Headquarters in the 1980s. In the event of nuclear war, this is where civil servants and military commanders would have lived and ruled north-west England. The surface bunker resembles an ordinary building, but once through the **massive blast doors** one is transported into the top-secret world of the Cold War.

Underground Level 2 is the **communications centre**, a BBC studio and a scientists' fallout centre. Visitors can experience a real 'four minute warning' and there are many interactive and educational displays for children to discover. Younger children can follow the Soviet Spy Mouse Trail. Brown Secret Bunker signs indicate the direction to the site.

HALE [Halton]

SJ4682: 4 miles (6km) SW of Widnes

Hale lies on the north bank of the Mersey and was of some importance in times past as the departure point of the ferry to Ince on the southern side. Like other fords over the Dee, this one was subject to the shiftings of the sands, and up-to-date local knowledge was essential for a safe crossing.

The village of Hale, which was formerly in Lancashire, faced a take-over by Merseyside in 1974. The villagers ran a successful campaign to be included in Cheshire. The settlement was recorded as 'Halas' in 1094. Its name is probably derived from the Old English 'halh' – 'a piece of flat alluvial land by the side of a river'.

The village has a number of interesting buildings, particularly its thatched cottages with overhanging eaves, some dating from the 1600s.

A stroll down a track from Church Road, at the south end of the village, brings one to **Hale Lighthouse** overlooking the estuary. It was first built in 1836 to help vessels to safely navigate around Hale Head. The present structure dates from 1906 and it ceased operations in 1955. This well-known landmark is well worth a visit for the wide-ranging views across the river estuary and towards the sandstone hills on the southern bank.

On the Widnes side of the village, lying in an isolated situation on marshy ground, is the ancient site of a 'duck decoy'. Established in 1631, ducks were lured along channels towards a pond and into cages; it has been operating until comparatively recent times. The five-sided, wooded area is surrounded by a moat and the central area can only be reached by a narrow swingbridge. The feature has now been taken over by the Cheshire Conservation Trust.

The **church of St Mary** has a 14th-century tower with the rest of the building of 1754; although inside only the west gallery remains of that date. The church has no separate chancel, and the west wall has two circular windows.

The Manor House lies to the north-west of the church. This is not the original house, but the present building dates from about 1700. It has a façade of five bays in red sandstone and brick.

An interesting character who lived in the village was John Middleton, better known as the 'Childe of Hale', (1578-1623). He was reputed to have grown to a height of 9ft 3ins before he was twenty. His grave lies in the churchyard within a railed enclosure.

An interesting village tradition that has been retained is the election of a Lord Mayor; a ceremony which appears to go back to the 14th century. The person is elected from among the Freemen of Hale, and is a local resident who has rendered service to the community.

HALTON [Halton]

SJ5382: ½ mile (1km) NE of Runcorn

In the Domesday Survey, the settlement of Halton was listed as 'Heletune' which became Halton in 1259. Orm held it and the lands were owned by William, son of Nigel. Domesday recorded a picture of extensive arable land, meadow and woodland, with a number of inhabitants including two priests.

Halton Castle stands on a sandstone outcrop with panoramic views stretching from Helsby and Frodsham to Runcorn Bridge. Originally a motte and bailey fortification with wooden palisades in the 11th century, it was rebuilt in stone during the next century. Over the years it was used as a fortress, court, administrative centre and prison. All the castle rooms were built into the walls and the gatehouse provided the only access to the inner ward. However, the gatehouse was demolished in the 18th century.

During the Civil War, the Royalist castle was besieged twice and considerable damages inflicted on the masonry before the Parliamentarian forces captured the castle.

The **church of St Mary** was built in the 13th-century style by Sir Gilbert Scott, (cf Scott, Chester) between 1851 and 1852. The church has no tower but there is a polygonal bell-turret. Inside the building is a monument to Sir Richard Brooke, 1889. The parish library (1733) is situated at the entrance to the churchyard.

The **Castle Hotel** (1737-8) was originally the duchy of Lancaster Court

House. There is an impressive Hanoverian coat of arms of George III decorating the doorway.

In the main street of Halton village are a number of interesting houses. The Seneschal's House (1598) with side bay windows continuing round the corner, Halton House (1779) and Hollybank House with an imposing doorway.

Norton Priory lies 2 miles (3km) north-west of Runcorn town centre. The Priory was founded by Augustinian Canons in 1134, and became an abbey in the 15th century. After the Reformation the priory was acquired by Vice-Admiral Sir Richard Brooke who demolished most of it, but used the remodelled abbot's quarters. A large Palladian house was built on the site in the 1730s, and later altered by the architect James Wyatt for another Sir Richard Brooke who died in 1781. From the 18th century onwards, the Brooke family fought a continuous battle against encroaching industry, new canals and railways crossing their land and chemical fumes. The family gave up the fight and left in 1928. The house was demolished, but the medieval work was kept.

Of the original monastic buildings, there is a Norman vaulted undercroft of seven and a half bays with a remarkable stone statue of St Christopher, a mosaic floor and a late Norman doorway. There is a museum on site with a fine exhibition of medieval monastic life. Nearby is a Georgian walled garden.

HANDBRIDGE [Chester]

SJ4065: 1 mile (1.6km) S of Chester

Handbridge is a residential suburb of Chester situated by the river loop on its southern bank. Handbridge is Chester's oldest suburb and existed in the 12th century. The settlement was attacked so many times that it has no medieval buildings. The Welsh called it 'Treboeth' – 'the burnt settlement'. Its inhabitants were no doubt thankful to escape across the Dee bridge to the protection of the city walls.

A timber bridge existed in Norman times and the first stone structure was erected in 1280. In fact, the Romans first exploited this important crossing-point. They found a ford here and later built a bridge. Over the years, the many wooden structures across the Dee were constantly being washed away and tolls were authorised by Richard II to pay for repairs. Those tolls were not abolished until 1885.

The settlement was mentioned in Domesday as 'Bruge' in Chester Hundred. Wulfnoth held it and the lands were owned by Hugh fitz Osbern for the Earl. There were two smallholders with three oxen. The settlement was described as 'Honebrugge' in 1260 and 'Hunebrugge' in 1289. The first element is a personal name 'Hana', giving the name of the place as 'Hana's bridge'.

Greenway Street used to be called Stye Lane by the fishermen who lived there. It is a cobbled way leading down to the river.

The **church of St Mary** -Without-The Walls (1855-7) was designed by T.B. Wade for the Duke of Westminster and is situated in Overleigh Road, Handbridge. This large building has a west steeple and many lancet windows. The interior is high with a high chancel arch. The piers are octagonal. The south-east chapel has two wooden tunnel vaults.

There is a fine reredos designed by Frederick Shields in 1888 and made in cloisonné (an enamel finish produced by forming areas of different colours separated by strips of wire placed edgeways on a metal backing). There are several stained-glass windows by Edward Frampton (1887 and 1896).

HANDLEY [Chester]

SJ4558: 7 miles (11km) SSE of Chester

Handley is a small village lying on the A41, Chester to Whitchurch road. It stands on high grounds above the Mere Brook, which becomes the Aldford Brook before joining the Dee.

The settlement is mentioned in Domesday as 'Hanlei' in Dudestan Hundred. Grimkel held it, and Earl Hugh owned the lands. There was land for four ploughs, and there were two villagers and one smallholder.

The settlement was described as 'Hanlegh' in 1175 and 'Handleg' in 1200. It is probably derived from the Old English 'Hea-leah' or 'high leah'. The element 'leah' means 'a pasture in a forest clearing'.

The **church of All Saints** has an inscription and the date 1512 on its west face. The south doorway is decorated with mouldings and the nave has a hammerbeam roof dated 1662. The remainder of the church was restored between 1853 and 1855. On the north side there is a stained-glass window by Wailes (1855).

During the Civil War the tower withstood a siege, but the Parliamentarians burned out the defenders. When Charles II was on the throne, the church was repaired and the handsome hammerbeam roof bears the date.

Golborne Old Hall (1682) lies a short distance to the north-north-west. The house has been much altered and has a splendid doorway, pilasters and a pediment.

Manor House Farm, Aldersley Green, is a black and white house with lattice and herringbone work.

HANKELOW [Crewe]

SJ6745: 7 miles (11km) SSW of Crewe

The village of Hankelow is situated on the A529, Audlem to Nantwich road. It lies just to the east of the River Weaver and the Shropshire Union Canal. The surroundings consist of extensive agricultural land.

The settlement is not mentioned in Domesday. In 1260 it was described as 'Honkyloue' and in 1282 as 'Honkelow'. The first element is probably a personal name and means 'Haneca's hill'.

Hankelow Mill on the right bank of the Weaver was the last mill to function in the Audlem area. Records state that there has been a mill on the site for over three hundred years. The river above the mill had been straightened and embanked to create a head of water. Some sections of the former river course are still noticeable behind the canal aqueduct.

Most of the existing mill appears to date from the mid-18th century, and the building was extended in 1882. This was in order to accommodate a steam engine. The mill was equipped with a waterwheel that was 16ft (5m) in diameter, 6ft 6ins (2m) wide with three rows of six cast-iron spokes. It last operated about 1940 and the mill closed in 1972. Today, the mill is intact and in good repair having been converted into two houses.

Hankelow Hall is an early Georgian brick house of ten bays built for Gabriel Wettenhall and altered for his son Nathaniel in 1755-7. A very tall parapet surmounts the three storeys. In this century it has suffered neglect and is now empty and becoming ruinous.

Hankelow Court is a large brick black and white house (1870s). It was enlarged in 1901 and altered in 1958. During the

Second World War it was taken over by the army.

In the mid-19th century there were two Methodist chapels in Hankelow. One built in 1838 remained in use until 1935, when it was replaced. The present building stands on the edge of the village green. The other chapel, known as William Green's Chapel, was registered in April 1825. Once closed it became a private dwelling.

HARGRAVE AND HUXLEY [Chester]

SJ4862: 6 miles (10km) SE of Chester

Hargrave and Huxley are scattered villages along byroads between the Shropshire Union Canal and the River Gowy. The surroundings consist of extensive farmland. The civil parish, which includes Hargrave, is known by the title of Foulk Stapleford.

The settlement was not mentioned in Domesday. The name was described as 'Haregrave' in 1287 and the name is possibly derived from 'Hares' grove' or 'grey grove'.

The **church of St Peter** is a 17th-century church with a Victorian bellcot. An inscription states that the church was founded in 1627 by Sir Thomas Moulson, later to be Lord Mayor of London. The building has mullioned windows with arched lights. The roof is of hammerbeam construction, but there is no chancel arch. A New Connection chapel was opened in Huxley in 1842.

Lower Huxley Hall lies to the north-west of the village. The house is the centre part of a larger original mansion. Constructed in brick, it is surrounded by a moat that is crossed by a bridge. At the end of the bridge is an archway with curvy decoration of typical Jacobean style. The house has a recessed centre with mullioned and transomed windows. During the Civil War, Colonel Thomas Croxton garrisoned the house for the Parliamentarians.

Higher Huxley House is another old mansion, which has a carved oak Elizabethan staircase. It has two presumed priest holes and it is said to be haunted by a ghostly lady who rides through the garden at midnight.

HARTFORD [Vale Royal]

SJ6372: 2 miles (3km) SW of Northwich

Hartford has a station on the main Crewe to Liverpool railway line. The settlement lies near to the Weaver Navigation Waterway, and it became a desirable area for the homes of wealthy local manufacturers. With the coming of Brunner Mond (later ICI) to Winnington, the nature of Hartford began to change. Housing developments took place and the village lost its rural character.

Included amongst the range of educational facilities is the Mid-Cheshire College of Further Education. It has a fine campus set in almost parkland surroundings.

Early Hartford dates from pre-Roman times when it was established on a route near the river. The route grew in importance, becoming a branch of Roman Watling Street but still surrounded by the wooded acres of Delamere Forest. The settlement was mentioned in Domesday as 'Herford' and described as 'Hertford' in 1278. Its name is derived from 'stag ford'.

The **church of St John the Baptist** (1874-5) was designed by John Douglas. The tower has a higher stair turret built in 1887-9. The aisles have five bays with a very low window. The church has an interesting interior, especially the chancel that has totally different sides.

Large houses were built for local industrialists such as Thomas Marshall and his sons John and Thomas who owned brine and rock salt works and the vast Dunkirk salt mine. Today, these houses are occupied by the utilities of gas and water, the Borough Council and a well-known hotel chain.

HARTHILL [Chester]

SJ5055: 9 miles (14km) SE of Chester

The picturesque village of Harthill stands in an elevated position on the slopes of a western outlier of Bickerton Hill. Its beautiful situation is enhanced by a range of wooded heights and the summit of Raw Head, 745ft (227m).

Harthill is not mentioned in Domesday but it certainly formed part of the original barony of Malpas. The church, the pleasantly designed grey sandstone estate houses and the school are clustered round the village green. There is a panoramic view from the church grounds, extending from the neighbourhood of Farndon, past Eaton and the city of Chester to the waters of the River Dee.

The village name was recorded as 'Herthil' or 'Harthil' in 1259, and means 'hill frequented by stags'.

The present **church of All Saints** is probably early 17th century, though the clock tower was added in Victorian times. The first reference to a place of worship occurs in 1280 when it was called 'the chapel of Harthil'. A reference to the medieval church states that a sum of money was bequeathed to Sir Thomas Belewe, 'parson of Harthil', in 1361. The amount was 2s 6d to celebrate a trental of Masses, and 12d towards the maintenance of the chapel.

The nave and chancel are in one with a clock turret added between 1862 and 1863. A hammerbeam roof surmounts the wide nave, where stone corbels hold up the wall posts supporting the hammerbeams.

The shields of arms on the roof timbers and screen record the influence and links with many local families. Vigorous restorations in the 19th century resulted in the removal of much old panelling and furnishings, including an orchestra gallery at the west end of the church. From records it appears that church music was provided using a variety of wind and string instruments on various dates between 1790 and 1847.

Over the south porch doorway is a stone bearing the arms of Sir William Brereton, Bart. of the Barony of Malpas, and the motto 'Opitulante Deo, 1506'. The carving above this in bold letters states, 'Rondvull Prickett, Churchwarden ever since 1606 until 1611.' This is surmounted by a smaller inscription reading 'John Webster, George Brown, Ch. 1779', Churchwardens. Inside the porch, a small slab bears the arms and name of Sir Marmaduke Drake, 1669. These Drakes acquired an estate at Malpas in the reign of Charles II, but originally came from Devonshire.

The interior of the church contains a Georgian pulpit with interesting panelling, Jacobean altar rails and an **unusual font** in the shape of an urn. In the churchyard there is the prominent **mausoleum** of the Barbour family of Bolesworth Castle.

A cobbled way leads down one side of the village green to reach **Harthill County Primary School.** The attractive gabled building, with a date of 1868, is complete with a coat of arms, bellcot, clock and modern flagpole; all splendid appurtenances for the well-being and tone of any school.

By the gate stands a once proud stone fountain complete with a coat of arms. Sadly, it lacks fittings, and more to the point there's no water!

Half a mile north-west of the village, Bolesworth Castle is set high on the western slope of the Broxton Hills and backed by rocky wooded escarpments. The house, built in 1830 by William Cole, is a two-storey castellated and turreted mansion. Between 1920 and 1923, Clough Williams Ellis changed the interior, removing the Gothic decoration, except the staircase, and giving it a much more classical appearance. There is a fine formal garden with terracing, steps and alcove seats.

HASLINGTON [Crewe]

SJ7456: 2 miles (3km) E of Crewe

The village is situated on the eastern approaches to Crewe and lies on both sides of the A534 Sandbach to Crewe road. The settlement was not mentioned in Domesday. It was described as 'Hasillinton' in 1280 and the name is derived from 'tun among hazels'.

In the time of Edward I, the Barony of Wich Malbank was divided among the heirs of William, the last Baron of that name, and Haslington became the property of Auda Vernon of Shipbrooke. One of her ancestors was Sir Ralph Vernon.

During the Civil War, there was a skirmish at the southern end of the village at a spot called Slaughter Hill. This engagement was fought on December 27 1642 with the honours going to the Roundheads.

Haslington Hall stands in open countryside to the east of the village. This large, attractive-looking timber-framed house was the home of the Vernon family until 1700. The central part was a late 15th-century Great Hall and its collared roof remains. Two cross wings were added in the 16th century, complete with splendid timber framing. The east side of the house includes a 17th-century brick service wing. Other fine features of this house are the several gables, herringbone bracing and the splendid decoration of **quatrefoils and lozenge patterns.**

It is said that the woodwork was salvaged from the great Spanish galleons of the Armada in 1586. To back up this statement, there is a plaque in London that states that 'Francis Vernon Esq. of Haslington House, Cheshire, is remembered for his part in the wars with Spain'.

The **church of St Matthew** was built in two parts at an interval of one hundred years. The west part (1810) is built of brick with arched windows. It has an arched doorway and there is a cupola on the gable of the nave. The east part was designed by Reginald T. Longden and built in 1909 in the Decorated style. This section has a seven-light east window.

The South Cheshire Way is a long-distance footpath of 34 miles (54km) from Grindley Brook on the Shropshire border to Mow Cop on the Staffordshire Way. It passes through the lush unchanging landscape of south Cheshire, passing south of Nantwich and skirting the villages of Wybunbury, Haslington and Wheelock. Eventually it makes the climb to the hilltop village of Mow Cop.

HATHERTON [Crewe]

SJ6847: 4 miles (6km) SE of Nantwich

Hatherton consists of a widely scattered collection of farms and cottages and was formerly part of the Delves-Broughton estate. The settlement was recorded in

Domesday as 'Haretone', and woodland and an enclosure were listed. It was described as 'Hatherton' in 1300, the name being derived from 'hawthorn tun'.

There were two Methodist chapels in Hatherton, one in Crewe Road and the other in Audlem Road. The latter closed for worship in 1968.

Stapeley Water Gardens are situated just off the A51, Nantwich to Woore road. The centre welcomes one and a half million visitors each year and is becoming the world's leading water garden attraction. There are tanks after tanks of cold water and tropical fish and their equipment and over three hundred and fifty varieties of water lily. Pools line up next to a maze of ponds, and a small lake contains blooming water lilies throughout the summer.

The Palms Tropical Oasis is an any-season visit to tropical and Mediterranean garden splendour. Beneath the palms are displays of flowering plants from around the world. Exotic flowers and lush foliage lead one past fountains and cascades to the silence of the Jungle Room. Here, piranhas and huge catfish lurk beneath the enormous leaves of the giant Amazon water lily.

HATTON [Warrington]

SJ5982: 4 miles (6km) S of Warrington

Hatton lies just north of the M56 and south of Warrington. In the past it was an entirely agricultural community. Now it is becoming a dormitory area for Warrington and the Warrington New Town development is reaching out across the fields to Hatton.

The settlement was described as 'Hatton' in 1230 and the name is derived from the Old English 'Haep-tun' meaning 'a tun on a heath'. The surrounding district contains a number of dwellings that were built in the early part of the 18th century. Gradually, over the years, they have been developed into successful modern farms.

HAUGHTON [Crewe]

SJ5856: 2 miles (3km) S of Bunbury

Haughton is a small village in the heart of a landscape devoted to dairy farming and general agriculture. Until the late 1950s, cheese was made on many of the surrounding farms.

The settlement was described as 'Halghton' in 1311 and the name is derived from the Old English 'Halh-tun' or 'a tun in or by a halh'. In this part of the country, the usual meaning of 'halh' is 'a remote place'.

Haughton Hall is thought to have been part of lands granted at the Conquest to one of the influential Norman barons, Robert fitz Hugh. By the time of Edward II's reign the estate had passed into the hands of Robert de Halghton, and it remained in this family until the 1750s.

A red brick house replaced the original timber building in 1891-4. This was for the shipowner Ralph Brocklebank and was noted for its tall chimneys and the variety of materials used in its construction. In 1950, the house was reduced from three storeys to two. Three large bays enliven the aspect of the building facing the garden. There is an attractive group of red-brick outbuildings with tile hangings and tile roofs.

The village has no church but the Brocklebanks built a mission room.

HELSBY [Vale Royal]

SJ4876: 7 miles (11km) NE of Chester

The northern crags of Helsby Hill bear a strong resemblance to a human face.

These sandstone escarpments, a favourite haunt of rock-climbers, bring the mid-Cheshire Ridge to an abrupt end. The hill summit affords a magnificent vantage point for views of the surrounding countryside. The panorama is extensive, ranging from the Bickerton Hills to the Clwydian Range, east to the Pennine moorlands and north to the industrial and townscape scenes along the River Mersey.

The settlement is mentioned in Domesday as 'Helesbe' in Roelau Hundred. Ernwy Foot held the settlement as a free man, and ploughland, meadowland and woodland are recorded. Three villagers with one smallholder have one plough. Helsby is described as 'Ellesbi' in 1186 and 'Hellesby' in 1216. The first element may be derived from Old Scandinavian *hellir* for 'a cave', or *hiallr* for 'a ledge on the side of a hill'. The second element, the Old English 'by', is derived from the Old Norse *byr*, which denotes a village or homestead.

Iron Age people constructed a stronghold on Helsby Hill overlooking the surrounding forest and marshland. The earthworks of the **promontory fort** consist of a bank 65ft (20m) wide and 4ft (1m) high, enclosing an area of 1.4 hectares (3.5 acres). Outside the main earthworks lie the ploughed-out remains of a second bank. The crags to the north complete the defences. The original entrance lay at the south-west corner. Helsby Hill is now under the guardianship of the National Trust.

The Saxons gradually cleared the forests and homesteads were established in the clearings. Norse colonists from Ireland and the Isle of Man settled on the Wirral and then moved inland up the Mersey. The settlement of Helsby grew up at the foot of the hill, above the level of the undrained marshland. The early inhabitants of the settlement kept their cattle on the marshes that stretched northwards to the Mersey. Now the area has been more extensively drained and turned into agricultural land. The M56 was built on this land in 1971.

The small, rock-faced **church of St Paul** was erected in 1868-70 and the south aisle and chapel in 1909. Situated on a buttress midway along the west front is a squat, slated bellcot with a slated spire.

In the 1870s, quarrying was a thriving industry on the south side of Helsby Hill. Good quality building stone was used in such projects as Liverpool Docks, for many churches in the area and for repairs to Chester Cathedral.

On Good Friday, the three local churches hold a service on the top of the escarpment and a wooden cross is erected. The old custom of maypole dancing has been revived at one of the village primary schools.

HENBURY [Macclesfield]
SJ8873: 3 miles (5km) W of Macclesfield

The village lies west of Macclesfield on the north side of the A537 and is surrounded by farmland. It is closely linked with the nearby village of Broken Cross, which is now part of the western suburbs of Macclesfield. The name, Broken Cross, probably derives from the shape of the crossroads which did not form a regular intersection.

The settlement is mentioned in Domesday as 'Hamedeberie' in Hamestan Hundred. It is recorded together with a number of other settlements, including Capesthorne, Tintwistle, Werneth and Romiley. The value of this Hundred before 1066 was 40s, but it had fallen to 10s. Earl Edwin held the lands. The settlement was described as 'Hendebury' in 1289. It is possible that the first element may be 'Hemede' or 'Hemede's burg'. 'Burg' is a common element, usually meaning a fortified place or fort.

Ancient remains have been discovered at two farms in the locality. At Bearhurst Farm in 1966, burial mounds were excavated, with the evidence of a burial urn containing male remains. In 1971, at Brickbank Farm, ploughing operations unearthed the site of a stone circle, measuring 20ft (6m) in diameter.

The **church of St Thomas** has a slender west tower with a broach spire. It was designed by Richard Lane and built between 1844 and 1845 as a daughter church of Prestbury. The church has a fine set of engraved glass doors in memory of Sir Vincent de Ferranti of Henbury Hall, founder of the electronics firm.

The present **Henbury Hall**, a Palladian villa, was built between 1984 and 1986. The old hall was erected in 1742; a classical block with giant pilasters. It was remodelled in a neoclassical style in the early 19th century. The old building was demolished in 1957 and a stable block converted into a house. Sebastian de Ferranti carried out the idea of rebuilding Henbury Hall. The building is a domed Palladian rotunda built of creamy French limestone, beautifully set on rising ground.

Whirley Hall is a brick house on the site of an older building. The late 17th-century front is composed of five bays with two large, shaped gables.

HIGHER HURDSFIELD [Macclesfield]

SJ9374: 2 miles (3km) NE of Macclesfield

The old part of Higher Hurdsfield straddles the A5002, Macclesfield to Whaley

Bridge road. Today, a large private estate is situated on the east side of the main road. The community lies at the foot of Kerridge Hill, as the former turnpike road begins its climb through the Pennine foothills to the county's eastern border with Derbyshire.

The name Hurdsfield was recorded in 1285 as 'Herdisfeld', as is derived from 'Hygered's feld', or 'Hygered's open country'.

In the past, industry has touched the settlement with local coal mining, stone quarrying, cotton and silk manufacture. The Macclesfield Canal, which was completed in 1831, arrived late and was soon overtaken by the coming of the railways. Nevertheless, many bulky and heavy loads were carried along this scenic waterway.

A Sunday school was started in 1808 in a local farm building and a school was built in 1811. The Sunday school is now a community church.

HIGHER WYCH [Chester]

SJ4943: 3 miles (5km) W of Whitchurch

Higher Wych is one of a number of small settlements that straggle along the Welsh border in the south-west of the county. The Wyche Brook is the demarcation line that separates Cheshire from Wrexham. This used to be shown on maps as Detached Flint, a situation that always proved confusing to travellers. This is fairly isolated border country, where numerous byroads and lanes connect farmsteads, cottages and hamlets in an extensive farming landscape.

The Wych Brook follows a winding course between steep-sided wooded banks, overlooked by defensive earthworks such as Castle Hill. The author came this way using little-used footpaths on his long-distance walk from Cape

Wrath to Land's End. This rather remote area is well worth exploring.

The nearest major roads are the A41 from Whitchurch to Chester and the B5395 Grindley Brook to Malpas. A convenient railway station is at Whitchurch on the Shrewsbury to Crewe line.

HIGH LEGH [Macclesfield]

SJ6883: 5 miles (8km) NW of Knutsford

This former farming community is situated on higher land between Knutsford and Warrington, between the M6 and M56. The older part consists of some 17th-century houses and farms and cottages mainly built in the 18th century. The settlement is mentioned in Domesday as 'Lege', and a priest, a church and woodland is recorded. The name is described as 'Legh' in 1286 and is derived from the Old English 'leah', 'an open place, a clearing, in a wood'.

The two halls, West Hall and East Hall (High Legh Hall), once stood very close together and were lived in by two branches of the Legh family. West Hall was a half-timbered building but was rebuilt in brick with a new chapel just after 1814. The chapel was destroyed by fire in 1891 and parts of the building were incorporated into the parish church of St John. The hall was demolished in 1935.

East or High Legh Hall was built in 1581 with a chapel. A Georgian residence replaced the Elizabethan house in 1782. Humphry Repton landscaped the grounds of both halls in the 1790s. Another lodge was built in stone in Italianate style in 1833-4 and only this building remained after the hall was demolished in 1963 and the land used for modern housing development. During the Second World War, the army used the house and grounds.

The **church of St John**, 1893, was designed by Edmund Kirby. This is a tim-ber-framed building with a tower that has a mullioned and transomed west window. The brick-faced interior illustrates the fact that the exterior half-timbering is a pretence. The walls of the previous chapel are incorporated into the building.

The Independent Methodist movement began in High Legh in 1783. The missionary Robert Moffat attended the chapel while employed as a gardener at High Legh Hall. His daughter, Mary, married David Livingstone.

HOLMES CHAPEL [Congleton]

SJ7667: 7 miles (11km) WNW of Congleton

Holmes Chapel lies at the intersection of the A50 from Knutsford to Stoke-on-Trent and the A54 from Middlewich to Congleton. This has been an important route junction since the 13th century. In a charter of between 1245 and 1269, the Abbot of Dieulacres (near Leek in Staffordshire) gave permission for the Abbot of Chester to conduct divine service at certain chapels belonging to the mother church of Sandbach. This indicates the early existence of a place of worship here.

From this parish come the names 'Cherche Hulm, Cherche Hulme, Hoolmes chappel, Humes chappel, Hulms chapel' and 'Church Hulme'. The element 'Holm(e)' derives from the Old English 'holm' and the Old Norse *holmr*, which means – ' a piece of dry land partly surrounded by streams or by a stream'. So the name Hulme became Church Hulme or Holmes Chapel.

The **church of St Luke** consists of a nave with two side aisles, a square tower at the west end and a small chancel. Externally, the 15th-century sandstone tower is now the oldest part of the building. However, the old aisles and chancel were of timbered construction and, had the building remained in this form, it would have been one of the largest examples of a timber-framed church in Cheshire.

In the 18th century, the oak framework was encased in brick, retaining the octagonal, slender wooden pillars that support the horizontal beams. These main rafters are of great strength and are supported by stout diagonal pieces. The beam timbering was hidden under a plaster ceiling for centuries and has only recently been rediscovered. It survived the depredations of Victorian restorers because they did not find the original medieval roof under the plaster. The screen has a top frieze with the date 1623 over the west door. The brass candelabrum, dated 1708, is the oldest in the county.

The Manchester – Crewe railway was opened as far as Stockport in 1840, reaching Crewe the following year. The **viaduct** over the River Dane at Holmes Chapel features twenty-three arches, each of a 63ft (19m) span, with an overall length of 1794ft (547m).

HOOTON [Ellesmere Port]

SJ3677: 3 miles (5km) NW of Ellesmere Port

Hooton is situated on the Wirral to the south of the M53 and straddles the county border with Merseyside. The settlement is mentioned in Domesday as 'Hotone'. It was described as 'Hoton' in 1260 and its name is probably derived from the Old English 'Ho-tun' from 'hoh', denoting 'a spur of a hill'.

The **church of St Paul** (1858-62) is a spectacular building designed by James Colling. It is notable for its bands of red and white sandstone and its octagonal crossing tower with an unusual dome. Granite columns support the arcades.

The **church of St Mary of the Angels** (RC), 1879, was designed by E.J. Tarver in the late 13th-century style. The building has no tower and no aisles but it has a polygonal apse.

Hooton Hall was a half-timbered courtyard house dating back to 1486. Samuel Wyatt designed a new house in 1778 and this replaced the earlier structure. In 1847 Hooton was purchased by R.C. Naylor, a wealthy Liverpool banker, who employed the architect James Colling to remodel the house in an Italianate style.

During the First World War the hall was used as a military hospital, and after many years of neglect was demolished around 1935. Only a pair of lodges by Wyatt remains. The surrounding parkland was used as an airfield for some time but then it became an industrial site. Now, the Vauxhall motor factory covers the area.

HOUGH [Crewe]

SJ7050: 3 miles (5km) S of Crewe

The small village of Hough lies in a farming area south of Crewe and a little to the east of the neighbouring villages of Shavington and Wybunbury. Hough is close to the main Crewe to Stafford railway line and convenient for a recent M6 link just a short distance from the village.

The settlement was described as 'Houcht' in 1287 and the name is derived from the Old English 'hoh', 'a spur of a hill'.

Dark deeds were afoot here in 1890, as two young brothers named Davies lay in wait for their drunken, brutal father. He was attacked and murdered in one of the local lanes. At their trial, the elder youth was condemned to death and the younger brother sent to gaol.

Parts of Hough Hall date from the 16th century and one room contains some fine

East Cheshire, gritstone country. Above: Windgather Rocks, Kettleshulme;
Below, from left: Jenkin Chapel, Saltersford; The Bowstones, Bowstonegate

Manchester Ship
Canal, Ellesmere Port

The Macclesfield
Canal, Bosley

Eaton Estate Lodge,
Aldford

Lamaload Reservoir – at the heart of walking country, near the Cheshire-Derbyshire border

St Edith's, Shocklach

Stretton Mill, near Tilston

High Lane, near Lyme, looking east

Malpas

Pott Shrigley: the church of St Christopher is of the Perpendicular style throughout and probably founded in the late 14th century.

Queen Anne panelling. The house, lying on the south side of the A500, is surrounded by well-kept grounds and mature trees. A set of splendid wrought-iron gates dating from the reign of James I, and made for the original hall, stand at the entrance of Hough Gates Farm.

HULME WALFIELD [Congleton]

SJ8465: 2 miles (3km) NW of Congleton

The small settlement of Hulme Walfield is situated on higher ground just north of the River Dane. A byroad connects the village to the busy A34, Congleton to Alderley Edge road. The surroundings consist of extensive farmland.

The **church of St Michael** was designed by Sir George Gilbert Scott and built between 1855 and 1856. The church is a surprising feature of this small community. It is an attractive, rock-faced building, which would have incurred considerable expense. The plan consists of a nave, a north aisle and a chancel. A bellcot is placed on the east gable of the nave.

HUNTINGTON [Chester]

SJ4264: 2 miles (3km) SSE of Chester

Huntington lies just south of Chester centre and for hundreds of years remained a small settlement surrounded by farming land. Earlier this century, many houses were built and further recent housing development has greatly increased the population.

The settlement is mentioned in Domesday as 'Hunditone', and the Survey records meadowland, a small boat and a net. It was described as 'Huntindun' in 1233 and its name may be derived from the Old English 'hunting-dun' or 'the hill for hunting'.

At the southern end of the village is situated a major water intake works. From here, water from mid-Wales is treated and piped to Liverpool and Merseyside. In 1987 the village became part of the new parish of St Luke's and worshippers welcomed the imminent construction of their own new church.

HURDSFIELD [Macclesfield]

SJ9374: 1 mile (1.6km) NE of Macclesfield

Hurdsfield is basically an outer industrial suburb of Macclesfield. It lies on the eastern side of the town, astride the A5002, Macclesfield to Whaley Bridge road. The line of the Macclesfield Canal provides the district's eastern boundary. The canal towpath is also an excellent vantage point for views of the town centre standing impressively above the River Bollin. On the other hand, and equally eye-catching, are the sweeping hill slopes and high moorlands of the Peak District National Park.

Set amongst a recent industrial estate are the buildings belonging to Ciba Geigy, the Swiss pharmaceutical firm, and Zeneca, another large pharmaceutical manufacturer.

Holy Trinity Church was designed by William Hayley and built between 1837 and 1839. The style was similar to a Commissioners' church, with a later Victorian east window. The church has a pinnacled west tower and lancet windows with slender pointed arches.

INCE [Ellesmere Port]

SJ4576: 3 miles (5km) E of Ellesmere Port

Ince is a small parish along the southern shore of the Mersey estuary. The settlement is situated on a small rise of land

and consists of the church, the village square, a number of houses and nearby meadows This peaceful haven is screened from the encroaching oil storage tanks of the Stanlow refinery by a fringe of trees. The village has a fine outlook across the river, views of distant mountains, glimpses of local churches and two cathedrals.

The village is a mixture of old and new houses with a patch of cobbled street near to the church. There is a large, five-bay brick house with a three-bay pediment and a central doorway. A lamp in the village square commemorates the coronation of King Edward VII.

In the Domesday Survey, the settlement is recorded as 'Inise'. The manor belonged to the canons of St Werburgh's, Chester. There is land for five ploughs and in the demesne there is one plough, two slaves, eight villagers and one smallholder. Its value had fallen from 30s to 15s. There are two acres of meadowland.

The settlement was described as 'Ynes' in 1100. The name is derived from the Welsh *ynys* for 'island, water meadow'.

On the edge of the village, the two ruined red-sandstone buildings are part of the late medieval hall of the manor of Ince. The side of the hall facing the road has four windows, and at right angles is a second longer building, buttressed on both sides. The lord of the manor was the abbot of St Werburgh's, Chester. The building of the manor house (1485-93) was by Simon Ripley, the twenty-third abbot of St Werburgh's.

In medieval times Ince was a place of some importance, being the southern end of a ford crossing the Mersey from Liverpool and Hale on the north bank. A safe journey relied very much on local and up-to-date knowledge of the unpredictable shifting sands.

The **church of St James** occupies the site of a Norman chapel of which there

are no traces. There was remodelling in the 16th century, but of this period only the tower and chancel remain. All else was rebuilt and reconsecrated in 1854. The church, as it survives today, reveals late Perpendicular work in the tower and the chancel. The chancel roof is dated 1671.

During the 1854 restoration, two courses of stone were added to the tower and new battlements erected. The chancel has two-light square-headed windows (1897) and the east window has three lights with 14th-century tracery. In the chancel is a fine two-tier brass chandelier with twelve branches (1724). There is a late 17th-century communion rail with twisted balusters.

A lane leads down to Ince Marshes, an area where islands of higher land were settled by Scandinavian colonists; these sites identifiable by the word 'holm'. One such example is Holme Farm, now a large brick farmhouse surrounded by lush low fields.

After the completion of the Manchester Ship Canal in 1894, Ince Marshes were permanently protected. This meant that the village was cut off from the shore, which made life difficult for local fishermen. North of the canal the marshes are the haunt of wild fowl and wild flowers, and further out in the estuary stretch barren wastes of sand.

In the last few decades, the Stanlow refinery has extended across the marshes right into the parish. Now the oil storage tanks have occupied the site and park of the former Ince Hall. All that remains is a sandstone archway by the road under which the hall drive once passed.

KELSALL [Chester]
SJ5168: 7 miles (11km) E of Chester

The straggling village of Kelsall nestles beneath the sandstone ridge which runs across Cheshire from Helsby to Beeston. The A54 leaves the higher land by the Kelsall Gap and runs west down to Stamford Bridge over the River Gowy. Stamford Bridge is the 'stane' or stony ford of Saxon times.

Kelsall is not listed in the Domesday Survey but the settlement's name in 1260 was 'Kelsale' and 'Keleshale' in 1297. The name is possibly derived from 'Cenles' or 'Keles halh', which is Old English for 'a corner, a secret place'. The first element is possibly a personal name.

The first inhabitants in the area appear to be Bronze Age Celts. There are traces of a settlement on Kelsborrow Hill, which was one of a line of early ridge forts on the main trackway from north to south. The hill fort was built to command the pass between the hills. When danger threatened, livestock and goods could be taken into the fort.

The **Kelsborrow hill fort** is oval in shape and has an area of 3 hectares (7 acres), with steep slopes on the west and south-east. Only on the north does the fort need the protection of a single bank and ditch 25ft (7.5m) wide. The entrance is a narrow gap between the eastern end of the rampart and the natural slope defining the promontory.

Just west of Longley Farm, lynchet banks run east to west across the ridge. Less well-defined banks, much reduced by ploughing, also run north to south, forming a group of small rectangular fields. The field system may either be Iron Age or Romano-British.

The principal **Roman road** from Chester to the north, for Carlisle and the frontier, seems first to have gone eastward to Manchester before turning to the north. Just before reaching Kelsall, the line of the road re-crosses the modern highway and a hedgerow marks it up to the north side of the village. Here the older main

road probably marks the course of the Roman route.

The **church of St Philip** is a rock-faced building of 1860. The nave and chancel are late 13th-century Gothic. The bellcot seems to sit uncomfortably on the east gable of the nave.

Opposite the Royal Oak Inn (1900) is a lockup, windowless and constructed of large blocks of stone.

KETTLESHULME
[Macclesfield]

SJ9879: 6 miles (10km) NE of Macclesfield

This small village nestles amongst the hills between Macclesfield and Whaley Bridge and it formed one of twenty-three townships in the Forest of Macclesfield. It lies in the north-western corner of the Peak District National Park and close to the border with Derbyshire.

This is typical Pennine hill country: a landscape of long, grassy upland slopes, rounded hills, steep-sided valleys with countless watercourses, patches of peat, gritstone outcrops and miles of stone walling. South of Kettleshulme the county boundary runs along Cats Tor 1706ft (520m) and Shining Tor 1834ft (559m).

The settlement is not mentioned in Domesday. It was described as 'Keteleshulm' in 1285 and is derived from 'Ketil's holm or island'. The element *holm* (hulme) is derived from the Old Danish and points to Scandinavian colonisation. For an explanation, the settlement was sited on a piece of land (an island) between the Todd Brook and one of its tributaries.

The Macclesfield-Fernilee Turnpike through Kettleshulme, authorised by Act of Parliament in 1770, completed a cross-Pennine link between Macclesfield and Sheffield. This was an important trade route previously used by packhorse trains carrying salt from Nantwich and Middlewich.

The Brocklehurst family of Gap Head was in business as chapmen by the early 18th century, trading in locally produced silk buttons. In the textile trade, chapmen were merchants who would buy and sell wool cloth, silk etc., sometimes travelling with two or three ponies, or with a train of packhorses, from cottage to village and from village to market. Brocklehursts started silk weaving and founded the firm of Brocklehurst Whiston in Macclesfield.

Lumbhole Mill lies in the valley of Todd Brook just north of the village of Kettleshulme. In 1798 it was a water-powered cotton mill, and in 1811 hand-loom weavers occupied it. George Brocklehurst bought the mill and extended the building in 1811. The factory was burnt down in 1822. In 1823-4 the ruins were purchased by John Sheldon, who reconstructed the mill. From this time until 1937, this was the scene of one of the few 'candlewick' fabric industries in England.

Kettleshulme has no parish church but **Glebe House**, designed by Ernest Newton, was built as the vicarage for a church never provided (1911-12). Until 1924, the parish church was St John's Saltersford, better known as **Jenkin Chapel**. Kettleshulme is now in Taxal Parish.

Methodism found followers in Kettleshulme as it did in other hill villages. In 1781, James Mellor of Rainow, farmer, builder and later mill owner, erected the first Methodist Chapel on Billinge Hill above Rainow to serve Methodists of Kettleshulme and other hill villages. From the 18th century there was a large following in the area and often Methodist preachers conducted meetings at Pym Chair in the open air. The establishment of a Sunday School in Kettleshulme occurred some years before the building of a chapel in the village in 1815. Collections were made to support the building of the chapel, which was completed in 1901.

The **Gritstone Trail** passes a short distance to the west of Kettleshulme. This upland area is particularly well served with footpaths and bridleways. Routes lead to Macclesfield Forest, Shutlingsloe, Three Shires Head, Shining Tor and Cats Tor, and over the border to the Goyt Valley. Just outside the village, the much-loved Windgather Youth Hostel was open until fairly recently. Nearby, the crags of Windgather Rocks attract many climbers.

KINGSLEY[Vale Royal]

SJ5475: 4 miles (6km) S of Runcorn

The ancient village of Kingsley lies to the north of Delamere Forest, just east of the B5152 Delamere to Frodsham road. This pleasantly situated rural community is a much sought after location for residence. Commuters have the advantage of the M56 to the north, and railway stations at Delamere and Frodsham.

Kingsley was mentioned in the Domesday Survey as 'Chingeslie' in Roelau Hundred. Dunning held Kingsley from the Earl as a free man. It would appear that the Saxon, Dunning, was allowed to keep the estate after the Norman Conquest. There was land for two ploughs, and the settlement had five serfs (slaves), one villager and three smallholders. Domesday records one and a half fisheries, a large tract of woodland that was taken by the Earl, a hawk's eyrie and four deer parks. In Norman eyes, also a very much sought after place.

The name is described as 'Kingisleg' in 1260. The word is derived from 'the King's leah'.

Delamere Forest (from de la Mara) stretched from Frodsham marshes almost to Nantwich. Not all was wooded terrain, there were some parts under pasture and some arable. At one time, Frodsham, Tarvin, Tarporley and Weaverham were all in Delamere Forest.

Once an area was declared a royal forest, the main concern of those in charge was the preservation of the forest animals, particularly deer and boar. Severe regulations were imposed forbidding the harming of the beasts. The carrying of bows and arrows was always restricted and the killing or injuring of any animal, such as deer or boar, would be punished at the court of the **'Forest Eyre'**.

However, increasing afforestation met growing protests and the barons forced King John to issue a Charter of the Forests, probably because of the increased need for agricultural use. In the 12th century, the appointment by the Earl of Chester of the Master Forestership of the forests of Mara and Mondrem was to be held by the tenure of an official horn.

In 1812, the remaining tracts of medieval forest were officially disafforested. The Crown retained some land, some went to private owners and the rest was planted with conifers to be controlled by the Surveyor of Forests (now the Forestry Commission).

Many dwellings have existed in and around the village since Saxon times. The present **Kingsley Hall** stands on the site of a Norman manor house, and another mansion that stood there until it was demolished early in Queen Victoria's reign. The present brick farmhouse was erected at that time.

Peel Hall in the Weaver Valley was once a fortified farmstead. A moat that surrounds the red-brick Victorian farmhouse gives a clue to the ancient history of the site.

The **church of St John the Evangelist** was designed by Sir George Gilbert Scott in the late 13th-century style, and built for the Commissioners between 1849 and 1850. It is a small building with a west tower with two side chambers. The north aisle is short with a timber arcade. Inside the church there is a formation of three arches.

KNUTSFORD [Macclesfield]
SJ7578: 6 miles (9km) W of Wilmslow

Knutsford is an attractive old market town on the edge of gently undulating lowland. At one time a staging post on the old Liverpool to London road, it now has the presence of Knutsford service station, Junction 19 on the M6.

Knutsford was listed in Domesday as 'Cunetesford'. Egbrand held the settlement and the lands were owned by William, son of Nigel. In 1282, the place was recorded as 'Knottisford'. The Norse presence in Cheshire was considerable and, although the founder may have been the famous ruler Canute as suggested locally, the name would be a fairly common one.

Edward I granted the town's charter in 1292, and its present day architectural character is complemented by two large open spaces within sight of the town centre.

A network of narrow streets and passages connects Knutsford's two main streets, Toft Road, the upper one, and King Street, the lower thoroughfare. Toft Road contains the thatched pub, the **White Bear,** and narrow King Street retains a number of interesting old houses. Here, many of the shops are black and white half-timbered buildings, some genuine, others Victorian creations. However, amongst these properties is an amazing building, a single square stone tower in the Italianate style – the **Gaskell Memorial Tower**;. This was commissioned by Richard Harding Watt, a Manchester glove manufacturer who used his wealth in engaging architects to carry out his ideas of fine building.

Elizabeth Gaskell's novel *Cranford* (1853) is a classic picture of old Knutsford society. It chronicles the daily events and lives of people and characters who lived in this small country town. In her novels *Wives and Daughters* and *Ruth*, Elizabeth Gaskell (1810-65) also charmingly portrayed the town and its inhabitants. She is buried in the churchyard of the Unitarian Chapel.

On the first Sunday in May, Knutsford celebrates the crowning of the **Royal May Queen**. This very happy and colourful occasion has the May Queen riding in a landau accompanied by an impressive retinue of pages and ladies-in-waiting. The whole town is decorated with bunting and the procession, led by 'Jack-in-the-Green', parades to Knutsford Heath for performances by brass bands, and Morris and maypole dancing.

The **church of John the Baptist**, Church Hill (1741-4) is a brick building with a tower and nave. The aisles are composed of five bays with two-tiered arched windows. The interior consists of Tuscan columns and two galleries. The font dates from the building of the church and is of marble with an oak cover. There is a fine two-tier brass candelabrum, the gift of the Hall family in 1768, and an interesting prayer book dated 1686. The children's chapel at the east end of the south aisle was formed in 1923.

The **Unitarian Chapel** , Adam's Hill was licensed in 1689. It is brick built with two-light windows. The front of the building has two entrances, one at each end, and the staircases, which lead to the galleries, are outside at each end of the building.

Tatton Hall lies 3 miles (5km) north of Knutsford. Its history goes back to a Saxon called Tata who established a homestead 'Tata's tun'. In Domesday the place is listed as 'Tatune'. Leofwin held it and the lands were owned by Ranulf Mainwaring. It was a small settlement with a little arable land and the inhabitants consisted of one rider, two slaves, two villagers and four smallholders.

Over the centuries, the estate passed from one family to another and eventually, from 1598, into the possession of the Egerton family. In 1958 the magnificent house and park was bequeathed to the National Trust. The present hall was designed by Samuel and Lewis Wyatt in the neoclassical style; it was begun in 1788-91 and completed around 1807.

The earlier house, the Old Hall, stands in the park together with the surrounding evidence of a deserted medieval village – the original settlement. The main block of the hall is of two storeys and the south front is of seven bays. Lewis Wyatt was responsible for the interior decoration, and Gillows of Lancaster executed many of the furniture designs.

The main entrance hall is in the classical Greek style with columns in marble and porphyry. The music room and the drawing room are more comfortable and intimate and the fine library constitutes an important room in the house. The dining room (c1750) is part of the earlier mansion that existed here.

The kitchens and the servants' quarters provide an excellent insight into what life was like below stairs. The gardens at

Tatton look out across many acres of parkland and over Tatton Mere. The gardens contain terraces, woodland areas, the Orangery, shrub borders and rose gardens, the Tower Garden and an attractive lake with a Shinto temple on an island.

The **Old Hall**, which lies on the east side of Tatton Park, is basically a timber-framed building. The Great Hall has a splendid roof with carved beams.

Tabley House lies 2 miles (3km) west of Knutsford. It was built between 1761 and 1777 as a replacement for Tabley Old Hall. The present building is a mansion of red brick with stone dressings. The Old Hall and Tabley House were built for the **Leicester family.** It was their seat from 1272 until 1975, when on the death of Lt Col John Leicester-Warren it passed to the University of Manchester.

The building is a Grade 1 listed Palladian mansion with a very fine entrance side. The house consists of seven bays and one and a half storeys above a basement. The latter is really a low ground floor with a roughened stone exterior surface.

The garden side, which was originally the main entrance, displays two fine curved outer staircases up to the main doorway. This side of the house has nine bays and the former entrance has a portico of Tuscan columns and pediment. The original entrance hall is now a fine room; there is a spacious staircase leading to a screen of columns on the upper landing. The drawing room is blessed with a splendid fireplace and a ceiling with plasterwork.

The first Lord de Tabley was a great patron and collector of British paintings. The famous gallery created for Sir John Fleming Leicester before 1809 has been restored (1988-90) to its appearance in the 1840s, when it was remodelled with lavish red flock wallpaper. Today, impor-

tant works by J.M.W. Turner, Henry Thomas and James Ward can be seen, together with fine paintings by Dobson, Lely, Reynolds, Cotes, Nothcote, Callcott, Fuseli, Lawrence and Martin. The collection is owned by the University of Manchester and administered by trustees.

The Chapel of St Peter, together with Tabley Old Hall, was originally built between 1675 and 1678 on an island in Tabley Mere. Subsidence caused the buildings to collapse but the chapel was rescued and re-erected west of Tabley House between 1927 and 1929. It has arched windows and inside the high pulpit has a sounding board and an hourglass. One window was designed by Edward Burne-Jones, (1895) and there is a collecting box of 1678.

LACH DENNIS [Vale Royal]
SJ6972: 3 miles (5km) ESE of Northwich

Lach Dennis is an attractive little village situated between the A530 and the M6. It consists of old cottages and more modern dwellings built in recent years. This is mainly a farming community surrounded by rich agricultural land and nearby farmsteads.

Lach (Dennis) is mentioned in Domesday as 'Lece', and was described as 'Lache Deneys' in 1260. The first element is derived from 'lache, leche' or 'a stream flowing through boggy land'. The element 'Dennis' is probably a personal or family name.

The village pub is the Duke of Portland. Its name was said to have been changed because King Edward VII used to travel under that title when he accompanied the Cheshire Hunt.

A story told and retold, tells how the notorious highwayman, **Dick Turpin**, used one of the village smithies. Nowadays, one engineer still attends to the farmers' agricultural machinery and equipment.

The **church of All Saints** was built in 1895.

LEDSHAM [Chester]

SJ3575: 6 miles (9km) NNW of Chester

This small village is mainly an agricultural community on the Wirral, on the north-west border of Cheshire. It lies between the A550 and the A41 to the west of Ellesmere Port.

The settlement was mentioned in Domesday as 'Levetesham', and was described as 'Leuedesham' in 1100. The name is derived from the personal element 'Leofede's ham'. The Old English element 'ham' can mean 'village, manor or homestead'.

After the Second World War, land was taken from local smallholdings for the needs of the Atomic Energy Authority at Capenhurst. This complex is now owned by the British Nuclear Fuels Limited, whose futuristic structures dominate the landscape. The factory not only provides employment but allows local people the use of its sports and social facilities.

A Calvinistic Methodist chapel was opened in 1855 and is now a branch of the Presbyterian Church of Wales.

LINDOW AND ROW OF TREES [Macclesfield]

SJ8381: 1 mile (1.5km) W of Wilmslow

Lindow is a small community surrounded by other villages and hamlets, just to the west and joined to the town of Wilmslow.

Lindow Bog was once a dangerous area for unwary travellers. It is said that thirty lime trees planted as a guide for people crossing the district gave rise to the name of Row of Trees.

Lindow Moss became famous when, on 1st August 1984, a man working a peat excavating machine uncovered part of a human foot. Other parts of the body were found and, after carbon dating tests, scientists calculated that the remains were some 2000 years old. The victim, nicknamed Peter Marsh, had been garrotted, beaten and stabbed and was naked apart from an armband of fox fur. It was concluded that Lindow Man had been a sacrificial victim of a ritual execution.

The name of the hamlet Lindow, may be derived from the Old Scandinavian *Linda* – 'lime tree'; and from the Old English second element 'hoh' – 'a wet depression'.

The immediate neighbourhood contains dwellings, farms and cottages representing styles from the Georgian, Victorian and Edwardian periods. Examples include Row of Trees Farm, a black and white building c1603, and the 18th-century Davenport House Farm.

The **church of St John Evangelist**, 1873-4, designed by J.W. Beaumont, is situated in Lindow.

LITTLE BOLLINGTON [Macclesfield]

SJ7286: 4 miles (6km) NW of Wilmslow

The village is situated in the north of the county between the Bridgewater Canal and the River Bollin; the latter is the border between Cheshire and Greater Manchester. Across the river lies the parkland and mansion of Dunham Hall.

The settlement was described as 'Bolington' in 1287; the etymology of the river name 'Bollin' is uncertain.

The sandstone **church of the Holy Trinity**, 1854, was designed by Anthony Salvin. The building has a nave, chancel and lancet windows, and a black and white porch.

There is a picnic area at the car park to the Bridgewater Canal. This is now a popular waterway for many types of leisure craft.

LITTLE BUDWORTH [Vale Royal]

SJ5965: 3½ miles (5.5km) W of Winsford

The village lies midway between Winsford and Tarporley, in the angle between the A49 and the A54. Budworth Pool is situated just north of the village and Little Budworth Common to the west.

The settlement is mentioned in Domesday as 'Bodeurde' and was described as 'Bodeurdeworth' in 1291. Its name is derived from a personal element – 'Bud(d)a's wor(p)th'. In the Middle Ages the area was part of the great forests of Mara and Mondrum. Of particular importance is the fact that Little Budworth Common remains as the last vestige of that great wooded area and is now designated as a Site of Special Scientific Interest.

The **church of St Peter**, circa 1526, has a square Perpendicular tower. The present building (1798-1800) was erected at the expense of a Manchester merchant. John Douglas restored the church in 1870. Arched windows illuminate an interior that contains an attractive pulpit of around 1800 and an 18th-century font. There is also a good painting entitled 'The Entombment' in the family pew.

Today, village people are still involved in agriculture but many others commute to the nearby large centres of population. The village has a set of almshouses near to the church. They are two-storeyed, brick-built structures with mullioned windows.

Oulton Park House was a Baroque mansion built for John Egerton in 1716 to replace a Tudor house destroyed by fire. The new building consisted of fifteen bays with an imposing Corinthian centrepiece. Alterations and additions were made by Lewis Wyatt in 1816-26. Sadly, this house was burned down on the 14th February 1926. During the removal of works of art, six people were killed when the ceiling collapsed. Today, all that remains are farm buildings, garden walls, a lodge, a pair of wrought-iron gates and a monument to John Francis Egerton.

In 1953, **Oulton Park** became a motor-racing circuit and other features include a racing school and a polo ground.

LITTLE SUTTON [Ellesmere Port]

SJ3777: 2 miles (3km) W of Ellesmere Port

The village is situated on the A41, Chester to Birkenhead road, and has a station on the Liverpool to Ellesmere Port railway line. At one time a rural community, the area has now become a residential suburb of Ellesmere Port.

Before the Norman Conquest, the settlement belonged to the canons of St Werburgh. Later the land was held by Benedictine monks until the Dissolution of the Monasteries. The settlement is mentioned in Domesday as 'Sudtone', and the name is commonly derived from the Old English 'Sup-tun' or 'Southern tun'.

LOSTOCK GRALAM [Vale Royal]

SJ6874: 3 miles (5km) ENE of Northwich

The village is situated to the north-east of Northwich, between Wincham Brook and the A559 Northwich to Altrincham road. The community is served by a railway station on the Northwich to Manchester line.

During the past century, brine pumping and salt mining have caused considerable subsidence around the area. Great sheets of water called **flashes** collected to the west of Lostock Gralam, between Wincham and Northwich. They are called Ashton's Flash, Dunkirk Flash, Neumann's Flash and Worthington Flash.

Holford Hall, now a farmhouse, is a moated, black and white-timbered house. The remaining sections are only part of a much larger house rebuilt for Mary Cholmondeley after the death of her husband, Sir Hugh, in 1601. There is a fine double-arched stone bridge opposite a timber-framed block, originally the centre of the larger dwelling. Carving and patterned timberwork decorate the three storeys and two broad gables.

The village of Lostock Gralam is not mentioned in Domesday. The settlement was described as 'Lostoch' in 1100 and 'le Lostoke Graliam' in 1288. One Gralamus held the manor of Lostock Gralam in 1200. 'Gralam' is no doubt a French personal name.

'Lostock' is an interesting name which could be explained from the Old English as 'hloc-stoc' or 'stoc with a pig-sty'. However, there may have been a Welsh connotation, *llost* 'trail' or *llostog* 'beaver'. So it could be a Welsh name meaning 'beaver stream'.

The **church of St John Evangelist** was built between 1844 and 1845 and has later Victorian features. It has an attractive spire.

LOWER PEOVER [Vale Royal/Macclesfield]

SJ7474: 6 miles (10km) E of Northwich

The countryside south of Knutsford seems to be composed of a flat, featureless landscape of green fields. But this part of the Cheshire Plain hides many a secret, sometimes hidden by trees and hedgerows. One such place is Lower Peover. Pronounced 'peever', the village consists of two sections half a mile apart. A church has stood on the site since medieval times and it dominates a handful of buildings around a green and its cobbled lane.

One of the buildings is the old school house, founded in 1710 by the vicar, Richard Comberbach. Not only did he endow the school with a sum of money, he also acted as the head teacher.

Another building is the public house whose official name was the Warren de Tabley Arms. In parts it dates back some 700 years and has been known for some time as The Bells of Peover. This has nothing to do with the church but gets its name from the Bell family who used to live there.

The **church of St Oswald** was formerly a chapel of ease of Great Budworth. The small church gradually increased in size, but the plan remains unchanged, consisting of a nave with aisles, a chancel with side chapels and a fine sandstone tower of around 1500. Inside, the huge timbers that support the roof rest on octagonal wooden pillars. This half-timbered church receives many visitors who come to admire its nave roof, box pews, some with crests on their doors, and all the richness of the 17th-century woodwork. The church originally had aisles under the same roof as that of the nave. The restoration by Salvin in 1852 gave the three aisles separate roofs. The ancient font is possibly early 14th century and has a Jacobean cover.

There is a fine Jacobean pulpit, thought to have been part of a three-decker model, Jacobean parclose screens and a massive dug-out wooden chest, bound with iron bands and secured by staples and locks dating from the 13th century.

Lower Peover church has many memorials to the Shakerley, Leicester and Cholmondeley families.

LOWER WITHINGTON [Macclesfield]

SJ8169: 7 miles (11km) S of Alderley Edge

This is a scattered community in mainly agricultural surroundings between the A535 and the A34. The manor of Lower Withington came into the possession of the Mainwarings who held it until the end of the 17th century. At the time of William the Conqueror, a Baskervyle came from Normandy and one of his descendants acquired the manor of Old Withington around the middle of the 13th century.

The settlement is mentioned in Domesday as 'Hungrewenitune' and described as 'Widinton' in 1186. The name is derived from the Old English 'wipig' (withig) meaning 'willow', so 'a tun among willows'.

Withington Hall consisted of two houses; one built in brick about the middle of the 18th century and a larger dwelling built in 1795 for John Baskervyle Glegg. The house was demolished in 1963 and replaced with a smaller brick residence.

The discovery of silica sand has resulted in vast quantities being extracted for use in glass making, abrasives, steel and other purposes. The retreating glaciers at the end of the Ice Ages deposited this area of sand.

The nearby **Jodrell Bank** complex was opened in 1957 to house Manchester University's radio telescope. There is a 250ft (76m) circular metal dish, fully steerable, supported on two 180ft (55m) metal towers. Close by are the Mark II and Mark III paraboloids, a small telescope for tracking space probes and a fifth bowl with a massive concrete pillar. There is an impressive visitor centre and many 'hands-on' exhibitions that are a great delight to children of all ages. Other attractions include Planetarium shows, an arboretum with paths and tree trails, a children's playground and a picnic area.

The Lower Withington Gooseberry Show has been an attractive local event for a number of years. It usually takes place at the end of July and is held in the parish hall.

The Methodist chapel was built in 1808 and the church of St Peter in 1892.

LYMM [Warrington]

SJ6887: 5 miles (8km) E of Warrington

Downstream from Warrington and close to the Manchester Ship Canal lies the town of Lymm; although it is still very much a village in character. Lymm's roots have traditionally rested in agriculture but it has had an industrial past with small industries such as tanning and fustian cutting. The settlement, centred around Bradley Brook, has now spread along the A56, the A6144 and along the sides, in parts, of the Bridgewater Canal.

Lymm is now primarily a residential commuter base for Warrington and Manchester, being very accessible to Junctions 9 and 21 of the M56 and M6. Also nearby is the famous and recently widened Thelwall Viaduct, which leaps across the Manchester Ship Canal and the Mersey Valley.

Lymm's shopping centre is situated next to the **Bridgewater Canal**. This canal, initially from Worsley to Manchester, took from 1758 to 1761 to build. The remaining twenty miles across North Cheshire were not completed until 1777. At Preston Brook it was joined by the Grand Trunk, now the Trent and Mersey Canal.

The cutting of fustian cloth began in three-storey cottages, with the top storey housing the cutting benches, which needed a long workshop. Such cottages may still be seen in Church Road in Lymm. The bulk cloth was transported from Manchester along the Bridgewater Canal. Nowadays, the canal is very busy with holiday craft.

The centre of the village is The Dingle, a pretty tree-lined area alongside Bradley Brook. A delightful footpath leads from the bottom of The Dingle to Lymm Dam. The lake is a man-made feature in a rocky ravine with wooded slopes.

Also in the centre of Lymm is **The Cross**. It stands on sandstone bedrock and is raised above street level and a surrounding cobbled area. The steps are actually cut into the sandstone and lead up to three sundials with inscriptions around them. These old inscriptions seem very appropriate to this day and age.

'Save Time

Think of the Past

We are a Shadow'

The present cross dates from the 17th century but it is believed that a cross has been here since the 14th century; it served as an open-air meeting and preaching point. It was restored in Queen Victoria's Jubilee Year (1897).

The **church of St Mary** was designed by John Dobson and built between 1850 and 1852. J.S. Crowther of Manchester built the high west tower (1888-90). It is a long building with transepts with galleries. The church contains an octagonal font, probably 1660s, and a 17th-century pulpit dated 1623. There is a good east window displaying Christ, Saints and Angels (1865). There are other examples of 19th-century stained glass to be found in the north aisle and the south aisle.

Lymm Hall, Rectory Lane, is a much restored Elizabethan house with a porch. The house is set in beautifully landscaped grounds. The approach to the hall is via a bridge with a decorated parapet.

MACCLESFIELD
[Macclesfield]

SJ8973: 31 miles (50km) E of Chester

The town of Macclesfield is situated at the foot of the south Pennine Hills on the banks of the River Bollin. The infant stream has its sources amongst the peat moors of Macclesfield Forest. The lively river and its tributaries flow round **Tegg's Nose Country Park** and contribute to a number of reservoirs in the Langley area. It continues through Macclesfield and flows in a north-west direction to join the **Manchester Ship Canal** at Bollin Point.

In the Domesday Survey the settlement is listed as 'Maclesfeld', which became 'Makelesfeld' in 1183. Macclesfield was the name of a great forest and the first element may be the old name of the forest. Earl Edwin held the settlement and the lands were owned by Earl Hugh. Domesday records considerable arable land, a mill, meadowland for oxen and an extensive area of woodland. Macclesfield grew rapidly and became a borough in 1220. In 1261 Prince Edward granted a Charter to the burgesses of the town, with the privileges of a free borough.

Good clues to a medieval past are to be found in street patterns and in street names such as Jordangate, Chestergate and Backwallgate. The word 'wall' is a corruption of 'well', and 'gate' is a medieval word for 'street'.

Macclesfield Forest was a tract of land that extended for some considerable distance along the flanks and foothills of the south Pennines. After 1237 it became a royal hunting forest for the kings of England and their eldest sons, who were also the earls of Chester.

The **church of St Michael** stands perched on an escarpment above the River Bollin. Queen Eleanor, first wife of Edward I, endowed the manor with a chapel which was consecrated in 1278. This was the beginning of the parish church, then called All Hallows. Over the west door can be seen the **arms of Queen Eleanor of Castile**. There are just two reminders of the 13th-century building in the form of medieval masonry in the tower and half pier supports bonded into a wall of the former nave.

Between 1898 and 1901, Sir Arthur Blomfield practically rebuilt the whole church by pulling down the mid-18th century structure. Sir Arthur William Blomfield, (1829-1899) was educated at Rugby School and Trinity College, Cambridge. He commenced practice in 1856.

He was architect to the Bank of England, 1883, and diocesan architect to Winchester. He carried out many commissions for Chester Cathedral, and for a considerable number of churches throughout the country. He was knighted in 1889 and was awarded a Royal Gold Medal in 1891. He was buried at Broadway, Worcestershire.

The principal interest in **St Michael's Church** is centred on the Savage and Legh Chapels and their very fine monuments. The Savage Chapel contains the Pardon Brass in memory of Roger Legh who died in 1506. It depicts Roger kneeling with his six sons. The middle section depicts the Mass of St Gregory. Originally there was a companion piece that portrayed his wife and seven daughters. On the south side, within the sanctuary, is the beautiful tomb in memory of Sir John Savage, died 1495, and his wife, Katherine; the effigies are splendid examples of late 15th-century craftsmanship. They had a large family of nine sons and six daughters. The Legh Chapel, founded in 1422 and rebuilt in 1620, is now used as the baptistery.

Two families were influential in this area during the 15th century: the Leghs of Lyme Hall and Adlington, and the Ridge and Savage family, who leased the Lord's Park throughout the 15th and 16th centuries. Thomas Savage became Archbishop of York. The family were related to the Stanleys who, after the Battle of Bosworth in 1485, were rewarded by Henry VIII with the title of Earl of Derby and the stewardship of the Macclesfield Forest.

Christ Church, Catherine Street is a large, brick, Georgian church in a rather severe classical style. It has a very high tower. The church was built in 1775-6 at the expense of **Charles Roe**, a local industrialist. The interior contains an important monument to the founder. This includes a female figure with a portrait medallion of the deceased in one hand and a cogwheel in the other. Below are reliefs of the church and the industrial works of the founder.

St Alban Roman Catholic Church, Chester Road is a Pugin church of considerable size. It was begun in 1839 and opened in 1841. The church contains a screen surmounted by a rood between the nave and chancel. Pugin also designed the altar. The Unitarian Chapel in King Edward Street was built in 1689.

The commencement of the **silk trade** in Macclesfield is obscure. Charles

Roe's silk mill built in 1743 was at the lower end of Mill Street. Production also took place in cottages or in small workshops. By the middle of the 18th century, mills began to use water-powered machinery, which was followed by steam.

Many of the new houses built at that time had garrets for the handloom weavers. There were spinners and weavers and throwsters, dyers and finishers, fringers and trimmers, printers by screen and block hemmers and embroiderers. There were also a number of delightful names given to some of the specialist jobs in the silk mill: bale breakers, draft pickers, uptwisters, multiple end cheese winders and gassers.

Paradise Mill, Roe Street is unique in Britain, being the only mill where silk handloom weaving survived on a factory scale. It continued until the 1980s, when it became a museum.

Tegg's Nose Country Park was the site of former stone quarrying operations. It is situated 1½ miles (2km) east of Macclesfield. Access is from the A537 Buxton road. There are many waymarked trails including the Gritstone Trail. The Park's situation on a valley side gives wide, open views.

Macclesfield Forest is a large attractive area of coniferous woodland, 3 miles (5km) east of Macclesfield. There are walking routes and picnic areas around the four reservoirs in the valley bottom.

MALPAS [Chester]

SJ4847: 5 miles (8km) NW of Whitchurch

Malpas is one of the delightful and compact small towns of Cheshire. It is situated in an agricultural area of the Cheshire Plain in the far south-west of the county. The countryside of the parish is mostly rural, gently undulating farmland

criss-crossed by narrow lanes. Lying along the route of the Roman road from Wroxeter to Chester, this settlement was always prone to incursions by the Welsh and became a strategic place guarding the route to the Welsh border.

When the Normans came this way on their wasting of the Cheshire countryside, they found the terrain hard going and named the settlement Malo Passu – meaning 'difficult passage'. Domesday lists the place as 'Depenbech' and records that Earl Edwin held the settlement and the lands owned by Robert son of Earl Hugh. The survey records meadowland, ploughland and that its inhabitants included five men-at-arms. A castle was constructed here by one of the Norman barons, the site of which can be seen behind the church as a grassy mound.

A village cross on stone steps stands at the crossing of the main street. This is not medieval but is of 1877.

In the 18th century, the little town was greatly influenced by the Cholmondeleys, who built the town's almshouses in 1721. From the junction of Church Street and High Street, one can see the **Market House** dating from 1762 and built of local brick; it has a recessed ground floor and eight Tuscan columns. Church Street contains a fine, three-bay brick house of 1733 and Church View, an example of 17th century architecture. The Red Lion is an old coaching inn visited by King James I.

The **church of St Oswald** is a large and handsome sandstone building of the 14th century; it stands to the south of the castle motte. The present church was largely remodelled in the second half of the 15th century, with late 15th and early 16th century additions. The church, with the exception of the chancel, is embattled and its complement of parapets and pinnacles give it a splendid appearance. The church interior is equally impressive, with fine timbered roofs to the nave and aisles. Most of the roof dates from the 15th century and the picture of rich moulding and elaborate bosses is a splendid sight.

The church contains many fine tombs and monuments. At the east end of the two aisles are the Brereton and Cholmondeley Chapels. The Brereton, or Egerton Chapel, possesses a magnificent alabaster altar tomb to Sir Randle Brereton and his wife, Eleanor (1522). The effigy of Sir Randle is depicted in plate armour and that of his wife is attired in an elegant, flowing cloak. The sides of the tomb have niches containing figures of the sons and daughters.

In the Cholmondeley Chapel there is a fine alabaster altar tomb to Sir Hugh Cholmondeley and his lady, 1596. The knight is shown in armour and with a moustache and neat beard. The lady is shown wearing a form of the French hood with a long-waisted bodice.

In the chancel and chapels are stalls, some with misericords; one is the figure of a mermaid with a brush and comb. There is a memorial in the east window to **Reginald Heber** who was born in Malpas in 1775, and who became Bishop of Calcutta. He was the author of many well-known hymns, including *Holy, Holy, Holy, Lord God Almighty* and *From Greenland's Icy Mountains*.

At the end of the Middle Ages, a branch of the influential Brereton family settled in Malpas. Sir Randle Brereton served Henry VII and Henry VIII in military posts of importance at home and abroad. He was appointed chamberlain of Chester, the earl's principal deputy in the county. He founded a school and almshouses as well. After his death the buildings decayed and disappeared.

Another influential family in the history of Malpas are the neighbouring Cholmondeleys. In 1488, Richard Cholmondeley left a sum of money in his will to the remodelling of the church. Sir Hugh Cholmondeley was Sheriff of Chester in 1589. In the 18th century, the Cholmondeleys revived the school and almshouses. In 1847, the Marquess of Cholmondeley presented 16th-17th-century Flemish roundels and panels from Cholmondeley Chapel to the church.

MARBURY [Crewe]

SJ5645: 3 miles (5km) NE of Whitchurch

The picturesque village of Marbury, sometimes winner of the Best Kept Village Competition, is set in a gently undulating landscape on the south-west border of the county, to the south of the Shropshire Union Canal.

Listed in the Domesday Book (1086) as 'Merberie', the lands were owned by William Malbank, but had previously belonged to King Harold. Domesday mentions wooded surroundings.

The village name became Merebury in 1260, which means 'the burg by a lake' – 'a burg' being an Anglo-Saxon fortified place or manor. The area is renowned for its meres or lakes, formed when water filled the numerous glacial depressions left following the last Ice Age. The Big Mere, which lies to the south-west of the village, has a maximum depth of 26ft (8m) and provides a safe habitat for a wide range of waterbirds, as does the nearby Little Mere, which is fringed with dense vegetation and reeds. Quoisley Meres, two small lakes with wooded banks, lie a short distance to the west of Marbury.

The oak tree on the village green was planted to commemorate the Battle of Waterloo (1815).

The village holds **Marbury Merry Days** on the second weekend in May to raise money towards the upkeep of the church. It is a two-day event of country entertainment with a variety of displays, attractions and competitions. Set beautifully above the Big Mere, the sandstone **church of St Michael** dated from the 13th century, although most of the present church is 15th century.

The western tower is of fine proportions. There are two good string-courses which display a frieze of carved animals and flowers. Gargoyles are a feature of the church design and present many curious figures carved by the medieval masons. These include faces of smiling twins, monkeys and humorous and grotesque faces.

The church possesses a fine and decorative 15th-century **wooden pulpit**, the oldest example in Cheshire. The oldest wooden example in England is to be found in the church of St Thomas at Mellor, near Marple in Stockport District.

There is a sundial plate now inside the church, and several cast-iron grave slabs in the graveyard near the east end of the church. These are thought to have been manufactured in neighbouring Staffordshire. One of the memorials in the church commemorates Captain William Halstead Poole of Marbury Hall, who fell at the storming of Sebastopol on the 8 September 1855.

At the approach to the church, on the left is a 17th-century, black and white house of timber-framed construction infilled with brick.

Facing the church on the far bank of Big Mere is **Marbury Hall**. This is a Regency house of white stucco with twin curved bows. It was built for the Poole family in 1810. They originally lived in Marley Hall a short distance to the east of Marbury.

The Shropshire Union Canal (Llangollen Branch) lies a short distance to the north of the village. The canal was cut in 1793 and provided a vital link to an isolated community. Nowadays, the canal has a brisk trade in holiday craft.

The Crewe to Shrewsbury Railway lies 1½ miles (2.5km) south-east of the village. It was opened in 1858 and at one time goods for the village were off-loaded at nearby Poole's Siding. At the present time, the nearest stations are at Whitchurch and Wrenbury.

The route of the South Cheshire Way passes close to the village.

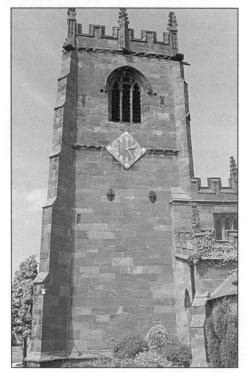

St Michael's, Marbury

MARSTON [Vale Royal]

SJ6676: 1 mile (1.6km) N of Northwich

Marston is a small village adjoining the Trent and Mersey Canal and the large sheets of water called flashes. They are called Dunkirk Flash, Neumann's Flash, Worthing Flash and Ashton's Flash. These were caused during the past century by brine pumping and salt mining.

There is a famous story that the Tsar of Russia visited the area and held a dinner party in the mines. It is said that the function was illuminated by the light of 10,000 candles, the light glittering and reflected ten-fold by the surrounding salt crystals.

The settlement was described as 'Merston' in 1304 and 'Merschton' in 1316. The name is derived from the Old English 'Mersc-tun' or 'tun by a marsh'.

MARTHALL [Macclesfield]

SJ7976: 4 miles (6km) SE of Knutsford

Marthall lies on the A537 Macclesfield to Knutsford road. This small village lies amongst an extensive farming area. Pastureland and arable land are part of a landscape of hedges, trees and patches of woodland. Although probably unnoticed, there is an **Ordnance Survey Triangulation Pillar** near to the village crossroads. For the records, this indicates that particular location as being 259ft (79m) above mean sea level. The pillar may be regarded as an object that should have listed status.

The **church of All Saints** was built in 1839 and enlarged in 1887. It is constructed in brick, with round-arched windows and an apse.

MARTON [Macclesfield]

SJ8468: 3 miles (4km) N of Congleton

The old village of Marton, with its distinctive black and white church, is situated close to the A34.

In Domesday, Marton is listed as 'Merutune', which became 'Merton' in

1248. The meaning is 'the tun (homestead) by a lake'. The settlement was named after Marton Mere, which has now been drained. Domesday records that it was held by Godric, and the lands owned by Earl Hugh.

The **church of St James and St Paul** was not built until the reign of Edward III, being founded by Sir John de Davenport about the middle of the 14th century. The head of the house of Davenport was the chief forester of Macclesfield Forest. It is one of the ancient timber-framed churches of Cheshire, and considered one of the oldest longitudinal timber churches of Europe.

The tower is unique and most interesting when seen from inside the belfry. There is a mass of huge, squared timbers piled into a framework to support the shingled turret. The ladder in the church is probably the original one and leads into the bell-ringers' loft. Four octagonal oak pillars which divide the nave and the side aisles rise to support the exposed roof beams. By the 18th century, the timbers of the chancel and side chapels had deteriorated and the decayed wood was replaced by brick.

The church interior includes a medieval wall painting on the west wall above the tower doorway; this is thought to represent the Last Judgement. There are also two painted panels of the 17th century. Two of the church windows contain fragments of medieval glass. The Jacobean pulpit, dated 1620, has good carving and a coat of arms. The parish chest is Elizabethan with heavy hinges and three locks.

The village inn, the **Davenport Arms**, was originally part of the Capesthorne Estate. It was once a courthouse and also a collection point where estate tenants paid their rent.

The giant village oak is now split into three parts.

One of the cottages was the birthplace of William Buckley (1780-1856). He was a bricklayer then joined the army, but was transported to Australia in 1802 for stealing. He escaped from prison at Port Phillip, near Melbourne, and lived with the native aborigines for the next 32 years. Known as the 'Wild White Man', following his 'discovery' he became a bodyguard to the colonel in command of the new colony, and later moved to Tasmania, where he died. Buckley's Cave and Buckley's Falls in Australia are named after him.

The village usually celebrates the **Wakes Féte** on the second weekend in July. The annual **Gooseberry Show** promotes intense competition for the largest fruit and takes place on the first weekend in August.

MICKLE TRAFFORD [Chester]

SJ4469: 3 miles (5km) NE of Chester

Mickle Trafford is situated just west of the River Gowy. Until recent housing developments, the community was scattered along the A56. Mickle Trafford is divided from Bridge Trafford by the River Gowy and the settlement lies around the junction of two embanked railway lines approaching Chester. Today, Mickle Trafford is a popular commuter village for Chester, the Wirral and Warrington.

The settlement is recorded in Domesday as 'Traford' and is described as 'Trocford' in 1190. The name means 'a ford in a valley'.

Mickle Trafford lies in the parish of Plemstall. The church of St Peter at Plemstall has a tower of 1826. The body of the church is Perpendicular in style and

has a six-bay north arcade. The interior is noted for its hammerbeam roof and for the extent of carved woodwork by a former incumbent, the Reverend J.H. Toogood, 1907 to 1946.

Trafford Heath lies to the north of Mickle Trafford. Here stood the old gallows where James Price who robbed the Warrington Mail in 1790 was executed. His body hung in chains for thirty years until the enclosure of the common land.

MIDDLEWICH [Congleton]

SJ7065: 6 miles (10km) SE of Northwich

The Keuper Marls underlie the Cheshire Plain for a considerable distance north and south, in fact salt springs have occurred close to the Lancashire and Shropshire borders. Middlewich was a borough in the 13th century and one of the trio of Cheshire wiches. There have been mixed fortunes for the salt towns, with Nantwich fading at the end of the 17th century and neighbouring Winsford beginning to develop.

The Roman site of Salinae (Middlewich) seems to straggle a little way along the Roman road, King Street, just north of the town. The position lies between the Trent and Mersey Canal and the railway line. On excavation, outlines of long, narrow timber buildings were discovered, together with a framework of fired clay for the heating of salt pans and vessels for the storing of brine. One exciting find was a jar with the letters 'AMYRCA' scratched on it; this was known to be the name given for a solution of brine waste, a cleaning product used by the Romans. Other evidence of the Roman presence came to light in the form of coins and shards of pottery. The excavations revealed that this important site was in use throughout the occupation of North West England.

Despite its growth as a salt town, Middlewich was just a handful of dwellings in the 17th century. Nevertheless, it is recorded that there were 107 salt houses in the town in 1605. As salt production increased, so came the problem of transportation. To connect the salt field more efficiently with the Mersey, the River Weaver was canalised in 1731. The Grand Trunk (Trent and Mersey) was authorised in 1766, connecting the salt field with the Mersey and the Humber, and later with the Potteries and Birmingham to carry coal, rock, salt and brine.

Nowadays, the King's Lock Inn, which lies just short of the junction with the Middlewich branch, is a popular stopping point for holiday craft traffic. Today, Middlewich is a quiet little town of neat red-brick houses and a short length of quiet shopping street. This road lies parallel to the thoroughfare of St Michael's Way, a route that appears to have arbitrarily slashed its way through the middle of the town.

Although Middlewich was an important place in Anglo-Saxon times, the settlement is not recorded in Domesday and neither is the mention of a church or priest. The name 'Mildestvic' was, however, recorded in Northwich Hundred. In 1185 the settlement's name is given as 'Middelwich'.

The **church of St Michael and All Angels** was badly damaged in the Civil War when Royalist troops, who had sought sanctuary inside the building, were killed.

It is certain that there was a Norman church on the site and that the church that exists today is a building dating in part from the 12th century. Built in sandstone, mainly Perpendicular in style, battlemented and pinnacled, the church consists of a nave, chancel and side aisles and a late 15th-century Perpendicular tower. It was rebuilt in the 14th century and the present building is of the 14th-century plan.

Sir William Brereton erected the timber roof in 1621. It is arch-braced with beautifully carved hammer beams. The only remaining section of the old roof has been renewed. There are finely carved Flemish panels in the screen and stalls and a splendid Jacobean screen with the Venables arms. Note the curious crest of the Venables – a dragon swallowing a child.

MILTON GREEN [Chester]

SJ4658: 1½ miles (2km) W of Tattenhall

Milton Green is a small village set amongst extensive farmland lying to the north of Broxton crossroads on the A41 Whitchurch to Chester road. This area of rich agricultural land is noted for its fine farmhouses and manor houses.

Calverley Hall is a late 17th-century house hidden behind a later plain façade. The interior contains a very fine, broad staircase with double twisted balusters. The quality of the carving is particularly good and suggests a craftsman of the Restoration period.

Lady Mary Calveley, the second wife of Sir Hugh Calveley, is known to have erected a domestic chapel in 1690. She died in 1705, and the estate passed to the Leghs of Lyme.

Other houses of note in the area are Clayley Hall, Russia Hall, Golborne Hall and Manor Farm, Aldersey.

The village was not mentioned in Domesday. Its name is probably derived from the Old English 'Middel-tun', 'middle tun'.

MINSHULL VERNON [Crewe]

SJ6860: 2 miles (3km) NNW of Crewe

Minshull Vernon is a scattered community on the A530, Nantwich to Middlewich road. The surroundings are mainly agricultural, with arable and pastureland. A short distance to the west lie the Shropshire Union Canal and the River Weaver.

In comparatively recent times, many of the local farmsteads were known for their cheesemaking. The hamlet of Bradfield Green lies on the line of the Roman road. Evidence of a section of road and a bridge have been discovered.

Minshull is mentioned in Domesday as 'Manessele' and records meadowland, woodland, enclosures and a hawk's eyrie. It was described as 'Munshull Vernoun' in 1309. The first element is derived from the Old English 'Monnes scylf' or 'Monn's ledge of land'. Vernon is a family name from Vernon in France.

The **church of St Peter**, c1847-9, was designed by John Matthews. It is a Commissioners' church with a nave and chancel, a bellcot and lancet windows.

The front of the Congregational church, 1809, in Cross Lane, received a Victorian restoration but one original arched window remains. A Wesleyan chapel was built in 1832.

MOBBERLEY [Macclesfield]

SJ7981: 2 miles (3km) E of Knutsford

The village is strung out along the B5085 Knutsford to Alderley Edge road, with the older part lying to the north. The settlement adjoins the Mobberley Brook and is east of the wide acres of Tatton Park. The surroundings consist of farmland and farmsteads. Mobberley is now a residential area and the local railway station on the Northwich to Manchester line serves commuters. The end of Manchester Airport's main runway lies across the River Bollin to the north-east.

The settlement is mentioned in Domesday as 'Motburlege' in Bochelau Hundred. Dot held it as a free man and the lands were owned by Bigot de Loges. There was land for four ploughs and the settlement contains a thane, one serf, one villager and two smallholders. Domesday records meadowland, an extensive area of woodland and two enclosures. The settlement was described as 'Modberleg' in 1260, and the name is derived from 'leah' or 'glade with a 'gemot-beorg' or 'assembly mound'.

In the first half of the 13th century Mobberley had an Augustinian priory, but no trace appears to remain.

The **church of St Wilfrid** has a broad west tower of 1533. The rest of the building is 14th to 15th century except for the east end, which is a Victorian addition (1889) by J.S. Crowther. Outside, the church shows its medieval origins in the square-headed windows in the aisles and clerestory.

The church is strongly linked with the Mallory family who acquired the estate in 1619. Since then, members of the family have served as squires and as rectors. The arcades consist of four bays with Decorated arch mouldings, but the chancel arch is of 1889.

A fine feature of the church is the medieval nave roof. This low-pitched covering is panelled and richly ornamented, particularly the section above the rood screen. This screen is probably the best example in the county with the uprights decorated with trails of foliage, and the ribs spreading out into vaulting under the coving. The whole is beautifully decorated with a rich tracery of leaves, fruit and various patterns.

The monuments include the

Leigh-Mallory memorial window. **George Leigh-Mallory** perished on Everest in 1924.

MOORE [Halton]

SJ5783: 3 miles (5km) SW of Warrington

Moore lies in the Mersey Valley, and the Manchester Ship Canal, opened by Queen Victoria in 1894, forms the northern boundary of the village. Hereabouts, the land that was drained is now used for agriculture. The name of the settlement was 'Mor' in 1311, and is derived from the Old English word 'mor' meaning 'moor, fen'.

Two railway lines pass through the area as well as the A558. The Duke of Bridgewater's canal, which runs along the village's southern boundary, was the first canal proper to reach Cheshire and the second in England. The section of this canal from Manchester to Worsley was completed in 1761 and the extension to Runcorn was completed in 1777.

The central part of the village is a conservation area. One of the old buildings situated close to the canal is Moore Hall. It is an early 18th-century house and said to be haunted. It is built of stone with a fine façade of five bays and a later Palladian porch. The house contains a fine staircase. One of the oldest dwellings in the village is Village Farm, a mid-17th-century stone building with three bays.

MOSSLEY [Congleton]

SJ8761: 2 miles (3km) SE of Congleton

The residential suburb of Mossley stretches out from Congleton beyond the Macclesfield Canal.The housing development follows the A527 Biddulph road and the road towards Dane in Shaw. To the east rise the gritstone escarpment of Congleton Edge and The Cloud, part of the dramatic boundary between the Pennines and the Cheshire Plain.

These gritstone ridges are part of the initial section of the Gritstone Trail and the Staffordshire Way. At Mossley, the path descends to follow the Dane in Shaw Brook and then climbs up to The Cloud, 1125ft (343m). The Cloud is formed of thick beds of Chatsworth Grit, which form a huge cliff right round the nose of the hill like the prow of a ship. There are magnificent all-round views from the summit.

The **church of Holy Trinity** was designed by C. and J. Trubshaw, and built between 1884 and 1885. This rock-faced building has a nave, chancel and bellcot. The interior of the church offers a lovely surprise in the form of the east window, which has excellent Morris glass (1889). The window depicts the Crucifixion above and three saints below. There are delightful floral quarries, also by Morris.

The first element of the place-name is possibly derived from the Old English 'mos' or the Old Norse *mosi* for 'a bog or swamp'. 'Leah' indicates 'a clearing'.

MOTTRAM ST ANDREW [Macclesfield]

SJ8778: 4 miles (6km) NW of Macclesfield

Mottram St Andrew lies on a byroad linking the A538 and the A34 east of Alderley Edge. The village, or ancient township, is in the ecclesiastical parish of Prestbury. To the west of the village rise the wooded sandstone hills of Alderley Edge, culminating in a fine escarpment. Copper and lead has been mined from these hills since the days of the Romans.

The settlement is mentioned in Domesday as 'Motre'. It records ploughland, extensive woodland, enclosures and a hawk's eyrie. The name was described as 'Mottrum' in 1248.

Some houses in Mottram have been farmhouse residences for many years; stone mullioned windows and traces of black and white work indicate their antiquity. The Mottershead family lived in Mottram and possibly this name bears some relationship with the name of Mottram. The first element of Mottershead was 'Moctresheved' in 1287, and the Welsh word *mochdre* means 'a pig farm'. The second element 'Andrew' possibly arises from a priest of that name who lived in the village during the Middle Ages.

Mottram Cross, an old butter cross, has steps and part of the shaft from the Middle Ages; the remainder of the shaft is 1832.

Mottram Old Hall was erected in the late Middle Ages as a semi-fortified house. One lower section of the house is part of the original building, and an L-shaped section on the other side is the remains of an early 17th-century, timber-framed extension. The house was originally surrounded by a moat.

Mottram New Hall, a short distance to the east, is a large brick mansion with a central block. It was built just before 1753 for William Wright, a Stockport landowner. With the chapel now converted into a banqueting suite, the hall is now established as a hotel and leisure centre.

MOULTON [Vale Royal]

SJ6569: 3 miles (5km) S of Northwich

The large village of Moulton lies between the Weaver Navigation and the River Dane, roughly equidistant between the salt towns of Winsford and Northwich. The surrounding area consists of farms and scattered patches of woodland. There is easy access to the A533, Northwich to Sandbach road.

The Crewe to Liverpool railway line passes alongside the village, but there is no station. The nearest stations are at Hartford and Winsford. The secluded site of the Vale Royal Abbey lies on the west bank of the Weaver, just across the river from Moulton.

The settlement is mentioned in Domesday as 'Moletune' in Middlewich Hundred. Richard of Vernon owned the lands, Leofnoth held it as a free man. There was land for two ploughs, with one villager and one smallholder. Domesday records meadowland, a large area of woodland and one enclosure.

The settlement was described as 'Multon' in 1260. The name may be derived form the personal name Mula, hence 'Mula's tun'. Or, another possibility, from the Old English 'Mul(a) tun', 'tun where there were mules'.

The **church of St Stephen** was designed by John Douglas and built between 1876 and 1877. The nave and chancel lie under one big timber roof and it has a slender west spire. The interior of the church has exposed surfaces of yellow and red brick, whereas the exterior is faced with small stones.

MOW COP [Congleton]

SJ8557: 2 miles (3km) NE of Kidsgrove

Cheshire's Pennine border runs from Disley to Mow Cop, a distance of nearly twenty miles. Here the range peters out into the North Staffordshire foothills. The higgledy-piggledy village perched on the escarpment is dominated by the mock ruin of **Mow Cop Castle** The folly, which sits astride the Cheshire/Staffordshire border at a height of 1099ft (335m), was built to enhance the view from Rode Hall by Randle Wilbraham in 1754. The village lies half in Staffordshire and half in Cheshire.

The outcropping rock is a hard sandstone of the Yoredale Series, a little older than Millstone Grit. Within Cheshire stands the Old Man of Mow, a pillar of rock some 65ft (20m) in height.

The name of the settlement was described as 'Mouhul' in 1317. The element 'Mow' is from the Old English 'muga' for 'a heap' and 'Cop' is Old English for 'a hill'. The 'heap' probably refers to a boundary cairn.

In the past smallholders, quarrymen and miners inhabited the village. The spot became celebrated as the place for the great revivalist meetings held by the **Primitive Methodists**. They drew their support from the Potteries and east Cheshire. Its principal founders, Hugh Bourne and William Clowes, believed in the fervent expression of faith and in open-air meetings. They did not wish to leave the Methodist church but were expelled by the authorities for their methods of spreading the gospel. In May 1807, Hugh Bourne and William Clowes called a camp meeting, which lasted 14 hours. In 1937, when Mow Cop Castle was given to the National Trust, 10,000 Methodists marked the occasion with a meeting on the hill.

In Staffordshire, the church of St Thomas, 1841-2, is a Commissioners' church designed by T. Stanley. It has a thin tower, a short chancel and lancet windows.

In Cheshire, the church of St Luke, 1875, has an aisleless nave and lancet windows. The interior contains a cruci-form stained-glass window depicting the Holy Spirit.

In Cheshire, a Wesleyan chapel, 1862, has a façade in the Georgian style. The building has three bays with arched windows.

NANTWICH [Crewe]

SJ6452: 4 miles (6km) SW of Crewe

The town is intersected by the River Weaver as it flows north to join the Mersey. Although no Roman site has been discovered, the Legionary fortress of Chester lay only some twenty miles to the north-west. A Roman road from Whitchurch ran north through Middlewich via King Street, and along Watling Street to Manchester.

The underlying geology is Keuper Marl with sediments of New Red Sandstone laid down in Triassic times. This particular strata has given rise to substantial deposits of salt. Its importance as a salt-producing settlement was clearly recorded in Domesday, and salt had been extracted in Saxon times.

In the Domesday survey, Nantwich is listed as 'Wich' (salt settlement) in the Hundred of **Warmundestrou**. The manor was held by William Malbank, hence it is sometimes called Wich Malbank. The element 'nant' is after the famous Malbank. The settlement became 'Nametwich' in 1194 and Nantwich in 1281.

Domesday records that before 1066 there were a saltpit and eight salthouses divided between the King and Earl Edwin. So valuable was the commodity that thefts of salt carried the death penalty.

Fire badly damaged the town in 1438 and again in 1583, when most of the town was destroyed. Queen Elizabeth donated a large sum of money and also issued a commission for a countrywide collection.

Nantwich was at the centre of fighting between the Royalists and Parliamentarians in the Civil War. The Royalists initially captured the town, but they subsequently lost it to the Parliamentarians who established it as their garrison. Later Royalist forces beseiged the town, which was relieved after the battle on 25 January 1644. The King's soldiers were trapped between the advancing Parliamentarian forces of Brereton and Fairfax.

In 1803 there were serious riots in the town when common land at Beam Heath was enclosed. After fences were torn down, troops from Chester arrested many townspeople, who were later tried and imprisoned.

The **church of St Mary** was built mostly in the 14th and 15th centuries. There was a chapel of Wych Malbank under Acton in the town in 1130. Later it became a chapel of ease to Acton and remained so until the 17th century. Standing impressively in the centre of town, it is basically of the 14th century. Its splendid octagonal tower is borne on four great pillars between the nave and chancel.

The chancel vaulting is very fine indeed, being the only medieval lierne vault in Cheshire. Lierne vault is a pattern of linked ribs that do not spring from the main supports or from the central boss. The chancel also has windows of the Decorated period, which have features of flowing decorated tracery. The east window above

the altar is of the more austere Perpendicular style.

The choir stalls, with beautifully carved canopies, are late 14th century. The misericords exhibit a delightful collection of subjects, including dragons, a mermaid, the Devil pulling a woman's mouth open, a woman beating her husband with a ladle, an angel with bagpipes, wrestlers and two dogs watching poachers skinning a deer.

The carved bosses in the vaulted roof of the chancel display designs of faces, animals and foliage. The church has a fine high-roofed nave, with four pointed arches on each side supported by tall fluted pillars. There is a very beautiful

Detail of the remarkable architecture of the church of St Mary

stone pulpit at the crossing, supported on an octagonal stem, with the pillar, body and back wall elaborately decorated with panels. The outside of the church has crocketed gables and pinnacles and openwork parapets.

The great attraction of the town is its fine architectural mixture of Tudor, Georgian and Victorian buildings.

The Grade 1 listed **Crown Hotel** in High Street was rebuilt soon after the fire of 1438. It is three storeys high with an impressive front of timber framing. The second storey has continuous gallery windows with oak-mullioned transoms and casements.

Welsh Row was called Frog Row in medieval times, and later named after Welsh traders' packhorse trains carrying away salt. The road continues out of town to meet the Telford aqueduct carrying the Shropshire Union Canal. Among the other buildings of interest: the Tollemache almshouses were built in 1878, the early Georgian Townwell House is now an antique shop, and the **Cheshire Cat pub** was formerly almshouses of 1675.

Crossing Welsh Bridge over the River Weaver back into town, the brine spring is on the left. In the town centre, the Lamb Hotel in Hospital Street, 1861, is built on the site of a previous Lamb Hotel which was the headquarters of the Parliamentary garrison during the siege of Nantwich. Further along Hospital Street, Sweetbriar Hall is timber-framed and probably the oldest inhabited building in town. Close by, the Rookery is a stately Georgian brick house of the 18th century.

Churche's Mansion is a Grade 1 listed building. This is an outstanding piece of decorated half-timbered architecture. Built in 1577, it has two gabled ends with a central part containing a hall and porch with three- to five-light mullioned and transomed windows. This splendid merchant's house was, until 1998, a restaurant but is at present (Aug. 1999) closed.

The battle for Nantwich is re-enacted every year on **'Holly Holy Day'**, on the Saturday nearest 25 January. There is the staging of a colourful and substantial mock battle, complete with cannons, banners, uniforms and standards.

NESS [Ellesmere Port]

SJ3075: 2 miles (4km) SE of Neston

In about 1761, Ness was the birthplace of a blacksmith's daughter who gained fame and fortune with her physical charms. She became **Lady Emma Hamilton** when she married Sir William Hamilton, the British Ambassador in Naples, in 1791. She became Lord Nelson's mistress, giving birth to his daughter in 1801. Widowed in 1803, she died in poverty in 1815. Swan Cottage, the house where she was born, still remains and is the tall building at the end of the village.

The **Ness Botanical Gardens** has one of the finest collections of trees and shrubs in the country. The gardens were planted by Arthur Kilpin Bulley, a man keen on conservation and one of the first people to collect plants from around the world. The gardens are now in the ownership of Liverpool University.

The settlement of Ness is recorded in Domesday as 'Nesse'. It was held by Erngeat and the lands were owned by Walter of Vernon. The survey lists ploughland and meadowland. 'Ness' is derived from the Old Norse *nes* or the Old English 'ness' and means 'headland, cape'. It may be a relic of the name Ness for the Wirral peninsula.

NESTON [Ellesmere Port]

SJ2877: 7 miles (11km) W of Ellesmere Port

At the beginning of the 19th century, Neston was a thriving small town and became an important place on the Wirral. Its prosperity had resulted from the decline of Chester as a port because of the silting of the River Dee. The port moved downstream to Neston, which became a market town and coaching station.

Neston's New Quay was built by public collections in the 18th century but this, in due course, was abandoned in favour of a quay at Parkgate. In Parkgate Road there are some early 18th-century houses. Vine House has two storeys of four bays with pilaster strips at the corners. Elmhurst is a two-storey house with a projecting wing at either end. Adjoining Elm Grove House is a three-story structure with four bays.

Neston is mentioned in Domesday as 'Nestone'. Arni held the settlement and the lands were owned by William, son of Nigel. Ploughland is recorded, with villagers, smallholders and one slave. A priest is also mentioned.

The **church of St Mary and St Helen** is situated to the south of the town centre. Built of sandstone, it has a short, square 14th-century tower. The top storey of the tower dates from the 19th century, when the rest of the church was rebuilt between 1874 and 1875. Inside the church and in the tower are preserved fragments of Saxon and Norman stonework. Careful examination of the fragmented shaft of a cross reveals two figures fighting on one side, a winged figure on the other and a priest on another. There is also a stone built into the belfry depicting two knights fighting on horseback.

NETHER ALDERLEY [Macclesfield]

SJ8476: 2 miles (3km) S of Alderley Edge

Alderley was divided into two manors before the Norman Conquest. A branch of the Stanley family inherited the manor of Over Alderley in 1602 from the Fittons. Nether or Lower Alderley was listed in Domesday as 'Aldredelie'. Godwin held it and the lands were owned by Bigot de Loges. The survey records arable land, meadowland, woodland and enclosures. It became 'Alderdelege' in 1275. The name is derived from 'Aldred's leah' or 'Aldred's clearing'.

The **church of St Mary** is a sizeable Perpendicular building of the late 14th century. It has a square embattled tower of the 16th century and a chancel rebuilt in 1856. From the churchyard a flight of steps enters a Jacobean gallery: this was the pew of the Stanleys of Alderley. Their coats of arms are painted on the arches at the front of the gallery. Further shields are painted on the musicians' gallery, now housing the organ at the west end of the church. A fine 16th-century timber roof covers the nave and four pointed arches on octagonal pillars support the walls.

On display are copies of the Breeches Bible (1560) and the Vinegar Bible (1717). In the former, Genesis 3 verse 7 reads 'They sewed fig leaves together and made themselves breeches'. The Authorised Version translates this as aprons. In the latter the print refers to 'the parable of the vinegar' (instead of vineyard).

At the east end, in niches, are two 19th-century tombs; a fine effigy of John Thomas Stanley, first Lord Stanley of Alderley (died 1850) and the other, his son, the second Lord Stanley (d1869).

The Stanley Mausoleum (1909) stands in the churchyard.

Nether Alderley Mill, dating from the 15th century, lies alongside the A34. It is under the care of the National Trust. Its Victorian machinery was restored in the 1960s and is now in full working order. Looking at the building from the outside, the striking feature is the very long, sloping flagged roof, which almost reaches the ground. The complex arrangement of wheels, cogs and shafts is powered by two 12ft (3.6m) diameter overshot wheels using water stored in a reservoir at the rear of the mill. There are two sets of grinding stones (French Burrs) and there are regular flour-grinding demonstrations.

Across the road from the mill is a 17th-century black and white, half-timbered cottage that used to be a coaching inn named the Eagle and Child – the crest of the Stanley family. The legend of the eagle and child is very old. A lord of the manor had an affair with a young gentlewoman who bore him a son. He wanted a son to inherit his name and fortune and worked out a plan to ensure the illegitimate child became his heir.

He told his trusted servant to place the infant at the foot of a particular tree on his estate that was frequented by an eagle. The idea was that as the lord and lady were strolling through the grounds, they would find the child by accident. The old lady would consider it a gift from heaven and adopt the boy as the heir. They were so overjoyed with the child that, from that time on, the crest of the eagle and child was used.

Soss Moss Hall is situated one mile (1.5km) to the west. This timber-framed building has the date 1583 on a chimney stack. The front of the building has three gables with herringbone bracing.

All that remains of Alderley Park

House, the former Stanley home, are the stables, dovecote and summerhouse.

NEWTON [Chester]
SJ4168: 1½ miles (2km) NE of Chester

Newton is now an extensive residential suburb of Chester. It stretches northwards towards Upton Heath and the Zoological Gardens. For commuters, there is a convenient railway station on the Chester to Birkenhead line at Upton. Also nearby are access points for the M53 and the M56.

The settlement is mentioned in Domesday as 'Newentone' in Chester Hundred. Arni held it and the lands were owned by Earl Hugh. There was land for three ploughs, and there are six villagers. The name is probably the most common for an English settlement and usually means 'new homestead or village' from the Old English 'neowa tun'.

The Roman Catholic **church of St Columba,**, Newton Lane, was designed by L.A.G. Prichard, Son & Partners. It is an interesting construction using the five sides of an octagon backed by a steep pyramidal steeple. The building contains attractive abstract glass by Hans Unger and E. Schulze.

NORLEY [Vale Royal]
SJ5772: 6 miles (10km) W of Northwich

The village of Norley lies on the eastern fringe of Delamere Forest. When the remainder of the medieval forest was officially disafforested in 1812, some of the crown lands were reserved for the Surveyor of Woods and Forests, now the Forestry Commission. In the Norley area, conifers were planted in an area north of Delamere station, which became the foundation of the modern forest.

Lines of marching conifers, orderly and disciplined, give little idea of what a medieval forest would look like.

Nevertheless, those times have left their imprint. In the heart of the old forest area there are no large centres of population, no towns, no villages of any size, no old halls and no old churches. The churches at Norley, Kingsley and Alvanley did not appear until after 1850.

Norley lies at the heart of a network of roads and lanes, another imprint of the wandering tracks and pathways of medieval times. Today, the surroundings are a patchwork quilt of farmland and woodland just to the south of the River Weaver.

The settlement was not mentioned in Domesday. Norley was described as 'Nortleg' in 1259 and 'Northle' in 1288. The name is derived from 'Northern land and leah'.

The **church of St John the Evangelist** was designed by J.L. Pearson and built between 1878 and 1889 in the 13th-century style. It has a broad, central tower with bell openings to each side. The north chancel has three long windows with tracery and four bays complete the north aisle.

Just to the south of Norley is Gallowsclough Hill. A tumulus in the form of a round barrow was investigated and found to contain a cremation burial. Ploughing has diminished what must have been a considerable monument. Measurements have recorded a mound 50ft (15m) in diameter and 5ft (1.5m) high. Higher land not only attracted early man for burial sites of their chiefs and leaders, but also as places for security and defence.

Situated on **Eddisbury Hill**, 2 miles (3km) south-west of Norley is a hill fort of 4.5 hectares (11 acres) surrounded by two lines of ramparts and ditch. Excavations in the 1930s showed four Iron Age phases. It started with a palisade, which was then replaced by a stone rampart and ditch with an entrance gap. Later the camp was extended, and a second entrance constructed at the north-west. In its final stage, the second outer bank and ditch were constructed with entrance walls refaced with drystone walling.

The Romans attacked the fort in the first century AD and slighted the defences. It is believed that the site was reoccupied in the tenth century, when the rampart was heightened and the outer ditch deepened.

The **Forest Centre** at the Delamere Forest park is open every day and is within easy reach of Chester, Liverpool and Manchester. The visitor centre contains an exhibition and a wildlife display. The forest classroom can be booked and there are guided walks and cycle routes. Other facilities include free parking and toilets.

NORTH RODE [Macclesfield]

SJ8867: 3 miles (5km) NE of Congleton

North Rode is a small community close to the Macclesfield Canal. There is access from the A54 Congleton to Buxton road. Prior to the Beeching era, North Rode was quite important. It had a station on the Stoke-on-Trent to Manchester line and was a junction for the Leek to Uttoxeter route. Now, both station and Leek line are no more. (However, on this route at Cheddleton, Staffordshire, the Churnet Valley Railway are now running trains down to Consall).

The line joining the Potteries with Macclesfield opened in 1849 with two viaducts – one at North Rode crossing the Dane valley by a series of twenty arches, and another at Congleton where the ten arches were 110ft (34m) above the river.

The settlement is mentioned in Domesday as 'Rodo' in Hamestan Hundred. Bernwulf held it as a free man. There was land for two ploughs. Domesday records an extensive tract of woodland. The settlement was described as 'Rode'. The name is derived from the Old English 'rod' meaning 'clearing'.

The **church of St Michael** was designed by C. and J. Trubshaw and built in 1845. The building is rock-faced, with a west tower with a higher stair turret.

NORTHWICH [Vale Royal]

SJ6573: 14 miles (22km) ENE of Chester

Northwich occupies a site in a flat area of the Cheshire Plain, although close to pleasant countryside with meres and undulating farmland. The town lies at the confluence of the Rivers Weaver and Dane and grew up as another important salt town, another Cheshire 'wich'.

In Domesday, this third wich is recorded as 'Norwich'. The king and Earl Hugh shared the returns from the sale of salt. The Romans set up an auxiliary fort here by the name of Condate. Much Roman material has been found at Castle Hill, which may originally have been a military site. The base would have guarded the Roman road and the supplies of salt.

In order to improve the transportation of salt from the salt fields, an Act of Parliament in 1721 allowed the River Weaver to be canalised. To understand the importance of salt: in one year alone, 1832, just over 200,000 tons of salt were shipped from Northwich. Today, much of the brine pumped from the salt beds is used at the nearby Winnington Chemical Works.

Brine pumping is potentially dangerous because the holes caused by extraction become filled with water. These collapse causing ground subsidence and the appearance of 'flashes' or small lakes. Brine pumping is now controlled but, in the past, subsidence was a great problem in the town. The timber-framed houses seen in the centre of Northwich are not medieval, but are 19th-and early 20th-century buildings. They are designed and constructed to withstand the effects of subsidence.

In Witton Street, the Post Office has a four-storey gabled frontage in black and white and was built in 1911. A little further along Whitton Street is the timber-framed Brunner Public Library of 1909.

The **church of St Helen** , Witton, at first gives the impression of being a Victorian church. However, it has a Perpendicular exterior and partly Decorated inside. There has been much restoration and rebuilding in 1842, 1861 and 1884. This included the rebuilding of the north arcade in order to create a wider nave. Of particular merit is the splendid nave and chancel roof, which is panelled and with different sized bosses. There are several initials by William Venables, Lord of the Manor at that time.

The **Anderton Boat Lift** was built in 1875 by E. Leader Williams. This massive iron structure enabled boats to be raised and lowered hydraulically between the Weaver Navigation Canal and the Trent and Mersey Canal.

The **Northwich Salt Museum** in London Road provides a unique journey through the history of Cheshire's oldest industry. It illustrates the startling effects that salt mining have had on the architecture, landscape and environment of Cheshire.

OLLERTON [Macclesfield]

SJ7776: 1½ miles (2km) SE of Knutsford

This settlement lies on the outer edge of Knutsford and to the south-east of the town. It straddles the A537, Knutsford to Macclesfield road, at an intersection with a minor road. The village is surrounded by farmland.

The settlement is mentioned in Domesday as 'Alretune' in Hamestan Hundred. Wulfric holds Ollerton from the Earl as a free man. There was land for three ploughs, with one villager and two smallholders. Domesday records some woodland. The settlement is described as 'Olreton' in 1288 and the name is derived form the Old English 'alder', 'the tun among alders'.

Kerfield House is a neo-Georgian building built in yellow brick and was originally called Beechwood. In 1912 it was remodelled by Sir Percy Worthington and re-cased in red brick, with the roofs hidden behind a parapet. Building additions made the house plan into a square. The entrance front of five bays is highlighted with a well-carved timber doorway.

Ollerton Grange is situated just north of the village of Ollerton, just off the A537. It was designed by J. Brooke and built in 1901.

OUGHTRINGTON [Warrington]

SJ6987: 1 mile (1.6km) E of Lymm

Oughtrington is a compact residential suburb situated at the eastern end of Lymm. The housing development occupies a narrow area of land between the A6144, Warrington to Sale road, and the Bridgewater Canal.

The **church of St Peter** was designed by Slater and Carpenter and built be-

tween 1871 and 1972. It is a substantial church with a thin spire and a large polygonal apse. There is a pleasing group of four lancet windows and a rose window, which combine well with the rib-vaulting of the chancel and the apse. There are stained-glass windows by Kempe (1894).

The settlement is not mentioned in Domesday.

OVER [Vale Royal]

SJ6366: ½ mile (1km) W of Winsford

In the Domesday Survey, Over was listed as 'Ovre'. Four free men held the settlement as four manors, and Earl Hugh owned the lands. The name was described as 'Ufre' in 1150 and Overe' in 1291. The name is derived, from Old English 'ufer, ofer' or 'slope or ridge'.

A charter of around1280, granted by the Abbot of Vale Royal and confirmed by Kind Edward I, created a free borough of Over. The burgesses were granted market rights along with several other Cheshire towns that gained borough status at that time.

Over never developed beyond village size, and in 1894 it was recognised as the smallest municipality in the country. The ex-officio title Mayor of Over was last used in 1974.

In medieval times Over was the mother church of Little Budworth and Whitegate, and both church and manor were of great local importance.

The **church of St Chad,**, Over is now the parish church of Winsford. It was one of the few churches where sanctuary was legally recognised, which suggests that the church was the senior, if not the oldest, in the forest of Mara. Documents from the 13th century indicate that the extensive forests of Mondrum and Mara extended into the Over district.

The church is approached by a fine avenue of trees some distance from Winsford town. St Chad's has the typical octagonal piers and embattled parapets of a Perpendicular church. It is a through church with a narrow north aisle and a wide south aisle, which reveal its 14th-century planning. Built of red sandstone, it is a two-gabled building with a fine tower at the west end.

Hugh Starkie of Oulton built the south aisle in 1543. There is a two-storey south porch, with the upper part reached by a handsome staircase. There is a font of 1641 with a plain octagonal bowl. In June there is a **well dressing** ceremony when two churchyard wells are decorated and floral panels are displayed in the church.

Tradition has it that Over was the birthplace of **Robert Nixon**, the Cheshire prophet who is supposed to have been born in the reign of Edward IV, about 1467. One prophecy arose when he was out in the fields ploughing on 22 August 1485. He fell into a trance, and when he awoke he told of a great battle and that the king had been overthrown. That was the day of the Battle of Bosworth. The prophecy was reported to the new king, Henry VII, who commanded Nixon to be brought to court.

The Cross, Delamere Street, Over, stands on a huge, stepped base. The cross was renewed as a market cross around 1840, when the market was revived nearby. The stepped base, which probably stands on the site of a medieval cross, has a blocked rear door to a cell inside. This was where drunks and petty criminals were held overnight. The Great Reform Bill of 1832 banned pillories and stocks, decreeing that lock-ups should be provided instead.

The site of **Vale Royal Abbey** lies 3 miles (5km) north of Winsford. On the 13 August 1277, King Edward I and Queen Eleanor came to lay the foundation stones of the abbey. He had vowed to found the abbey while in danger of shipwreck crossing the Channel. It was never completed due to Edward's other commitments – Welsh castles and the rebuilding of Chester's walls. The original church, at 420ft (128m) long, was the largest Cistercian church in England.

Vale Royal was always under endowed and impoverished, but was finally completed by the Black Prince. In 1360 a great gale demolished the central tower, which fell and destroyed the nave.

Documents give evidence of great unrest and dissatisfaction – relations between landowners and the Abbot were decidedly uncomfortable. At the Dissolution the site went to Sir Thomas Holcroft who demolished the abbey church but kept most of the cloister ranges.

A large house was built on the site, and in 1616 it came into the possession of Lady Cholmondeley. The Cholmondeleys, Lords of Delamere, held it into the 20th century. Hardly anything is now visible above ground of this once great abbey, just a collection of pier bases and the head of a churchyard cross.

The **Whitegate Way** runs for a distance of 6 miles (10km) from just north of Winsford through to Cuddington; along the route of a former railway. This lovely linear walk passes meres, pools and woodland in an historic area where the Cistercian Abbey at nearby Vale Royal at one time owned much of the land.

OVER PEOVER [Macclesfield]
SJ7874: 2 miles (3km) SSE of Knutsford

Over Peover is set in rich farmland, completely secluded, and reached by a winding country lane. The road south from

Knutsford, the A50, gives access to a side road that leads to Parkgate with its small scatter of houses. In the area in the centre of Over Peover lies extensive parkland. This is dominated by **Over Peover Hall**, the ancient seat of the Mainwaring family and the nearby church.

The Leicesters of Tabley Old Hall were patrons of the living. The Shakerleys of Hulme Hall, Allostock and the Holfords of Holford Hall, Plumley were landowners and possessed family chapels in the church. Mary Holford married Sir Hugh Cholmondeley. Mary Cholmondeley lived at Holford before moving to Vale Royal in 1616.

Peover was listed as 'Pevre' in the Domesday Survey but little information is recorded. Ranulf Mainwaring owned the land around Over Peover.

The name is derived from the Welsh *pefr* meaning 'radiant or bright', and to this was added the Old English 'ea' for a 'river'. Sir Randle Mainwaring replaced the old half-timbered hall standing in a moated enclosure with the present brick building in 1585-6. It is part of a larger house that has probably been demolished. Today, the hall's beautifully mellowed brick is highlighted with buff-coloured stone quoins, doorways and mullions. At the rear of the building, the stables date from 1654 and exhibit a splendid interior of decorated woodwork and plasterwork ceilings. The coach house is dated 1764.

The **church of St Lawrence** is a daughter of the mother church of Rostherne and seems to have been first erected in the 14th century. Although the nave and chancel were rebuilt in brick in 1811, the two ancient Mainwaring Chapels were preserved. The south chapel dates from the 15th century, and contains the fine canopied tomb of Randle Mainwaring and his wife, Margery

The church of St Lawrence
(Graham Beech)

(1456). Randle Mainwaring is depicted in a full suit of plate armour and his wife is elegantly dressed in a long, flowing robe.

The north chapel was erected in 1648 and contains an elaborate tomb chest with the reclining figures of Philip and Ellen Mainwaring. This monument is in a good state of preservation. In the chancel of the new church, near to the north chapel, are the effigies of John Mainwaring and his wife, Margaret, or it may possibly be his second wife, Joan. The knight is wearing rich armour and his wife is attired in a long, loose, sleeveless cloak.

A treasured possession of the church is the American flag and a bronze plaque which commemorate the fact that General George Patten of the American Third Army worshipped here during the Second World War when he lived at Peover Hall.

OVER TABLEY [Macclesfield]

SJ7279: 2½ miles (4km) N of Knutsford

The dwellings of this small village line the road linking Northwich and Altrincham, the A556. The settlement adjoins Junction 19 of the M6 but the surroundings are farmland.

The settlement is mentioned in Domesday as 'Stabelei' in Bochelau Hundred. Leofwin held it as a free man. There was land for one plough and an area of woodland. The settlement was described as 'Over Tabbele' in 1289, which is derived from 'Taebba's leah'.

The **church of St Paul** was designed by Anthony Salvin and built between 1855 and 1856. It is a small rock-faced building with a later bell turret.

Over Tabley Hall lies just north of the motorway junction. The present building is part of a larger Gothic house, probably built before 1780. It is built in brick and has pointed windows. The doorway has a gable top with pinnacles. The side wings are two bays-long and surmounted by a frieze.

PARKGATE [Ellesmere Port]

SJ2778: 1 mile (1.6km) N of Neston

The village still has the atmosphere of a seaside resort, with cottages, terraced houses and a pleasant parade with 17th- to early 19th-century houses and cottages.

In the 18th century, Parkgate had become a principal packet port to and from Ireland. By 1830 it had, like Chester, succumbed to the silting of the River Dee. Nevertheless, it managed to continue as a holiday resort for some time afterwards. Now, looking out to the Dee estuary, Parkgate can view only the extensive salt marshes. The name is derived from Neston Park, an area enclosed in 1250 as a deer park. The village only became an established settlement in 1720.

The Wirral Country Park follows the track bed of the old railway which once linked Hooton to West Kirby. The Wirral Way is now a pleasant country walk. The sands at Parkgate, Gayton Sands, belong to the RSPB and attract many bird watchers.

PECKFORTON [Crewe]

SJ5358: 2 miles (3km) W of Bunbury

The scattered settlement of Peckforton nestles at the foot of the eastern slopes of the Peckforton Hills. These impressive hills in the centre of the Cheshire Plain are crowned by fortifications both ancient and modern.

Listed in Domesday Book as 'Pevretone', it was held by Wulfric, a free man, and the lands owned by Robert, son of Hugh (Robert fitz Hugh). In 1100 the settlement's name became 'Pecfortuna' or 'a tun by Peacford'. A ford near the Peckforton Hills must have been called 'Peac' (peak). Peckforton Castle is magnificently set amongst tall trees on the lower hill across the valley from the medieval castle on Beeston Crag.

Peckforton Castle, a Victorian structure, was erected between 1841 and 1850 by John (later 1st Baron) Tollemache as his country residence. He served as a Member of Parliament for over thirty years, but it was his concern for his tenantry that brought him great renown as a reforming landlord. He divided his estate into small units and built over fifty new farmsteads. Each farm worker was provided with a cottage and three acres of land.

The building of Peckforton Castle was started under George Latham, but he was dismissed and Anthony Salvin was en-

Peckforton Castle

gaged as the architect. Peckforton looks convincingly medieval as Salvin was determined to design a castle of the time of Edward I. The whole structure is a fascinating geometrical plan, with the accommodation set round a courtyard enclosed by a curtain wall with battlements and towers. Access to the courtyard is through a gateway on the west side. The interior is plainly designed with no frills or ornamentation regarding the walls and ceilings. There are spectacular features in the form of the great fireplace, the bands of Minton floor tiles and the grand main staircase.

The chapel is a separate building to the south of the gateway. Although the family lived in the castle to some extent until the Second World War, it has since then remained largely empty. It has been used by film companies and documentary makers and, more recently, as one of the country's most romantic wedding venues.

PENKETH [Warrington]

SJ5687: 2 miles (3km) W of Warrington

Penketh lies on the western edge of Warrington, chiefly between the A57 and A562. The area mainly consists of residential development with expensive houses. There is a shopping centre with all facilities, including a fine branch library. The local churches include St Peter's Church of England and the Methodist church. The Friends' Meeting House, Meeting Lane, was founded in 1681 and rebuilt in 1736. The building is now a community centre. The nearest railway station is Sankey, on the Werrington, Widnes and Liverpool line.

South of Penketh lies Fiddler's Ferry, a crossing point of the St Helen's Canal. Fiddler's Ferry is also an ancient crossing point of the River Mersey. At Fiddler's Ferry stands the Ferry Inn dated 1762. The derivation of the name Fiddler's Ferry is believed to come from the landowner, Adam le Vicleur, which was gradually altered to Violer. This became a player of the viol or fiddle, hence 'Fiddler'.

At one time the major employer in the village of Penketh was the local tannery. Other industries were quite diverse; including brewers, cabinetmakers, toolmakers and a family of shoemakers called Gandy.

In 1757 England's first canal was in operation from St Helens to Sankey Bridges. It was a common sight at that time to observe the coal barges or 'flats' lining the canal waiting for the tide.

A little to the west lies **Fiddler's Ferry Power Station**. This giant complex, commissioned in 1968, uses poor quality coal from Britain, South America and Australia. It has its own dock at Liverpool and the coal is transported in bulk by rail and by road. There are eight cooling towers, their steam emissions visible for miles around. The power station generates 6 to 8 mgw for the National Grid.

The settlement was not mentioned in Domesday. The name was described as 'Penket' in 1242 and 'Penketh' in 1259. The name is derived from the Welsh *pen coed* or 'end of the wood'.

PICKMERE [Macclesfield]

SJ6977: 3 miles (5km) NE of Northwich

The village hugs the eastern shore of Pick Mere just north of Northwich. The surrounding area consists of agricultural land. Pickmere has developed into a popular location with the siting of a campsite and caravan site.

PICTON [Chester]

SJ4371: 3½ miles (5.5km) NNE of Chester

Picton is a small village situated between the River Gowy and the M53. The surrounding land consists of low-lying pasture and water-meadows. Just to the west of the motorway lies the Shropshire Union Canal. The village may be reached by narrow lanes from the A56 or from the A41.

The **Manor Farm** is built in brick but has been given a half-timber decoration. There are two slightly projecting end sections with large Dutch gables. The date of the house is probably between 1660 and 1670.

The settlement was mentioned in Domesday as 'Pichetone' in Wilaveston Hundred. Toki held it as a free man, and Richard of Vernon owned the lands. There was land for three ploughs and the settlement had one rider and three smallholders. Domesday records meadowland. The settlement was described as 'Picketone' in 1150, and the name is derived from 'Pica's worp and tun'.

PLUMLEY [Macclesfield]

SJ7274: 3 miles (5km) SW of Knutsford

The village of Plumley lies on the north bank of a small stream called Peover Eye. A network of mature streams drain the surrounding area, which is mainly agricultural land dotted with some sizeable patches of woodland. The streams eventually flow on to join the River Weaver. A byroad connects Plumley with the A556, and the village has a railway station on the line from Northwich to Manchester.

Holford Hall, which lies on the banks of the Peover Eye, is the remaining part of a moated, timber-framed mansion rebuilt for Mary Cholmondeley after the death of her husband, Sir Hugh, in 1601. There is a fine double-arched bridge.

The house of three storeys and two

broad gables is decorated with carving and patterned timberwork. Mary Cholmondeley lived at Holford Hall before moving to Vale Royal in 1616.

The village was not mentioned in Domesday. It was described as 'Plumleia' in 1119 and the name is derived from 'plum-tree leah or wood'.

PLEMSTALL [Chester]

SJ4570: 4 miles (6km) NE of Chester

The small hamlet of Plemstall is situated near to the divergence of the two North Cheshire railway routes: Chester to Warrington and Chester to Northwich. The cluster of buildings sits on the banks of the River Gowy, with the church on the north side of the railway and Holme Farm on the south side. The surroundings consist of water-meadows and agricultural land.

The **church of St Peter** is completely Georgian in style, with the tower of 1826. The Perpendicular aspects of the church are the side window with tracery, the north arcade and the hammerbeam roof. The vicar of Plemstall, the Reverend J.H. Toogood, who was here from 1907 to 1946, actually carved most of the woodwork. He crafted the rood screen, the top of the parclose screen, and also carved the reredos, the choir stalls, the lectern and other pieces.

The church contains a three-decker pulpit dated 1722 and an octagonal font of the late 17th century. There are old fragments of stained glass in the south window and a painted tablet referring to gifts given to the church from 1660 onwards.

POTT SHRIGLEY
[Macclesfield]

SJ9380: 4 miles (6km) NE of Macclesfield

A minor road heads north-east from Bollington and soon reaches the small village of Pott Shrigley. The inn and a small collection of houses cluster round the old church in leafy surroundings. At the end of the green valley the encroaching high land seems to shelter this quiet fold in the east Cheshire hills.

For much of the 19th century the hamlet was influenced by the Lowther family of Shrigley Hall, who owned much of the land and property. The coal and clay mines of Bakestonedale were under the township of Pott Shrigley and were part of the Shrigley Hall estate. The settlement is not listed in Domesday but its name was recorded as 'Shriggeleg' in 1288. It is an interesting word derived from the Old English 'shrike' – a bird. Hence, 'Shriggeleg' – 'a wood frequented by shrikes'. Pott is a family name.

The **church of St Christopher** is of the Perpendicular style throughout and probably founded in the late 14th century. It was completed in its present form by the erection of the Downes' chantry chapel, which was endowed by Geoffrey Downes in the 15th century. Geoffrey Downes, brother of the local squire, was a Fellow of Queens' College, Cambridge and left a collection of religious books, printed and in manuscript form, in the chantry that he had just founded. Specific information relating to the foundation of this is found in Geoffrey Downes' will, dated 7th June 1492. Any gentleman who wished could borrow any of the collection for a period of thirteen weeks, 'soe that he Leave sufficient pledge to keep them safe and bring them again' - an early form of lending library.

Of particular note is the massive tower, battlemented and pinnacled, which has a clock face on each side. Thomas Schofield of Manchester made this church clock in 1809. The body of the church is considerably larger in width than in length.

The building is favoured with a fine roof, probably of the late 15th century, with the nave camber-beamed and divided into two bays. Some of the box pews came from Gawsworth and the grey marble font is probably 18th century. Of particular interest is the finely carved and gilded Royal coat of arms of George III. In the south wall of the chancel is a small priest's doorway. The monuments are chiefly to the Downes and Lowther families.

Below the church, a footpath leads to the local cricket ground. The well-tended circular area containing the hallowed square seems to epitomise an English country scene: peaceful, pastoral surroundings; tall trees with cawing rooks; a medieval church and the satisfying sound of ball on willow. Then there's the enjoyment in a general hunt for the ball after a massive hit. South-west of the village rises the prominent hill of Nab Head, 935ft (285m). The summit, a fine viewpoint, includes a survey pillar standing in the centre of a circular bank. This is the prehistoric burial site of a great local chief.

Shrigley Hall is a fine Regency house erected for William Turner, a mill owner from Blackburn, who acquired the Shrigley estate in 1818. His architect was Thomas Emetts, a member of a family of timber merchants from Preston. The house has eleven bays and two storeys, with an attic floor added later. It has a porch of unfluted, Ionic columns and the centre of the house has a three-bay pediment. Two large ground floor rooms contain fine neoclassical plasterwork.

The Salesian Mission formerly used the house as a school. They also built the chapel dedicated to St John Bosco in 1936. The architect was Philip Tilden, a late Arts and Crafts architect. After a period of neglect, the house is now a hotel and the chapel is used as a health club. The wide entrance drive to the hotel swings round in a sharp bend and passes a honey-coloured rock face.

POYNTON [Macclesfield]

SJ9184: 5 miles (8km) S of Stockport

Poynton lies in the north of the county of the border with Greater Manchester. It is situated on either side of the A523 and its junction with the A5149. The village nestles close to the foothills of the Peak District National Park and the wide acres of open parkland around Lyme Hall.

Poynton is not mentioned in Domesday. The settlement is described as 'Poninton' in 1248. The first element 'pun' may be related to the Old English 'punian' meaning 'to pound' (with a pestle).

Poynton is very much a commuter village with a station on the Macclesfield to Manchester railway line. A local beauty spot is Poynton Lake, where once The Towers, the Vernon family manor house, was situated. The fine stone house was demolished after the estate was sold.

Until the 1930s, Poynton was a coal-mining village with the mines situated on land belonging to Lord Vernon. Many of the local menfolk were employed in the collieries. Over the years, the old tramways and mineral lines to the pits, the old gig railway inclines have been developed by the **Groundwork Trust** into attractive walkways.

Just east of the village are the **Middlewood Way** and the Macclesfield Canal. The former is now a route for walkers and cyclists and follows the old track bed of the former Macclesfield and

Marple railway line. The railway was opened in 1869 and closed in 1970.

The **Macclesfield Canal** was the last of the waterways to be built in England. It was surveyed by Telford, engineered by Crosley and completed during 1831. The canal runs from Red Bull near Kidsgrove to join the Peak Forest Canal at Marple. Its pretty, meandering route is very popular with leisure craft and ramblers who walk along the towpath.

The **Anson Museum** in Anson Road, Poynton contains items recording the area's history. It also houses an impressive collection of steam and gas engines and other examples of machinery.

The **church of St George** (1858-9) was designed by J.S. Crowther in the late 13th-century style. Medland and Henry Taylor designed the south steeple (1884-5). The church has a fine west front with two very slim lancets and a small rose window. There is a splendid example of stained glass in the north aisle (1885) – a remarkably attractive object derived from the Pre-Raphaelites.

On a traffic island by St George's Church is an ornate piece of cast-iron work, which at one time combined the function of lamp standard, signpost and drinking fountain. It was erected to commemorate Queen Victoria's Diamond Jubilee in 1897.

Numbers 44 and 46 London Road North are two delightful Victorian cottages. Originally a single building, it was designed as a library and reading room. In 1854, John Hadwen, a mine manager, donated money to set up an institution. Lord Vernon provided the building, and in 1855 the library had five hundred volumes. After the First World War, the Vernon Estate retained the building, converted it into cottages and added a second storey.

PRESTBURY [Macclesfield]

SJ8977: 2 miles (3km) NW of Macclesfield

Prestbury's church and manor were granted by Hugh, Earl of Chester. The settlement lay at the centre of one of the largest medieval parishes in Cheshire; at one time it included Macclesfield and over thirty other townships.

In time, the village developed as a linear settlement focusing on the village green and the main street. From the mid-17th century to the start of the 20th century, the main street was the scene of twice-yearly cattle fairs. Imagine the sedate main street of today thronged with animals and farmers, with the accompanying noise and bustle; also, no doubt, with considerable inconvenience to the residents.

Before the 20th century, Prestbury was known for its parish church and the attractive village that had grown up around it. Then, as prosperous businessmen were looking for new homes out of the towns and moving to Alderley Edge and other pleasant rural areas, Prestbury also became a desirable place to live. It is now probably the best-known commuter village in the county.

The village is approached along leafy narrow roads that appear to wind round every field boundary. Along these roads are to be found the large villas and elegant houses upon which Prestbury's reputation is based. The very name Prestbury means 'the priests' manor or burgh'. Strangely, it is not mentioned in Domesday, probably because the settlement lay on the route the Normans took when they wasted Cheshire. However, its meaning is ample evidence of the early establishment of Christian worship here. Its name was recorded as

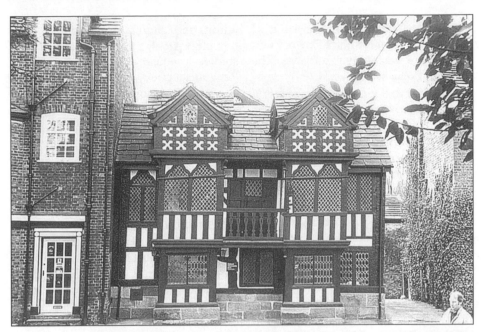

The Priest's House (now the National Westminster Bank), Prestbury *(Graham Beech)*

'Presteb[uria]' in 1175 and 'Presteburi' in 1221.

From the earliest times, a church has occupied its site in the village. The discovery of an Anglo-Saxon cross in 1841, built into the walls of the present structure, would date the first primitive church about AD900. It was most likely a wattle and daub building by the side of the River Bollin. The Norman chapel standing on the south side of the present church came into existence in the early 12th century.

The **church of St Peter** was evidently first established in its present scale in the 13th century, except for the north aisle which was rebuilt in the 18th century. The west tower and porch as they exist today are of 1480 and the square-headed windows of the south aisle are of the early 14th century. The Jacobean pulpit of 1607 was once a 'three-decker'. It was cut down and replaced in 1787.

A new roof was constructed in 1675, lower in pitch than the old covering. The font is possibly 13th century and has rather crude faces on the sides above four supporting columns. The paintings over the arches are of the Apostles and dated 1719. The chancel screen is a fine piece of workmanship with fluted pillars and a pediment, 1739. There are two, two-tiered brass chandeliers; the one in the chancel is dated 1712 and the other, an elegant piece, is in the nave and from 1814.

Reginald Legh was the son of Robert Legh, formerly Lord of Adlington. He was the chief helper in the building of the tower and porch of the church. He died on the 13 July 1482. This information is of special interest as it not only commemorates one who helped to build the church, but it helps to fix the approximate date when the tower and south porch were erected. The monuments include a carved slab to Reginald Legh, dated 1482. Another is to the memory of Robert Downes and his son who died in 1489 and 1495 respectively. Both are buried with their wives. The monument contains two shields of the arms of Downes and Booth. Robert Downes was a member of the family that founded the church at Pott Shrigley.

On the north wall of the chancel is a stone commemorating Sir Edward Warren of Poynton. He is depicted in full armour with his head resting on a helmet and dated 1558. In 1544, he and Edmund Savage of Macclesfield, took part in the expedition to Scotland to demand the surrender of Mary Queen of Scots, with the object of effecting her marriage to the King's son, Edward, Earl of Chester, afterwards King Edward VI. The Earl of Hertford, commander of the invading army, knighted both Sir Edward Warren and Sir Edmund Savage at Leith.

Possibly the finest monument in the church is affixed to the south wall of the Worth or Tytherington Chapel. It is the incised alabaster slab to the memory of Jasper Worth, who died in 1572, and Alice, his wife, who survived him by twenty-four years. He is dressed in plate armour and his wife attired in the costume usually worn by ladies of the 16th century. Beneath the feet of the lady, three children are depicted, and between the heads of the husband and wife is a shield bearing the arms of the families of Worth and Draycott. At the foot of the slab is another shield bearing the arms of Worth and Downes, indicating that a son of Jasper Worth married a daughter of a Downes.

In the churchyard stands the nave and chancel of the Norman predecessor of the church. The chapel was probably built on the site of a more ancient Saxon building. The structure was repaired and roofed in 1747. The beautiful doorway has a tympanum of seven carved figures, which are now greatly weatherworn and difficult to understand. However, the sixth figure holding a large key represents St Peter, to whom the church is dedicated. The complete panel is thought to represent a soldier, a monarch, the Holy Trinity, St Peter and a priest. There is the usual zig-zag ornamentation on the round-headed arch – a very fine example.

Prestbury is an especially handsome village and a tremendous effort has been made to preserve its character. At the south end of the main street is Prestbury Hall, a large, white, three-storey mansion.

In Bollin Grove on the other side of the river was the site of a corn mill. This was later transformed into a cotton mill, then a silk weaving mill. In Pearl Street, there is a row of weavers' cottages dated 1686. The main street of Prestbury has a fine range of brick town houses, where most of the ground floors have been converted into shops.

Originally a vicarage, the Priest's House is a black and white timber-framed building and now occupied by the National Westminster Bank. It dates from the mid-15th century.

The Legh Arms was built as an inn during 1423. It used to be known as the Saracen's Head in commemoration of the Holy Crusade. In 1719 a new sign was made but the painter made a mistake and put a black person's head on the board. So the inn acquired the names of the Blackmoor Head and the Black Boy. Today, there is still a sign depicting different designs – The Legh Arms and The Black Boy.

PRESTON BROOK [Halton]

SJ5780: 3 miles (5km) E of Runcorn

Preston Brook lies on the junction of the Trent and Mersey Canal and the Bridgewater Canal, as the former emerges from the Dutton tunnel. On the canal banks by the tunnel are the leggers' houses. These men lay on the top of the barges and pushed them along by using their feet on the tunnel roof. The horses were walked along the track over the top.

Lord Francis Egerton had a barge converted into a mission church round about 1840. It was placed on dry land and became known as the 'waterman's church'. Nowadays there is a marina at Preston Brook and this mooring area and the canal are greatly used by leisure craft.

The element 'Preston' in the name is commonly derived from the Old English 'Preosta-tun', 'the tun of the priests'.

PUDDINGTON [Chester]

SJ3273: 6 miles (10km) NW of Chester

Puddington is a small village on low-lying land in the Wirral. It lies to the north of the Dee estuary with a good view of the marshes, creeks, mud-banks and sands of the estuary. At the heart of the village is a tiny green that was handed over to the Parish Council when the Stanley estate was sold off.

The settlement was mentioned in Domesday as 'Potitone'. Hamo de Mascy held Puddington from Earl Hugh. There was land for three ploughs, and in the settlement were four villagers, four smallholders and one rider. The settlement was described as 'Podinton' in 1260 and the name is derived from 'the tun of Puta's (or Putta's) people'.

The village's most famous family were **the Masseys**, a prominent Cheshire family who lived in Puddington Old Hall. It was purported that William the Conqueror granted the lands and estate round Puddington to the Masseys. After the Reformation, the family remained Catholic and suffered social banishment. An ordained priest, **John Plessington**, tutor to the Massey children, was arrested in 1679 and nine weeks later was executed. His head was displayed on a pole at Chester.

The village consists of a small group of houses lining the road, a few modern dwellings and some outlying farms. Commuters have found this quiet haven in the Wirral and travel to Chester, Merseyside and further afield.

Puddington Old Hall was the ancient home of the Masseys, a leading Jacobite family. The house, which was formerly moated, overlooks the Dee estuary. Three sides of the timber-framed hall remain and the outside has been roughcast. An internal courtyard displays the late 15th-century timber framing.

PULFORD [Chester]

SJ3758: 5 miles (8km) SW of Chester

The village of Pulford lies in an extensive farming area on the Pulford Brook, which is the border with Wales. Pulford Castle was one of the motte and bailey fortifications built as a defence against the Welsh. Originally built of wood, it was replaced by a stone structure. The remains survive as semi-circular earthworks in a field next to the churchyard.

The settlement was mentioned in Domesday as 'Pulford' in Dudestan Hundred. Wulfric held it as a free man. The lands were owned by Hugh fitz Osbern. There was land for one plough, with two riders, one villager and two smallholders. The settlement was described as 'Pulford' in 1100 and is derived from 'a ford by the pool or pools'.

The village contains a **variety of architectural styles,** including the later distinctive examples of houses, farms and cottages built by the Second Duke of Westminster. There is the use of characteristic hand-made bricks, Dutch gables or black and white gables with decorative chimneys. There are particularly delightful farmhouses designed by John Douglas.

Green Paddocks is a fine example, built in 1872, and designed with flair and inventiveness. It has three bays, a steep roof, shaped gables and heavy dormers. Brick is very well used, especially for panelling in the gables. A little further north is **Belgrave**, now famous for having given its name to a square and a district in London. Council houses and a number of terraced houses have been built in the village and the former school turned into dwellings,.

The village is by no means spoilt by the estate architecture, but the estate influence is visible in other ways. The Pulford approach runs parallel with Old Lane to Poulton and finally emerges on the A483 from Wrexham to Chester by Pulford Church. Two stone lodges complete with the Grosvenor arms form the gateway here.

The **church of St Mary** was designed by John Douglas and built between 1881 and 1884 at the partial expense of the first Duke of Westminster. Red sandstone was used together with bands of lighter-coloured stone. The building has a north-west tower with a distinctive shingled spire. There are no aisles to the nave and the transepts open off the choir. The nave has noticeable rectangular windows

RAINOW [Macclesfield]

SJ9676: 3 miles (5km) NE of Macclesfield

The settlement is not listed in Domesday, but in 1290 its name was recorded as 'Ravenouh'. This is derived from 'hraefn hoh' or 'raven hill'.

Rainow lies at the foot of the east Cheshire hills on the border of the Peak District National Park. The rounded hills are a distinct contrast to the red brick and lush farmlands of the Cheshire Plain. In early medieval times it was part of the royal hunting forest of Macclesfield, and over the centuries man has transformed the rough upland slopes into a green pastoral landscape.

Originally a farming community, the settlement was established round the turnpike road that was built in the late 18th and early 19th centuries. Then came another transformation. Water-powered cotton spinning mills sprang up along the banks of the **River Dean** and its tributaries. Locally mined coal and locally quarried stone were much in demand. The stone was a buff-coloured carboniferous sandstone and many of the older houses are built of this material. The Dean Valley echoed to the non-stop sounds of mills and over twenty of them were packed into the environs of Rainow. Their specialities included cotton spinning, fulling, silk weaving, calico printing and engineering. Even workers from Macclesfield and Bollington would make their way across the fields – the soft ground was overcome by the use of flagged footpaths. Today, only one or two ruins and a mill pool remain.

Gin Clough Hall became a sawmill and is now part of a private house.

Hough Hole Mill was built around 1803 by James Mellor. From 1860 the mill was used as an engineering workshop. James Mellor senior was a farmer and builder. He built the first Methodist chapel in Rainow on Billinge Hill in 1781. At times in the 1820s he worked the cotton-spinning mill, assisted by his two sons, James and William. James Mellor senior died in 1828. William set up business elsewhere, but he returned to the mill in 1860 and, with his four sons, set up an engineering business.

John Turner, the great uncle of James Mellor junior, died in a snowstorm leading a packhorse train along Irwin's Lane towards Saltersford on Christmas Eve 1735. When a search party found the body, mysteriously there was a lady's footprint in the snow alongside. A copy of the memorial tablet that James Mellor erected is at the spot today.

James Mellor junior retired from business and devoted himself to the philosophy and religious ideas of a Swedish scientist, Emanuel Swedenborg. At his home, **Hough Hole House**, Mellor created an allegorical garden based on *A Pilgrim's Progress*. The walk through the garden takes in many features mentioned in the book, including the Slough of Despond, the Hill of Difficulty and the Delectable Mountains. It finally reaches the Celestial City, Mellor's own private chapel.

The first Saturday in June is **Rainow féte day**. The procession winds through the village, carrying the newly appointed 'Mayor' to the féte field.

The **church of Holy Trinity** was built between 1845 and 1846 as a Commissioners' church. These churches were built all over the country to supply the needs of the rising populations in industrial communities. The building has two slender, pointed arched windows and an east window with intersecting ribwork. The interior contains a west gallery and there are box pews.

The **Chapel of John the Baptist** , or **Jenkin Chapel**, Saltersford (1733) lies some 2 miles (3km) distant from Rainow and is reached by steep minor roads. It stands, windswept and alone, at the junction of three routes that were ancient packhorse trails or salters' ways across the hills. A track marker that came to be known as Jenkin Cross marked this point.

The junction became a convenient meeting place for local farmers, as the number of footpaths that meet at the crossroads confirms. The local farming population built their own chapel, and it is easy to recognise the basic style of a moorland farmhouse with the addition of a tower.

The tower has a saddleback roof and an outside flight of steps to the belfry. The building has square, Georgian cottage windows with small glass panes. The interior contains box pews, a two-decker pulpit and a carved reading desk. There is a small chancel and above the chancel arch is a modern stained-glass window.

ROSTHERNE [Macclesfield]

SJ7483: 3 miles (5km) N of Knutsford

It is a joy to wander down tree-lined lanes to the village of Rostherne, which is situated in the angle between the M56 and the A556, Northwich to Altrincham road. The settlement consists of a group of well-kept brick houses and one or two thatched cottages. One of the prettiest houses is Apple Tree Cottage, with a brick exterior and with wattle and daub underneath.

The church and village were linked with the Egertons of nearby Tatton Hall. At one time the community was a classic example of an estate village, where many of the inhabitants were dependent on the lord of the manor for their livelihood.

On the northern edge of the village lies secluded **Rostherne Mere**, Cheshire's largest and deepest mere. This fine stretch of water, with steep banks and woodland fringing the northern and western shores, was formed in the intermediate post-glacial age. The mere is a bird sanctuary and nature reserve; it is not open to the public.

The settlement is mentioned in Domesday as 'Rodestorne'. It was described as 'Roudestorn' in 1226, and is derived from the Old Norse personal name *Raudr*, so 'Raud's thornbush'.

The **church of St Mary** is beautifully situated on the south bank of Rostherne Mere with extensive views across the water. The church site has been occupied from the earliest times and it was once the parish church for Knutsford. The building is of dressed sandstone with a tower of 1742-4, replacing one of 1533. There is an interesting and unusual lychgate.

The interior contains side aisles separated from the nave by four pointed arches on Early English piers. The octagonal piers of the south arcade may be early 14th century.

In 1741 the tower of Rostherne church collapsed. During the rebuilding, an effigy and a coffin came to light. The effigy, holding a shield bearing the Venables coat of arms, is now in the chancel of the church. The chancel and the vestry were built in the latter part of the 19th century by Sir Arthur Blomfield. The roof of the church is decorated with shields bearing many coats of arms of local families, including those of Venables and Egerton.

Other monuments inside the church include one to Lady Charlotte Lucy Beatrix Egerton, died 1845, aged 21. This is a fine work in white marble; she is shown asleep and an angel kneels by her.

RUDHEATH [Vale Royal]

SJ6772: 7 miles (11km) NW of Holmes Chapel

Rudheath is the south-eastern suburb of Northwich, and lies between the River Dane and the Trent and Mersey Canal and is bordered in the south by the A556, Altrincham to Chester road. There is a convenient station at Northwich on the Manchester to Chester railway line.

The name of the settlement was described as 'Ruddheth' in 1271, and the name may be derived from 'Rudda's heath' or 'marigold heath'. The 14th-century word 'rud' means 'marigold'.

With the coming of the Trent and Mersey Canal in the late 1770s, a wharf and storage facilities were established at Broken Cross to store pottery from Staffordshire. Nearby the old Broken Cross Inn had stabling quarters for the horses which pulled the barges. There was a convenient blacksmith to hand for shoeing and general repairs. Today, there is an engineering business and the canal is now a popular waterway for leisure craft.

A chapel of ease was built in 1835 in King Street, with a chancel added to the building in 1902. It became known as Rudheath Church.

Housing development now occupies the area between the railway to the west and the encircling main roads.

RUNCORN [Halton]

SJ5182: 8 miles (13km) W of Warrington

The Romans built a fortification overlooking the river close to the present railway bridge. A strongpoint was built on Halton Hill in the 11th century and strengthened in stone during the 12th century. The summit was a good defensive position, with far-reaching views along the River Mersey.

It was the advent of the canal in the 18th century that dramatically changed the lives of the people in this thinly populated area. In 1766, the Duke of Bridgewater was given permission by

Act of Parliament to construct an extension of his canal from Worsley to Runcorn. This connection to the sea brought immediate success, attracting industry, bringing prosperity and a large growth in population in the surrounding district.

By the mid-19th century, Runcorn had a variety of industries, including timberyards, slate works, shipyards and a large tanning business. Soap and chemicals followed later.

The **Manchester Ship Canal** was built between 1887 and 1894 and, as a result, the Bridgewater Canal began a long, slow decline. Later its fortunes would be restored as the canal was used for pleasure craft.

The first structure to cross the Runcorn Gap was the railway bridge, built in 1868, when a walkway enabled pedestrians to walk from one side of the Mersey to the other. Gradually, it became increasingly necessary to have a road connection. In 1905 the transporter bridge was constructed. However, this became inadequate and in 1961 a modern road bridge, an elegant steel-arched suspension bridge, replaced it. On completion, it was the third largest bridge in the world and the largest steel arch in Europe.

The plan for Runcorn New Town was announced in 1964 with an area east of the town being developed. Halton Castle would overlook the new housing, and the new town centre would be to the south. An expressway and a busway now link the old town and the new development. The town park contains the red sandstone Norton Water Tower, 1890, walking routes, a ski slope and a miniature railway.

SAIGHTON [Chester]

SJ4462: 4 miles (6km) SE of Chester

Saighton is a separate farmland community on the southern outer approaches to Chester.

Saighton Grange was once the principal country house of the Abbots of Chester. The remaining part is the gatehouse, which was rebuilt by Abbot Ripley in 1400. The present house was built in 1861 for the second Marquess of Westminster and enlarged in 1874.

SANDBACH [Congleton]

SJ7460: 5 miles (8km) NE of Crewe

Sandbach is an ancient market town lying close to the Trent and Mersey Canal, which forms part of the Cheshire Ring. A feature of the town is the lovely cobbled market place; surrounded by old buildings and the famous **Saxon cross shafts**.

Sandbach was listed in Domesday as 'Sanbeco'. Dunning held the settlement and the lands were owned by Bigot de Loges. Its name became 'Sonbache' in 1260 and means 'sandy stream or valley'. Domesday records woodland and some arable land, and included amongst the inhabitants were three slaves. A priest and a church are mentioned.

The two fine crosses that stand on a base in the market place date from the ninth century. The taller cross is almost complete apart from the upper section of the head. All sides of the shaft are richly decorated with scenes from the New Testament. On the east face they include the Crucifixion of Christ surrounded by signs of the four Evangelists, a nativity scene and Christ as one of three figures in a circle. The opposite side includes a scene of Christ before Pilate. The north face displays a dragon at the top and below are small figure panels. There is some vinescroll ornamentation on the south side, accompanied by a panel of interlaced work.

The other cross is also richly carved and displays a pattern of triangles at the base of the shaft, which is also found at the foot of the taller cross. The west side carries a number of panels containing figures, the details of which are obscure due to weathering. However, part of the central section may represent the resurrection of Christ. The east face presents a number of scenes, possibly depicting the coming of Christianity to Mercia. Both the east and west faces include a decorative plaited border.

It is interesting to note that the crosses are mentioned as being in the market place in Elizabethan times. They were badly damaged by religious extremists in the 17th century and finally reinstated in 1816, after pieces scattered over the area were recovered.

An area just to the north of the town is called Scots' Common. In 1651 a troop of Scots retreating after the Battle of Worcester reached Sandbach and rested on open ground. The townspeople set upon them and many Scots were taken prisoner.

By the early 19th century, Sandbach's geographical position in the south-east of the county allowed it to become a busy coaching point. Coaches ran to London, Birmingham, Liverpool and Manchester.

The **church of St Mary** stands on rising ground near the River Wheelock. Sir Gilbert Scott largely rebuilt it between 1847 and 1849. The prominent west tower is said to be a reproduction of the original Perpendicular one that was erected about the time of Henry VII. The tower is built over a footpath passing through the churchyard and has open arches on three sides.

The interior of the church is spacious and handsome, with the panelled aisle and nave roofs retained from the original church.

Around the attractive cobbled market square stand two timber-framed houses. One is the former Williams Deacons Bank and the other is the **Black Bear**, dated 1634, with a thatched roof and a half-timbered upper storey.

Opposite the church of St Mary and across the High Street is the Old Hall Hotel. This is a beautiful black and white building built in 1656. This oak-framed house has the attractions of a secret door next to one of the fireplaces and a little door on the landing in which hides a spiral staircase leading to the attic.

SANDIWAY [Vale Royal]

SJ6070: 4 miles (6km) SW of Northwich

see CUDDINGTON AND SANDIWAY

SAUGHALL [Chester]

SJ3670: 3 miles (5km) NW of Chester

The village of Saughall is divided into Great and Little Saughall. This small settlement was at one time a fishing village, when nearby Chester was a busy port. However, the silting up of the estuary and the later channelling of the River Dee allow the village to look out now across a flat reclaimed area. The village is now mostly suburban Chester.

Saughall is mentioned in Domesday as 'Salhale' in Wilaveston Hundred. Leofing held it as a free man. There was land for six ploughs and the settlement contained seven villagers, one rider and four smallholders. Domesday records a fishery.

The settlement is described as 'Salchale' in 1100 and 'Parua Salighale' in 1271. The name is derived from the Old English 'salh-halh' or 'halh where sallows grew'.

The **church of All Saints** was designed by Medland and Henry Taylor and built between 1895 and 1901. It was constructed of bright red Ruabon brick. The central tower is rectangular in shape and carries a low spire. The design incorporates a fine contrast between the height and depth of the south transept and the extension of the nave roof by the south porch roof.

Modern development, such as shops and housing estates, group round the older buildings in the centre of the village. There is a black and white timbered farmhouse dating from the mid-16th century and the Charity House, a 16th-century building partly built with stones from Shotwick Castle.

The former Swinging Gate Inn, which stands opposite the Greyhound Inn, is now a private residence but is said to be of c1490. Built of brick, it has a stone spiral staircase.

Shotwick Park by John Douglas (1872) is a large, imposing, brick-built house with a tiled roof in a neo-Elizabethan style.

The annual ceremony of crowning of the Rose Queen takes place in June.

SHAVINGTON CUM GRESTY [Crewe]

SJ6952: 2 miles (3km) S of Crewe

The village lies on the north side of the A500 just south of Crewe. The B5071 road links the community with Crewe and byroads connect with the neighbouring villages of Willaston, Weston and Wybunbury.

The settlement is mentioned in Domesday as 'Santune'. It was described as 'Shawynton' in 1260 and the name is derived from a personal element – 'the tun of Sceafa's people'. For centuries, one of the settlement's two manors were held by the Woodnoth family and the site of their manor house was on or near the present Shavington Hall, which was rebuilt in 1661. In the late 19th century, the hall was leased to the Earl of Shrewsbury as a hunting lodge.

Housing developments have spread along the roads towards Crewe and the population has increased considerably. A wooden mission church, built about 1886, was destroyed by fire in 1892. This was replaced and a church hall built. The community is also well served by a social club and a bowling green.

A number of footpaths link Shavington with surrounding farmsteads and with the nearby villages of Hough and Wybunbury.

SHOCKLACH [Chester]

SJ4449: 3 miles (5km) NW of Malpas

Shocklach village was once a border stronghold, as indicated by the mounds upon which Shocklach Castle once stood. The earthworks lie on either side of the road just north of the village. The motte of the original strongpoint stands on the western side of the road and the castle **earthworks** are to be found on the eastern side, near to Castletown Farm. There are no ancient buildings in the village of Shocklach and it is probable that the original settlement lay close to the castle – hence the surviving name of Castletown. The ancient stone church is situated between the present village and Castletown Farm.

The parish of Shocklach lies between the parish of Tilston and the River Dee and consists of three townships – Caldecott, Church Shocklach and Shocklach Oviatt. The church was erected by the Lord of the Manor near his castle in about 1150.

The village is recorded in Domesday as 'Socheliche'. It mentions that Drogo held it and the lands were owned by Robert fitz Hugh (Robert, son of Hugh). Domesday lists ploughland and meadowland.

Records in 1260 show the name of the settlement as 'Schoclache'. Its meaning is very intriguing, because it can be translated as 'Goblin stream'. A study of the large-scale map shows a present-day stream running past the castle mounds. That is a pointer to the original site of the village.

The **church of St Edith**, stands about 1 mile (1.5km) north of the village, at the end of a small side lane; appropriately called Church Road. This lane continues towards the River Dee but there is no longer any crossing here to the Welsh side of the river.

The church is built of irregular blocks of sandstone and is set among firs. The main structure is a simple 12th-century chapel with a fine **Norman south doorway**. Built about 1150, it is one of the best Norman examples in the country. The doorway is round-headed in three courses: the outer of a chevron pattern, the middle in a cable design and the inner another chevron motif. There are stout ancient doors studded with iron. The building has a double bellcot, with the bell chains partly hanging outside.

Two large buttresses support the west wall. These were roofed over in the 17th century to provide a small baptistry. Inside the building the nave has a **coved plaster ceiling** of the 18th century. The furniture consists of pews from 1697, late 18th-century altar rails and old Elizabethan chairs.

The church is situated in a lonely area of border country and, perhaps because of its remoteness, it was not found by would-be restorers. This has resulted in the early 12th-century church surviving largely intact. This lovely church can offer one more surprise which verifies its lonely border setting. **A message** was scratched **on a window pane** with a diamond (now framed for safety): "I Robt. Aldersey was here the 31st day of October 1756 along with John Massie and Mr Derbyshire. N.B. The roads were so bad we were in danger of our lives."

SHOTWICK [Chester]

SHJ3473: 5½ miles (9km) NW of Chester

The isolated village of Shotwick was a fording point across the Dee on a main trading route from England to Wales. At one time the sea came right up to the boundary walls of the church. In the Middle Ages, Shotwick was an important port from whose quay Henry II left for Ireland and Edward I for Wales. Chester suffered when the River Dee silted up and Shotwick took over as the new port.

Sitting on the church wall, one can imagine the tidal waters beyond, where now there are acres of reclaimed land. However, look at the south-west corner of the churchyard wall to discover an iron ring that was used to tie up the boats so long ago.

Shotwick lies almost secretly just off the main A550, Queensferry to Birkenhead road. Its rambling cottages, ancient church and 17th-century mansion are well worth investigation.

The settlement is mentioned in Domesday as 'Sotowiche' and ploughland and meadowland are listed. It also records the fact that the land was held by the secular canons of St Werburgh, Chester. In 1100 it was described as 'Sotewica' and in 1214 as 'Schotewic'. The name could be derived from 'the wic at Sceothoh', or 'the wic (a dairy farm) on a ridge'.

The sandstone **church of St Michael** continues to stand guard, looking out across the Dee as it has done for centuries past. Then its tower would have been used as fortress, watch tower and beacon. The Perpendicular tower dates from around 1500 but the south doorway is Norman with chevron patterns on the arch stones. Note the deep score marks in the stone of the porch which were probably caused by soldiers sharpening their weapons.

The interior contains fine woodwork. Especially notable are the rare Georgian three-decker pulpit, the Churchwardens' Pew dated 1709 and late 16th or early 17th-century altar rails. In 1971, an appeal was successfully promoted to save the church from wet and dry rot.

Shotwick Hall, c1662, is an attractive red-brick house built in the shape of a letter 'E'. It has gabled wings, a noble façade facing on to the front garden and stands at the end of the lane leading to Puddington.

It was in the parish of Shotwick that Mrs Mary Davies, the celebrated **horned woman,** was born. Her horns were like a ram's, solid and wrinkled. Her horns are preserved in the Ashmolean and British Museums. Her portrait is given in Leigh's Natural History of Cheshire, taken in the 72nd year of her age, 1668.

In 1674 Ralph Heath, curate and schoolmaster, attended the Bishop's Court for illegally marrying two people from other parishes in a Shotwick alehouse without banns or licence.

SIDDINGTON [Macclesfield]

SJ8471: 5 miles (8km) N of Congleton

The hamlet of Siddington is composed of a few houses in the area where the B5392 crosses the A34. The nearby brick farm-house of **Siddington Hall** is the site where the family of de Sydinton lived during the reign of Henry III.

Siddington was listed in Domesday as 'Sudendune' and became 'Sudingdone' in 1286. It is derived from the Old English 'sup in tune' or 'a place south of the hill'.

Brown held the settlement and the lands were owned by Bigot (of Loges). Domesday records a substantial area of woodland.

The **church of All Saints** is an interesting medieval church located on a hill near the junction of the A34 and B5392. It is approached along a tree-lined avenue from the lane. On first sighting, it looks as much a black and white timber church as Marton. It was, in fact, a timber-framed building, but was partly rebuilt in brick in 1815. The front section is black painted on whitened brick. The brickwork is exposed in the nave, but on closer examination the **chancel** reveals true half-timbered construction.

At the time of the rebuilding, the chancel and the porch must have been in better condition than the nave. The chancel has two narrow bays with timber wall shafts and timber arched braces with herringbone bracing in the walls. The quaint little bell turret adds much to the charm of this little church. The interior contains a **pulpit** dated 1633 and an attractive 14th-century screen.

Nearby, to the north-east, lies **Redes Mere**, a shallow artificial lake that contains 'islands' of dead vegetation. These floating masses inspired the mysterious 'floating island' in Alan Garner's novel *The Weirdstone of Brisingamen.*

Capesthorne Hall lies two miles (2km) north of Siddington. Capesthorne is mentioned in the Domesday Survey of 1086 as 'Copestor' in the Hundred of Macclesfield. The name became

'Capestorne' in 1285. The second element of the word derives from 'thorn-bush', the first element is obscure.

In 1153, the Davenport family were granted the Chief Forestership over the surrounding great forests. They upheld the harsh forest laws and their **crest** was a felon's head with a halter of gold around his neck.

The family trace their descent in the male line from Ormus de Davenporte, a Saxon who lived at the time of the Conquest. The name Bromley was added to their name when they succeeded to the property of the Bromley family in 1822.

The Ward family settled at Capesthorne in the reign of Edward IV. A brick column in the park marks the site of their earlier house. In 1719 John Ward engaged William Smith to build a house and the first phase completed was two wings. Finally, the house was finished in 1732; a seven-bay structure of classical design, in brick with stone dressings.

In 1748, on John Ward's death, Capesthorne passed to the Davenports of Woodford and Marton through the marriage of John's daughter Penelope. In 1837, Edward Davies Davenport called in Edward Blore to remodel the house. The grand Elizabethan style was Blore's speciality and he joined the three parts of the old Capesthorne into one. He extended the central block, widened the wings, applied a façade of brick and stone and enhanced the skyline with turrets, gables and bellcot.

A disastrous fire of 1861 destroyed most of the central part of the house and Anthony Salvin rebuilt that section. He made a number of changes that altered the character of the house.

Holy Trinity Chapel, built in 1720-2, is a simple building of three bays. The panelling and carving on the west gallery was originally on the east wall. The reredos behind and above the altar are of the Italian style and executed in mosaic. The pulpit is Flemish, with carved panels depicting sacred stories.

In the grounds and, closing the entrance to the gardens, is a set of extremely handsome, Early Rococo Milanese gates of around 1750.

SMALLWOOD [Congleton]
SJ8060: 4 miles (6km) SW of Congleton

Smallwood is situated on a byroad that connects the A34 with the A50 to the south-west of Congleton. This settlement close to Staffordshire is surrounded by agricultural land. A small residential development, it has good access with the M6 junction 17 and is convenient for the Potteries.

The **church of St John the Baptist** was designed by C. and J, Trubshaw and built in 1845. It consists of a nave and lower chancel. At the east end are three stepped lancet windows. The building has a hammerbeam roof and the roof carries a bellcot.

The settlement was described as 'Smaleuuod' in 1252, which is derived from 'narrow leah and wood'.

STOAK [Chester]
SJ4273: 4 miles (6km) N of Chester

The small village of Stoak is situated between Chester and Ellesmere Port and adjoins the busy motorway interchange of the M53 and M56. The Shropshire Union Canal passes right by the village.

The name of the settlement is a variant of 'stoke' from the Old English 'stoc'. This word generally indicated a 'cattle-farm' or a 'dairy-farm'. Another meaning of 'stoc' is 'stockade'.

The **church of St Lawrence** was designed by George Edgecumbe and rebuilt in 1827. The small chancel and nave roof of the previous church remain. The interior of the building contains a late 17th-century pulpit. There is a west gallery and a communion rail with twisted balusters from the late 17th century. There is a large marble tablet in memory of Henry Bunbury (1668). Many of the decorated heraldic tablets were painted by one of the Randle Holmes 1627 to 1702. The church dates back to the Norman period and restoration took place in 1827.

During the Second World War, the Victorian stained-glass window was damaged by bombs. This was replaced with plain glass.

STOCKTON HEATH [Warrington]

SJ6185: 2 miles (3km) S of Warrington

Stockton Heath is a large residential suburb of Warrington and is really outer Warrington.

The **church of St Thomas** was designed by E. G. Paley and built in 1868. A large church with a big south-east tower, the exterior is faced with small stones. The north chapel has two bays, with odd details at the level at which the arch rises from its supports. There is a notable example of tile decoration in the chancel.

STRETTON [Warrington]

SJ6282: 4 miles (6km) S of Warrington

The small community of Stretton lies at the busy junction of the A49 and the B5356 Northwich to Warrington and Appleton Thorn to Daresbury roads. At the southern end of the village, nearer to Lower Stretton, is Junction 10, the intersection of the M56 with the A49 and the A559. The surroundings are mainly agricultural, particularly dairy and arable farming.

Slightly to the east of the northerly road junction is the line of the old Roman road, King Street, that ran from Sandbach to Wilderspool (Warrington). Stretton church is almost on the line of the road, and northwards for the next half mile, a hedgerow and footpath mark the approximate course.

The name of the settlement is probably derived from the Old English 'straettun' or 'strettun' meaning 'a tun on a Roman road'.

The sandstone **church of St Matthew**, 1870, was designed by Sir George Gilbert Scott to replace a Commissioners' church of 1826-7. The Early English style tower, nave and aisles were probably the work of Scott. The church clock face was refurbished in 1963 and carries the following inscription – "Time is not all" and "Forget not God".

Stretton Hall is a Georgian brick house erected around 1763 for John Leche, son of the rector of Tilston. It has a central block of two storeys over a basement and two single-storey wings. Sir John Leche moved here after Carden Hall, Clutton, was destroyed by fire in 1912.

Nearby are two 17th-century brick houses with attractively shaped gables: Stretton Old Hall and the previously moated Stretton Lower Hall.

STYAL [Macclesfield]

SJ8383: 2 miles (3km) N of Wilmslow

The village of Styal is sandwiched between Wilmslow and Manchester Airport. Styal has a station on the Wilmslow, Gatley, Manchester railway line.

The name of the settlement was described as 'Styhale' in 120 and 'Stihal' in
1286. The first element is the Old English
'stig' and means, 'a halh with a pigsty' or
'a halh by a path'.

Quarry Bank Mill at Styal, now under
the care of the National Trust, became
one of the water-powered mills to survive. Samuel Greg, originally from Bel-
fast, was the pioneer of a factory system
that largely replaced the cottage workshop.

He founded the mill in the wooded valley of the Bollin in 1784. There was a
good fall of water and a local supply of
cheap labour. The pauper children came
from orphanages. Indentures were signed
committing the apprentices to work for
the employer until they reached the age of
eighteen. For his part, the employer
agreed to feed, clothe and educate the
children.

Although this seemed to buck the trend
and the conditions were less harsh at
Quarry Bank Mill, life for the apprentices
could not be described as pleasant. Their
working hours extended from 5.30am to
8.00pm. In 1790, Samuel Greg built the
apprentices' house to accommodate the
child labourers.

As well as the factory buildings, a shop
and a school were built in the early part of
the 19th century. Most of the attractive
cottages in Styal village were built in the
1820s after a period of great expansion.
There is a pleasant mix of red-brick terraced houses, individual thatched cottages and two tiny chapels.

Weaving was introduced in 1834 and
the use of water turbines came into operation in 1904.

Footpaths lead away from the southern
end of the village down to the river. The
Styal Country Park covers the extent of
Samuel Greg's original estate. This em-
braces the village, Quarry Bank Mill and

woodlands along the riverbanks to the
north and south of the mill.

The HM Prison Styal was originally
built as cottage homes for children in
1898. This was an attempt to replace the
typical workhouse style of accommodation.

SUTTON LANE ENDS
[Macclesfield]

SJ9271: 2 miles (3km) SE of Macclesfield

The parish of Sutton lies south-east of
Macclesfield and is composed of three
districts – Langley, Sutton Lane Ends
and Lyme Green. Sutton Lane Ends lies
on rising ground at the edge of the Peak
District National Park. In medieval
times, this area was part of the royal forest of Macclesfield. Today, quiet byroads travel into the recesses of this
lovely hill country to explore Tegg's
Nose Country Park. Here, the **Gritstone
Trail** passes through on its way to Lyme
Park.

Other attractions in this area are the
group of reservoirs near to Langley.
They are Tegg's Nose, Bottoms,
Ridgegate and Trentabank. The latter
two are situated in the modern **Macclesfield Forest**, a large area of coniferous
woodland. Footpaths, forest tracks and
minor roads enable the visitor to explore
this beautiful landscape.

Sutton is a very common name that
goes back to the Old English 'Sup-tun' or
'southern tun or homestead'. Lane Ends
refers to the old routes out of Macclesfield before they became rough hill
tracks.

Nearby, C.F. Tunnicliffe RA, the artist, was born in 1902 in Langley. His father was a shoemaker in the village.

The **church of St James** was designed
by W. Hayley, and built in 1840. The

lower chancel and apse were designed by C. Hodgson Fowler and built in 1871. The low tower with its four gables at the front by the spire is Hayley's. There are lancet windows in the church.

SUTTON WEAVER [Vale Royal]

SJ5479: 3 miles (5km) SE of Runcorn

This former farming community is now a suburb of nearby Runcorn and effectively separated by the M56. The former surroundings of agricultural land, north of the River Weaver, are covered by roads, railways and residential development. This is in contrast to the valley of the Weaver Navigation, with its farmsteads and large tracts of woodland.

Sutton is a very common name that here indicates a 'southern tun or farmstead by the River Weaver'.

SWETTENHAM [Congleton]

SJ7968: 3 miles (5km) E of Holmes Chapel

Swettenham is a tiny village surrounded by rich agricultural land, a rural retreat in lovely countryside. It lies in peaceful seclusion in the valley of the Swettenham Brook, just north of the River Dane. The village is a cul-de-sac at the end of a winding country road and consists of a church, a handful of houses, a public house and a community building with a bowling green. Just east of the village, where the Midge Brook runs through a secluded valley, the area is known as **Daffodil Dell**, because of the mass of flowers that appear each spring.

The settlement is not listed in Domesday but its name was recorded as 'Suetenhala' in 1183 and 'Swetenham' in 1259 and 1288. The name is derived from

'Sweta's ham' – 'a homestead belonging to Sweta'.

Swettenham Church, whose dedication is unknown, seems to have been a dependency of Astbury. One suggestion proposed was that the church might be dedicated to St Peter because the first Lord of Swettenham was Peter de Swettenham.

The history of the church probably began in pre-Conquest times, as indicated by the Saxon cross that was discovered when the south aisle was rebuilt. Then it is thought a Norman chapel occupied the present site, later followed by a timber-framed building. In 1720, as the timberwork had rotted away, the frame was cased in brick. It is thought that the tower was erected in brick (c1717-22).

During the restoration, the original timber framing of the chancel was spared and the wooden features are probably the best part of the building. The oval windows in the chancel are a surprising find in a church. In 1846 the old wooden piers in the nave were removed and replaced with round 'Norman' pillars.

At the south side of the altar is a fine piece of medieval stained glass in an oval centrepiece; it is either of Flemish or Italian workmanship. The church contains a raised pulpit with painted panels thought to date from the time of Queen Anne. There is an elegant 18th-century font with a fluted bowl.

In this part of south-east Cheshire, annual **gooseberry shows** are held in several villages. Swettenham has two such events. The first is on the last Saturday in July, with the competition only open to gooseberries grown in the parish. Secondly, on the first Saturday in August there is an open show, when anyone from in or out of the parish may enter.

Swettenham Hall is situated to the east of the village, occupying a fine position overlooking the valley of the River Dane. It is a 17th-century house with late Georgian alterations towards the Gothic style. The entrance side is castellated and there are good examples of 17th-century outbuildings. The old manor house of Swettenham Hall, with its own chapel, is reputed to have a ghost. The apparition is that of a lady dressed in black, who appears to members of the Swettenham family as a sign of bad times.

TARPORLEY [Vale Royal]

SJ5463: 9 miles (14km) NW of Nantwich

The buildings that closely line the High Street reflect numerous architectural styles, particularly fine Georgian façades. At the south end of the High Street is the Manor House, dated 1586 and probably rebuilt on the site of an older house. The house was placed on the corner of the village triangle, which may mean that the village ended here at one time in the past.

The Swan Hotel was built in 1769. It has three storeys with two sloping bay windows. The building probably contains some medieval fabric within. The Swan Hotel is the headquarters of the Tarporley Hunt, with the meetings being held in the famous **Hunt Room**. This particular room has large windows as it is over the former market hall, which was the site of the famous Cabbage Fair. The old coaching inn was a staging post on the Chester to London route.

Tarporley is recorded in Domesday as 'Torpelei'. Wulfgeat held the settlement and the lands were owned by Gilbert of Venables. Domesday mentions ploughland, meadowland and a large tract of woodland. The name of the settlement was 'Torperleg' in 1282, 'Torperley' in 1293.

The meaning of the name Tarporley may be 'a place that stands by a prominent hill'. The hill may well have been called torr. The Old English for pear wood or glade is 'per-leah', hence 'perley by the hill called Torr'.

At one time Tarporley lay in **Delamere Forest**. There were areas where animals could be pastured and even some arable land. Special courts enforced the strict forest laws with regulations imposed forbidding the harming of deer and wild boar. In the end, the growing demand for land for agricultural use meant more forest being ploughed up and the inhabitants resisting the heavy fines that were imposed.

In 1812, what was left of the medieval forest was officially disafforested. Some of the crown lands were reserved for a governmental body that later became the Forestry Commission. The planting of conifers was the foundation of many modern forests such as Delamere. Here we have an official body welcoming visitors, but the orderly and regimental coniferous forest really gives little idea of what a medieval hunting preserve would have looked like.

The **church of St Helen** has a history of continuous alteration and rebuilding, yet it is basically a medieval church. In 1785 the west end was rebuilt, followed by work on the chapels, the chancel, the tower and the nave in the 19th century.

Mention should be made of the **Done family** of Utkinton Hall who were the hereditary Foresters of Delamere. In the early days they carried out the forest laws with utmost severity. There are several monuments to the Done family in Tarporley church. Sir John Done's monument depicts the knight in forester's dress which is richly embroidered. In his left hand he holds the famous horn. In the 12th century, Ranulf, 3rd Earl of Chester, conferred the Master Forestership on Ralph de Kingsley, to hold by tenure of a horn, which was to be blown when the earl attended the forest chase. The Dones of Utkinton succeeded the Kingsleys as Master Foresters through the marriage of Henry Done and Joan de Kingsley. The horn is described as 'black, carved, with silver gilt mouthpiece'.

The memorial to John Crewe has an effigy wearing a wig and with his shoulders enveloped in a loose garment. The handsome monument to Sir John Crewe, who died in 1711, shows a full-length figure in white marble. The finest of the Done monuments is the 17th-century altar tomb of Jane Done, Mrs Mary Crewe, and her young granddaughter, Mary Knightly. The complete memorial is very beautifully sculptured.

Oulton Park lies some three miles north-east of Tarporley. In 1926 a fire destroyed the ancient hall, which was not rebuilt. In 1952 the family leased part of the park and the Cheshire Car Circuit, Oulton Park, was established.

TARVIN [Chester]

SJ4967: 5 miles (8km) E of Chester

To the west of Kelsall, the sandy hills of the mid-Cheshire ridge fall down to the low-lying lands around the Dee estuary. The line of the Roman road, the principal route from Chester to Manchester, is followed east of Chester by the A51, passing near to the hamlet of Stamford Bridge. In the Dark Ages this was disputed territory, where the kingdoms of Powys and Mercia came together. The River Gowy, which is a name of Welsh origin, was the frontier between the Welsh and the English. Tarvin, unlike most of the surrounding settlements, which have an Anglo-Saxon origin, is also thought to be an Anglicised form of the Welsh word *terfyn* meaning 'a boundary'.

In the Domesday Survey, Tarvin is mentioned as 'Terve' in Risetone Hundred. The Bishop held Tarvin. Domesday records considerable ploughland with riders, villagers and smallholders, as well as a large stretch of woodland. William held two hides (a hide is a unit of land measurement reckoned at 120 acres) of this manor's land from the Bishop. Interestingly, its value before 1066 was £8 but this had fallen to £4.10s. It was laid waste, which means land gone out of cultivation or land ravished by the Normans. At the Conquest, the manor of Tarvin belonged to the Bishops of Lichfield and Coventry.

The **church of St Andrew** is approached from the street through 18th-century gate piers with urns and a short avenue of lime trees. There is a splendid Tudor doorway in the great west tower with particularly fine mouldings. The late 15th-century sandstone tower has a clock face on all four sides, and there are a variety of gargoyles and carved figures on the top stringcourse.

The north aisle was constructed after the tower, with a nave arcade of pointed arches resting on octagonal piers. The fine east window is original, having been bricked up during the 18th century and resurrected again after the removal of the vestry.

The **Bruen Chapel**, which is situated at the eastern end of the south aisle, is divided by a 14th-century screen and entered through a massive doorway. The Bruen family of Stapleford, just south of Tarvin, were local landowners. John Bruen acquired a great reputation as a Calvinistic Puritan who called in at various houses in the locality to preach the gospel. He was also known to befriend the poor and hungry with shelter, food and clothing. John Bruen removed all the pre-Reformation stained glass, with its dark, painted images, from the Bruen Chapel and replaced it with plain glass in the first part of the 17th century.

There is a fine 'squint' built to enable those in the aisle or side chapel to see the altar. On the south wall is the '**Church Imp**', supposedly spying through the squint. The splendid nave roof is of the arch-brace and hammerbeam design. There is a carving on the oak beams. The inscription reads, 'This Roofe was made ANNO DOMINI 1650 Raphe Wright, John Bruen, Churchwardens, Charls Boovth, Will Venables, Carpintrs.' In the 18th century the roof was covered by a lath and plaster ceiling, but the 1650 work came to light after the 1891 restoration.

The church contains a handsome 15th-century font, octagonal in shape, with panels, a decorated shaft and a base with beautifully carved roses. There is a fine two-tier 18th-century brass chandelier. A showcase displays interesting exhibits including cannon balls.

During the Civil War, there was a brisk engagement in the neighbourhood of the church in August 1644. One of the monuments has a ragged bullet hole in the brass plate. The village was the operational headquarters for the Parliamentarians during the siege of Chester.

On the outside south wall of the church are three medieval '**Scratch**' sundials – one with the hours marked in Roman numerals. The custom of **rush-bearing** is continued here on a Sunday in July, when the occasion is celebrated by decorating the graves in the churchyard.

In the Middle Ages, Tarvin lay on the edge of the royal forest. By the 14th century the church stood at the centre of a large parish and the settlement had a market in Tudor and Stuart times. In the 18th century, a fire destroyed much of old Tarvin, including many of the timber-framed cottages. Hence, the Georgian rebuilding in the village centre. At about that time the street market died out.

The Flaggs and Hamilton House are part of the rebuilding dated 1756. They were built of brick, each of four bays and two and a half storeys high. Along the High Street is Tarvin Hall, a Georgian replacement in brick.

Due to the fire in 1752, there are no earlier buildings except those round the church, which formerly included the local grammar school and the schoolmaster's house. Prior to his death in 1740, the schoolmaster was **John Thomasen.** His monument lies in the south porch of the church. He was particularly renowned for his beautiful handwriting and his penmanship brought him commissions from distinguished patrons including Queen Anne, for whom he transcribed the Icon Basilike of her grandfather.

Until the 1920s, there was a Tarvin **souling play** performed annually on All Souls' Eve. The play, which was enacted in a number of Cheshire villages, had variations in the characters. In some versions there was a Hodening Horse, in others there was King George and the Black Prince. In Tarvin, the latter character was called the Cheshire Champion.

At one time church bells rang out on All Saints' Eve and it was believed that this would give aid to all the souls in purgatory. Custom decreed that the soulers entered a house to sing two verses of the souling song. Then there were requests for ale, strong beer or money and, after these were dispensed, the party moved on to the next house. Gradually the state of the participants became open to doubt and progress round the village was governed by the level of hospitality received.

Children who went souling followed a

similar pattern, except for requests of a different nature. Their souling song was as follows:

'Soul, soul, for a soul cake!
I pray, good missus, for a soul cake!
An apple or pear, a plum or a cherry,
Any good thing to make us merry'.

The custom of ringing the **Pancake Bell** is still observed each Shrove Tuesday at 11.00am.

From medieval times, an important road from Lichfield to Chester crossed the River Gowy just south of Tarvin at **Hockenhull Platts**. Of stone and brick construction with a cobbled surface, the middle bridge spans the Gowy itself, the side ones are for flood waters. The bridges are medieval in origin and used by pedestrians and packhorse traffic, but the crossing was not wide enough for carts and coaches. Not until the 1770s was the official Chester-London road re-routed through Tarvin and the old route and bridges at Hockenhull Platts allowed to relapse into obscurity. Nowadays, this is a quiet atmospheric place visited by ramblers.

TATTENHALL [Chester]

SJ4858: 7 miles (11km) SE of Chester

Tattenhall is a well developed village lying a short distance to the north-west of the Peckforton Hills and just off the A41, Whitchurch to Chester road. An extensive area of farmland surrounds the village.

Tattenhall contains a variety of buildings, and this is a very pleasing aspect of the village. Architectural styles include brick terraces, timber-framed dwellings and Victorian imitation timber-framing.

The settlement was mentioned in Domesday as 'Tatenale' in Dudestan Hundred. Ernwin held it as a free man and

the lands were owned by William Malbank from Earl Hugh. There was land for six ploughs with two villagers, two smallholders and one Frenchman. There was a large tract of woodland. The settlement was described as 'Tatenhala' in 1100, which means 'Tata's halh'.

The **church of St Alban** was designed by John Douglas, except for the Perpendicular west tower. The **stained glass** includes two very fine early 14th-century figures of saints. The colours of yellow, green and red are of a splendidly bright quality. Other examples of stained glass include one in the south aisle by Kempe (1897). There is a beautiful brass candelabra dated 1755.

The church is one of a number that have stood on this site and some believe that in early times this was a pagan site.

At one period there were two Methodist Chapels in the village, but now there are none. Nowadays, a number of followers attend the chapel in Brown Knowl.

Tattenhall Hall is a Jacobean building with an irregular front and with mullioned and transomed windows. The doorway is placed in the gabled part.

THELWALL [Warrington]

SJ6487: 2½ miles (4km) ESE of Warrington

Thelwall lies on the southern bank of the Manchester Ship Canal, just to the west of the famous viaduct of the M6 that takes its name. The community is sandwiched between the Ship Canal and the Bridgewater Canal. The village is now a residential area for Warrington and district.

The Manchester Ship Canal is duty-bound to provide a daily ferry, a rowing boat, across the canal. Passengers are taken across to Thelwall Eyes for a fare that is fixed by Act of Parliament. The area on the northern bank is a dumping ground for silt and also a bird sanctuary.

Archaeologists believe that the River Mersey was one of the routes by which prehistoric cultures from Ireland entered Britain. The Saxons built burhs (usually means a fortified place or manor) at Runcorn and Thelwall. The Norsemen from Ireland and the Isle of Man also used the Mersey as one of their lines of communication.

In AD923, the name of the settlement was 'P(Th)elwael', and 'Thelewell' in 1241. The first element is the Old English 'thel' meaning plank. The second element is 'wael', a deep pool. So the derivation of the name is 'a deep pool by a plank bridge'.

Standing on the site of an earlier chapel, the rock-faced church of All Saints, 1843, was designed by J Mountford Allen. The building has a nave, a bellcot and a side of single lancet windows. The chancel was built in 1857 and the north aisle in 1890.

The interior of the church contains a memorial to the Saxon, Edward the Elder, who founded Thelwall. Eric Gill designed the memorial and two of the stained-glass windows.

Thelwall Hall was originally a brick Georgian house of around 1747, with seven bays and a central pediment. Now Chaigeley School, the building has been extensively altered with bay windows and a number of extensions.

THORNTON-LE-MOORS [Chester]

SJ4374: 3 miles (5km) SE of Ellesmere Port

The village is situated south of the massive Stanlow Oil Refinery complex. Beyond the welter of oil storage tanks and futuristic-looking equipment and plant lies the Manchester Ship Canal. The village stands on higher ground beyond the east bank of the River Gowy. The houses and farmhouses cluster closely together just off the A5117, but it remains a quiet location away from the hurly-burly of the main trunk road. However, the M56 crosses the area just to the south of the village.

Originally, the surrounding area consisted of low-lying heath and fen land until the Enclosure Acts. Some of the lower-lying tracts of land were only drained comparatively recently. An ancient footpath across the valley links with the neighbouring village of Stoak.

The settlement was mentioned in Domesday as 'Torentune', and the survey records a church, a priest and an area of meadowland. Its name is derived from 'a tun where thorn bushes grew'.

The **church of St Mary** has Decorated and Perpendicular features. The former style includes the tower, the south aisle doorway and the chancel's east window. The south window of the chancel and the fine hammerbeam roof are Perpendicular. The interior contains a 17th-century font and a splendid communion rail dated 1695. There are also a number of painted heraldic monuments, probably by Randle Holme, and dated between 1634 and 1687.

TILSTON [Chester]

SJ4551: 3 miles (5km) NW of Malpas

Tilston lies at the heart of a quiet rural landscape in the border country of south-west Cheshire. Tilston is recorded in Domesday as 'Tillestone'. The settlement was held by Earl Edwin and the lands owned by Robert fitz Hugh. The survey lists a mill and ploughland and, included among the villagers, was a reeve or factor, a blacksmith and a miller. Another entry states that Ranulf holds part of the land but that the Bishop of Chester claims part of it. Tilston is recorded as 'Tilleston' in 1291. This is derived from a personal name, so 'Tilli's tun'.

The **Roman road** Watling Street (West) passes through Wroxeter from north to south and this road was the base road for the military operations against Wales, connecting the main legionary fortresses at Chester and Caerleon. From Aldford, the line of the Roman road takes a south-south-east alignment, where a hedgerow line continues for some distance towards the south, almost to the Farndon – Barton road. In a short distance it reaches Stretton Hall, whose modern drive is on the alignment, then the road continues through Tilston and on via Kidnall Hill and Malpas.

The village consists of a small group of houses at the intersection of a number of meandering roads between the River Dee and the A41; with other dwellings tucked away down side lanes. There is an excellent community hall that caters for many of the village's organisations. These include the Tilston WI Group that holds regular meetings and maintains an interesting programme of events.

The **church of St Mary** stands rather isolated at the southern approaches to the village. Studying the network of footpaths that meet in the neighbourhood of the church, it is possible that this was the site of the original medieval settlement. The church is a handsome building in sandstone of various colours and with a fine tower sporting a weathercock.

St Mary's was rebuilt between 1877 and 1888, except for the tower and the north chapel. The tower is Perpendicular, with some fine gargoyles, and the chapel is of 1659 with Perpendicular windows. But the clues to older materials lie in the south and north doorways. The pulpit is of plain 18th-century design and the wooden communion rail is Jacobean, 1677.

Tilston once had a poet of local renown named Hopley. Quotations from his work can be seen carved on some of the tombstones in the churchyard.

The inhabitants of Tilston area could, at one time, catch a train from Malpas or Broxton. The line from **Tattenhall Junction** to Whitchurch, opened by the LNWR on 1 October 1872, sadly closed to passengers on 16 September 1957. There was potential in this line for local residents and commuters as it gave access to Chester and Liverpool. It would have been a simple matter to install a wayside halt on the line just east of Tilston.

Edge Hall, $1\frac{1}{2}$ miles (2km) east of Tilston, is a Jacobean house with five gables built around 1700. It has a fine large doorway and an entrance hall with a screen of Ionic columns.

Stretton Mill lies $1\frac{1}{2}$ miles (2km) north of Tilston and is approached by quiet lanes or from the A534 at Barton. The present mill dates from the 17th century, although there has been a mill here since the 14th century. The mill fell into disuse in 1959 and was restored to working order in 1975. Water-powered wheels using water from the Carden Brook drive the millstones. This is an attractive place to visit with a renovated barn providing an interesting exhibition. (Open Tuesdays to Sundays, 14.00 to 18.00 from 1 March to 31 October. Shop and picnic area.)

TILSTONE BANK [Chester]

SJ5659: $2\frac{1}{2}$ miles (4km) S of Tarporley

Tilstone Bank is a small settlement at a

crossing point on the Shropshire Union Canal. The River Gowy, having accompanied the canal for some distance, now turns away towards its source on the Peckforton Hills. A narrow country lane links Tilstone Bank with the large, attractive village of Bunbury. The name Tilstone is derived from 'Tidwulf's stone'.

TILSTONE FEARNALL [Chester]

SJ5660: 1 mile (1.6km) SE of Tarporley

Tilstone Fearnall is a small farming community surrounded by agricultural land. The landscape is one of woodland, numerous small ponds and parkland to the south of Tarporley. The village is served by the A51 Chester to Nantwich road.

The settlement is mentioned in Domesday as 'Tidulstane' in Risedon Hundred. William held the lands from Robert fitz Hugh. There was land for two ploughs with one smallholder. Domesday records a small wood. The settlement was described as 'Tideluestan' in 1150 and 'Tiduluestan' in 1190. The name is derived from 'Tidwulf's stone' and Fearnall means 'ferny halh'.

The church of St Jude was built in 1836 at the expense of Lord Tollemache of Peckforton Castle. It is of the Commissioners' type of church. There is a lancet window at the front and pairs of lancet windows along the sides. The building has a bellcot but no aisles or chancel. There is a Gothic tablet to Vice-Admiral J. R. Delap Tollemache (died 1837) and one to his wife (died 1846).

Tilstone Hall Folly is a structure just south of Tilstone Hall. It can be likened to the ruin of a Jacobean gatehouse, with an archway in the middle and mullioned windows.

TIVERTON [Chester]

SJ5560: 9 miles (14km) SE of Chester

Tiverton is an attractive linear village along a byroad joining the A49 Whitchurch to Chester road. The River Gowy and the Shropshire Union Canal run side by side just to the south of the village. This is a farming community set in an agricultural landscape of meadows, small ponds and extensive acres of farmland.

At the entrance to the village stands an attractive group of brick estate cottages set at right angles. The Methodist Chapel (1864), with a pleasing font, stands between the cottages.

The settlement was mentioned in Domesday as 'Tevretone' in Risedon Hundred. Dedol and Hundulf held it as two manors as free men. The lands were owned by Robert fitz Hugh. There was land for two ploughs, with three villagers and two smallholders. Domesday records a wide tract of woodland.

The settlement was described as 'Teverton' in 1260. The name is derived form the Old English 'teafor' meaning 'red pigment, vermilion'.

TOFT [Macclesfield]

SJ7576: 1 mile (1.6km) S of Knutsford

Toft is a small hamlet centred on Toft Hall. The surrounding area is composed of woodland and agricultural land. It lies just off the A50 south of Knutsford.

The settlement is not mentioned in Domesday. The name is derived from the Old Scandinavian word *toft* or *topt* meaning the 'site of a house'.

The church of St John the Evangelist was designed by W. and G. Habershon and built between 1854 and 1855 in the late 13th-century style. The building has a nave, a chancel and a north aisle under a nave roof, and a small south-west steeple.

Toft Hall has a thirteen-bay front in the shape of an 'E'. The porch design is continued up to a tower. On the opposite side, behind it, is a second tower. The outside was cement-rendered early in the 19th century. Before that time, the house was of brick and stone quoins, giving the appearance of a 17th-century house.

pyramidal roof. The windows are straight-headed except the east window, which is round-headed. There are tie beams inside with lovely openwork panels. The font is Jacobean and there is a three-decker pulpit. There is a monument to Thomas Vernon (died 1833).

There is a story that white owls fly down the tower as a sign to parishioners that they are going to die.

TUSHINGHAM CUM GRINDLEY [Chester]

SJ5246: 2 miles (3km) SE of Malpas

This small village is situated on the border both with Shropshire and with Wales. The surroundings consist of agricultural land. The village stands mainly on a by-road just off the A41 Whitchurch to Chester road.

The settlement was mentioned in Domesday as 'Tusigeham' in Dudestan Hundred. Humphrey held the lands from Robert fitz Hugh. There was land for two ploughs with one smallholder. Domesday records some woodland. The settlement was described as 'Tussinhgham' in 1260 and 'Tussingham' in 1288. It probably means 'the ham of Tunsige's people'.

The **church of St Chad** was built with walls of crazy paving between 1862 and 1863. The building has a nave, a chancel and transepts. The west tower is later, 1896. There are examples of stained glass by Kempe (1897) and in the north transept (1904).

Situated in fields in an east-south-east direction is the **Old St Chad Church**. It was built between 1689 and 1691 by gifts of money, particularly from John Dod, a London dealer in textile fabrics. Constructed in brick, it has a nave and chancel in one. It has a narrow west tower with a

UPTON-BY-CHESTER [Chester]

SJ4069: 2 miles (3km) N of Chester

Upton lies to the north-west of the city and is now part of suburban Chester sandwiched between the A5116 and the A41. Upton is served by a station on the Chester to Birkenhead railway line.

The settlement is mentioned in Domesday as 'Optone', and considerable ploughland and some meadowland are recorded. It was described in AD958 as 'Hupton' and 'Uptuna' in 1125. The most likely derivation is from the Old English 'Upptun' or 'a higher tun'.

Chester Zoo started from small beginnings after the Second World War and has now become a superb internationally known zoo. With spacious enclosures and delightful gardens, there is a marvellous collection of mammals, reptiles, birds and fish from all over the world. Major attractions are the Tropical House and the Aquarium.

The **church of Holy Ascension**, (1852-4), was designed by James Harrison. It has a tower with a recessed spire, a nave and a chancel. The transepts are later work, with dates of 1958 and 1967, completed in the early 14th-century style. The stained-glass work in the church is by Kempe and of various dates from 1871 to 1885.

UTKINTON [Vale Royal]

SJ5565: 2 miles (3km) N of Tarporley

Utkinton lies in rural surroundings at the foot of the Willington Hills. Nearby, tree-covered Billinge Hill, overlooking the Cheshire Plain, is the site of a Bronze Age tumulus.

Utkinton Hall was the home of the Done family, until the 17th century hereditary Foresters of Delamere. The Horn of Delamere symbolised the right of Forestership since 1123. This polished curved horn with ornamental hoops is kept at the Linmere Forest Museum.

At its greatest extent, Delamere Forest stretched from Frodsham marsh almost to Nantwich, and from the Weaver to the Gowy. Once an area was declared a special preserve, those officials in charge became responsible for the preservation of all the wild beasts. These mainly included three types of deer and the boar. Initially, severe restrictions were imposed, such as all household dogs living in or near the forest had to be lamed so that they couldn't jump at the beasts. Harsh punishments were decreed for killing or injuring the wild animals. Special courts called the 'Forest Eyre' were organised to try any misdemeanours.

The settlement of Utkinton was described as 'Utkynton' in 1303 and its name is derived from 'the tun of Uttoc's people'.

Utkinton Hall is now a much smaller building than it was originally. Now a farm, the hall was supposedly built round an oak tree. This was shaped into an octagonal pillar that ran up both floors to support the roof.

The Done family line terminated in 1629 with the demise of Sir John Done, whose daughter married Sir John Crewe. During the Civil War, the house was ransacked by the Royalists in 1644. In the 18th century, the splendid staircase with twisted small pillars was removed to Tarporley Rectory.

The area around the village has always been known for the number of wells, all with a good supply of water. Rain and spring water percolating through sandstone layers was often found to contain medicinal properties.

The village school was built in 1893 and the building is also used as the community's church.

WALTON [Warrington]

SJ5884: 2 miles (3km) S of Warrington

Walton is situated to the south of Warrington and lies between the A56 and alongside the Bridgewater Canal. North of the village is the Manchester Ship Canal and the River Mersey.

The settlement was described as 'Waletona' in the 12th century. It is a common name taken from the Old English and may mean 'the tun of the Britons', 'a tun in a wood' or 'a tun by a stream'.

Under a mile to the north at Wilderspool is an extensive Roman site, now largely situated between the Ship Canal and the Mersey. Excavations have indicated that occupation first began as a defensive position, probably in the time of Gnaeus Julius Agricola. He arrived in Britain in AD78 and became the best known governor; it was he who placed the seal on the occupation of Britain.

Later (AD85-90) this was followed by buildings that indicated extensive industrial activities on the site, including iron, bronze and lead working and the production of glass, pottery and enamelling.

Walton Hall was the home of Sir Gilbert Greenall, a Warrington brewer. It was built in the early Elizabethan style in brick with stone dressings between 1836 and 1838. Additions and enlargements were made in 1870, including a billiard room that formed the end of a wing. In 1941 part of the estate known as Walton Gardens was sold to Warrington Corporation and is now a popular area for recreation.

The gardens, parkland and the Victorian house are open to the public and the attractions include lawns, a children's zoo, ornamental gardens and a heritage centre.

The **church of St John the Evangelist** was designed by Paley and Austin and built in 1885 at the expense of Sir Gilbert Greenall MP. This attractive church has an impressive crossing tower surmounted by a recessed spire. The south side is noteworthy, with a vestry, transept and porch. The church contains some attractive stained-glass windows and a fine oak reredos.

WARMINGHAM [Crewe]

SJ7061: 3 miles (5km) W of Sandbach

The village lies on the winding River Wheelock to the west of Elworth and Sandbach. This small community is fairly remotely situated in an area of rich farmland. The river is the main drainage agent of this wedge of land between the A350 and the Trent and Mersey Canal. It quickly becomes a sizeable river as it bends and twists its way to join the River Dane at Middlewich. The area also contains many wide stretches of water in the form of ponds and flashes.

The **church of St Leonard** stands on the site of a Norman church. The west tower is built of dark brick with stone dressings and very much an 18th-century church. In 1870, the timber-framed church was rebuilt to designs by R.C.

Hussey. The interior was constructed in the Perpendicular style with narrow aisles.

The stained glass in the south transept is by Meréchal and Champigneule of Metz (1870); and in the north transept by Heaton, Butler and Bayne (1878). The church contains a monument to William Vernon (died 1732).

Some modern houses have been built in the village over the past few years, including council houses and bungalows for the elderly. The old corn mill in the centre of the village, which in later years used to grind coconut shells, is now a craft centre. Would-be photographers will find the river weir in the village ideal for attractive pictures.

An old legend tells the story of how, in Norman times, a savage dragon once roamed the area, killing and eating children. Baron Venables of Kinderton finally killed it. One of the nearby lanes in the village is known as Dragon's Lane.

WARRINGTON [Warrington]

SJ6088: 10 miles (16km) N of Northwich

Formerly part of the county of Lancashire, Warrington lies at the head of the Mersey Estuary. Early man established a crossing point here and small settlements grew up on drier land to the north and south.

The Romans established a fortified base at Veratinum (Wilderspool) and the Roman road crossed the ford at Latchford and continued north to Coccium (Wigan). The base and settlement became important as a meeting point for other Roman roads – west to Chester, south to Northwich and east to Manchester. Later, in the Saxon period, a settlement was established at Thelwall and was fortified as a protection against Scandinavian raiders.

Domesday listed the former Roman settlement as 'Walintune', which was held by King Edward and the lands were owned by Roger de Poitou. This was seemingly a prosperous area with many manors and considerable tracts of land. The place became 'Werinton' in 1259 and in Old English the word may be derived from the settlement or 'tun of Waer's people' or it could mean 'tun at a weir or ford'.

Since early times, Warrington has been noted for its diversity of industries, from ore smelting and glass making by the Romans up to the manufactured goods of modern times. It is on this range of successful industries that Warrington's prosperity has grown. There's a long list of products illustrating the point – sailcloth manufacture, fustian cutting, pin making, paper making, tanning, soap making, copper smelting, glass making, wire making, brewing and chemicals. The town had a linen market every week, as well as a strong retail trade. The heavy clays and damp climate were particularly suitable for growing flax, used in the production of sailcloth.

During the 1950s, Warrington suffered an apparent decline in its population (-6%, to 75,000), but the loss was mainly due to the removal of people to outer suburbs.

Before the 18th century, the main transporters of goods were packhorses, which were superseded in the 1750s by carriers' carts. As turnpike roads improved, travellers took advantage of stage coaches and mail coaches. Thus, by the middle of the 18th century, Warrington had a bi-weekly stage coach service to London. In 1820, existing turnpike roads south of the Mersey to Warrington ran from Chester, Knutsford, Davenham, Ashton and

Holford. Warrington is now surrounded on three sides by motorways – M62, M6 and M56.

Railways came to Warrington in 1831. A line to Crewe was opened in 1837, and three years later a passenger line from Warrington to Altrincham was completed. Warrington Central was opened in 1878. The **Crosfields Transporter Bridge** was used from 1916 to 1964, the only bridge of its type built for rail traffic. It still stands as a 'listed' building.

Inland waterways have played an important part in the growth and prosperity of the town. In 1698, Thomas Patten was responsible for making the River Mersey navigable from Runcorn to Warrington as far as Bank Quay. He was one of the large landowners in Warrington at that time. A port was established at Bank Quay, and this same Thomas Patten (father of Thomas Patten who built the town hall) established his copper smelting business at Bank Quay in 1717, using ore from Alderley Edge at first.

The River Mersey has been bridged at Bridge Foot ever since the 13th century. The present bridge is the sixth one to stand on the site. In 1757, the **Sankey Canal** was cut from Warrington to St Helens for the purpose of transporting coal.

In 1761, James Brindley engineered the **Bridgewater Canal**. It was built from Worsley to Stockton Heath to carry coal and raw cotton. The Runcorn section was added in 1776.

The **Manchester Ship Canal** was opened in 1894 by Queen Victoria. It stretched for a distance of thirty-six miles from Eastham to Salford in Manchester. At Warrington the Mersey had to be diverted and there is a junction of canal and river at Walton Locks.

In the 13th century, the Order of St Augustine built a friary church in the present area between St Austin's Lane and Bridge Street. A plaque now marks the site.

The **church of Holy Trinity**, Sankey Street dates from 1760. Built in the classical style, the galleries around three sides are lit by two tiers of windows. Fine gilded Corinthian columns support a flat ceiling.

The **church of St Elphin** was the town's first parish church and a simple wooden building was thought to have been built in AD675. St Elphin's was mentioned in Domesday as holding an area of land that was exempt from all usual dues except tax. The present church dates from 1226, the oldest part being at the east end. In fact the church has been altered many times, parts replaced and rebuilt. The present chancel, built in the Decorated style, belongs to the third church that was constructed in 1354 by Sir William Boteler.

There is one memorial of note: a tomb chest of Sir John Boteler and his wife, 1463, which is decorated with fine alabaster statuettes.

One of the oldest parts of St Elphin's Church is the crypt beneath the east end. The spire was added as comparatively recently as 1860 and is the third tallest spire in England. In 1943 the former Boteler Chapel, with fine oak panelling, became the South Lancashire Regimental Chapel.

Warrington Town Hall is an imposing Georgian mansion built in 1750 for the Patten family. It was purchased in 1873 for the Borough Council. Facing the building are the magnificent cast-iron gates, considered to be one of the finest sets in the country.

Sankey Valley Park lies on the western side of Warrington, alongside the old St Helen's Canal. Parts of Bewsey Old Hall date back to 1597.

Risley Moss Country Park and Nature Reserve is located to the east of Warrington. Risley Moss is one of the last remaining areas of post-glacial mossland in the country. From the visitors centre there are paths through woodland interspersed with ponds and there is also the chance to visit an observation tower.

Warrington Rugby League Club was formed in 1879 when it rented a local field. After several moves the Wires ended up at their present ground at Wilderspool. Warrington's best Rugby season to date was in 1973-4, when the Club won the Rugby League Challenge Cup at Wembley. They ended the season by winning the club championship.

WAVERTON [Chester]

SJ4663: 4 miles (6km) SE of Chester

Waverton is a well established village situated on both sides of the Shropshire Union Canal to the south-east of Chester. The surrounding area is fine agricultural land.

The settlement was mentioned in Domesday as 'Wavretone' in Dudestan Hundred. Ilbert held the land for Earl Hugh. There was land for four ploughs with three Frenchmen and three villagers. The settlement was described as 'Wauertone' in 1100, 'Waueretone' in 1150 and 'Waverton' in 1260. The meaning of the element 'Waver' is unknown, but may be associated with woodland i.e. brushwood, hence 'the tun amongst surroundings of brushwood'.

Just outside Waverton is Rowton Moor. Chester supported King Charles and he himself witnessed the defeat of his army at Rowton Moor. By the evening of 24 September 1645, over one thousand Royalist troops were dead or captured.

The **church of St Peter** has a Perpendicular west tower with a 19th-century recessed pyramidal roof. The church was restored in 1888. The timber framing of the chancel is probably original, as are the windows and also the clerestory. The roof of the nave is dated 1635.

The school was built in 1877 at the expense of the first Duke of Westminster, and designed by John Douglas. The three gables set against the high roof give an attractive aspect.

South of the church are some Eaton Estate cottages dating from the 1860s and built for the second Marquess. To the north of Waverton lies Cotton Abbots Farm (1873), also designed by Douglas.

WEAVERHAM [Vale Royal]

SJ6073: 3 miles (5km) W of Northwich

Weaverham lies just west of Northwich on the B5135 road to Kingsley. Convenient stations are at Greenbank and Hartford on the Manchester to Chester and Crewe to Liverpool lines respectively.

In the 14th century, the district around Weaverham experienced many bitter disputes between the smallholders and landowners and the abbot and monks of Vale Royal Abbey.

At one time Weaverham lay on the fringe of Delamere Forest, and it was around the edges of the great hunting preserve that settlements, churches and manor houses became established. It is believed that a medieval road ran along the line of the A49, a route along the old Roman road utilised by the Saxons.

This apparently thriving settlement is mentioned in Domesday as 'Wivreham' and its details record an excellent picture of that time. The survey lists extensive ploughland, a church, a priest, a mill, woodland, meadowland and deer enclosures. It was described as 'Weueresham' in 1100. Weaver is a British river name which is derived from the Latin root *vibrare*. The name would mean 'winding river'.

The **church of St Mary** lies on the north side of the village. It is a light and airy building due to large windows and the absence of a screen or arch between the nave and the chancel.

The late Perpendicular building has a large, square 15th-century tower with massive gargoyles and a clock. There are five bays of arcades and octagonal piers, with a low-pitched panelled roof in the north aisle. There were restorations by Anthony Salvin in 1855 and by John Douglas in 1877. The original oak pews, installed in 1634, were dismantled in 1877 and sections of them used in the present pews.

A chilling reminder of troubled times came to light when excavations in the churchyard in the 1930s revealed a mass grave. Skeletons were found, each with a hole in the forehead, and it is thought they were the victims of summary executions during the Civil War.

The former Weaverham Grammar School, founded in 1638, is a two-storeyed sandstone building with mullioned windows.

Since the time that Brunner Mond of the Winnington works began building model homes, in what was then the rural surroundings of Weaverham village, the settlement has expanded to increasingly become a suburb of Northwich.

WESTON [Crewe]

SJ7351: 3 miles (5km) SE of Crewe

The village lies adjacent to the A5020

Crewe road and the A500 Nantwich to Stoke-on-Trent road. North-west of the village lies the complex of railway sidings and the important junction of Crewe Station. The village is situated in the shallow valley of the little Basford Brook, amongst surroundings of arable land and pastureland.

The church of All Saints was built in brick in either 1838 or 1842. The structure has no tower. The nave has lancet windows and the arched chancel was built in 1893.

Weston Hall lies to the south of the village. It is a two-storeyed building of five bays and is dated 1677. North of the village stands Hollyhedge Farm, 1647, a timber-framed house with a small amount of lozenge-type decoration.

WESTON [Halton]

SJ5080: 1 mile (1.6km) S of Runcorn old town

Weston is a large industrial and dockland suburb of Runcorn overlooking the Mersey estuary. Considerable residential development has taken place in the area. Weston was not mentioned in Domesday.

The **church of St John the Evangelist** was built of blackened stone between 1895 and 1898. Douglas and Fordham designed the church. The building has a very short west tower with a short broach spire. The chancel is set higher than the nave. There is a narrow north passage aisle. The stained glass in the east window is by Kempe (1898).

Christ Church, Weston Point, is right in the dockland area. It was built in 1841 by the Trustees of the Weaver Navigation for the use of the watermen. It has a slender west tower with a broach spire. The interior consists of a nave and transepts.

The docks at Weston Point are close by the Manchester Ship Canal. The Weaver Navigation dates from 1721, and the canal was extended from Frodsham to Weston by means of Telford's Weaver Cut. This section was authorised in 1807.

WETTENHALL [Crewe]

SJ6261: 4 miles (6km) SW of Winsford

Wettenhall is an isolated rural community situated deep in the heart of farming country to the south of Winsford. Access is via twisting country lanes and past solitary farmsteads from the B5074, Winsford to Nantwich road.

The settlement was mentioned in Domesday as 'Watenhale' in Risedon Hundred. Glewin held it as a free man and the lands were owned by Gilbert of Venables. There was land for two ploughs, with one rider, one villager and two smallholders. Domesday records meadowland and woodland.

The settlement was described as 'Wetenhala' in 1150 and 'Wetinhale' in 1260. The name is derived from 'wet halh'.

The **church of St David** is a brick building designed by J. Redford and J. A. Davenport. It was built in 1870.

WHEELOCK [Congleton]

SJ7559: 2 miles (3km) S of Sandbach

Wheelock is a compact residential village on the southern edge of Sandbach, adjoining the Trent and Mersey Canal. The village lies on the A534, Crewe to Sandbach road, and the nearest station is Elworth on the Crewe to Manchester line. The River Wheelock flows through the village and continues on to meet the Dane at Middlewich.

The settlement was mentioned in Domesday as 'Hoiloch' in Middlewich

Hundred. Earl Morcar held it and the lands were owned by Ranulf Mainwaring. There was land for four ploughs, with two riders. Domesday records an extensive area of woodland.

The settlement was described as 'Qwelok' in 1321 and 'Whelok' in 1440. Wheelock is a British river name similar to Chwilogen and derived from the Welsh *chwel, chwyl* or 'turn'. The Wheelock is a very winding river.

The **Christ Church** was built between 1836 and 1837. It is of brick construction and has a chancel by Alfred Price (1903).

WHITEGATE [Vale Royal]

SJ6369: 3 miles (5km) NW of Winsford

Whitegate lies just west of the Weaver Navigation in an undulating, well-wooded farming landscape between Winsford and Northwich. The neighbouring villages of Whitegate and Marton have now been combined by the Boundaries Commission.

Both communities, together with manors, granges and lodges, prospered during the time of the influential Vale Royal Abbey, the largest Cistercian house in England. The name of the settlement was described as 'Whitegate' in 1545 and means 'white gate'. It is likely to have had its origin from being near to the gates of Vale Royal Abbey.

The prettily situated **church of St Mary**, (1874-5), was designed by John Douglas and built at the expense of Lord Delamere. The present structure replaced a previous church of 1728, of which the south portal and gate piers remain. Interestingly, the interior contains the octagonal timber piers that date back to the original Perpendicular timber-framed church. The roof, with its strong roof timbers, covers the nave and aisles. The

building has a short tower with a shingled spire.

The extraction of sand in the neighbourhood has resulted in new lakes, which attract large numbers of wild fowl and other birds. Lying to the north-west of the village is a large stretch of water called **Petty Pool**. This has now been designated as a Site of Special Scientific Interest. The pool is almost surrounded by an extensive area of Forestry Commission woodland.

The Whitegate Way runs along the trackbed of an old railway that once served the salt industry in the 19th century. The passenger service lasted until 1930 and all traffic ceased in 1963. In 1970 Cheshire County Council bought it from British Rail and converted it into a footpath and bridleway about 5½ miles (8.8km) long. The old station area has been provided with a car park, toilets and picnic site.

WHITLEY [Vale Royal]

SJ6079: 5 miles (8km) NW of Northwich

This scattered community is situated in a rural landscape with numerous ponds. Agriculture is still important, with arable farming and stock rearing. Lower Whitley lies just off the A49, Whitchurch to Warrington road. Higher Whitley is located to the north on a side road east of the A49.

The names of these villages have changed at various times in the past, including, Over and Nether Whitley, Whitley Superior and Inferior and now as Lower and Higher Whitley.

The settlement is mentioned in Domesday as 'Witelei' and ploughland, meadowland and woodland are recorded. It was described as 'Wytele' in 1288 and the name is derived from 'white leah'. Names ending in 'leah' are most common in old woodland districts. So in this context 'leah' means 'a glade' or 'natural open space in a wood'.

The **church of St Luke** at Lower Whitley is a small, low building built of brick with a north-west tower. It has mullioned windows and is thought to have been built in the early 17th century. The interior contains a particularly fine hammerbeam roof with richly carved oak beams. The church was restored in 1864 and at other times in the 19th century.

There is a Methodist chapel dating from 1802 that is thought to be the oldest Methodist chapel in regular use in Cheshire. The interior is laid out with terraced seating.

WIDNES [Halton]

SJ5185: 12 miles (19km) SE of Liverpool

Although not mentioned in Domesday, Widnes was said to be located in the Saxon Wapentake of 'Walintune' (Warrington). The settlement is described as 'Wydnes' in 1200 and 'Wydenes' in 1242 and means 'wide promontory'. The place is by a headland jutting into the Mersey.

Evidence of early occupation in the area came to light when several carved heads, said to be in the Celtic tradition, were discovered during excavations in Derby Road and Birchfield Road, Widnes in 1968. The heads were 12 inches (0.30m) high, and were probably images of the gods worshipped by the Brigantes tribe that lived in the area.

The Romans would have used the river for the transportation of materials to their auxiliary fort and industrial centre at Wilderspool.

The River Mersey was described as 'Maerse' in 1002, 'Merse' in 1142. The word is derived from the Old English 'Maeres-ea' and means 'boundary river'. The Mersey was virtually the boundary between Cheshire and Lancashire prior to reorganisation in 1974, and in distant times was the demarcation line between Mercia and Northumbria.

By the beginning of the 11th century, the settlements that first came into existence in Saxon times, for example, Farnworth, Upton, Ditton, Dutton and Denton, were populated by people of Anglo-Scandinavian descent. Although Farnworth was to become the most important of the Widnes villages, and later to have its own church, Halton Castle on the other side of the Mersey was the main administrative centre of the Barony of Widnes and Halton. In 1178 the sixth baron of Halton was granted a charter for a ferry at Runcorn Gap.

The eleventh baron of Halton, who was also earl of Lancaster, rebelled against his sovereign Edward II. The rebel earl was defeated in battle and executed in 1322. As a consequence, the Crown sequestrated the earl's titles and land, including the manor of Widnes. These were restored to the thirteenth baron in 1350.

Between the latter part of the fifteenth century and the beginning of the seventeenth century, Widnes was but the name for a loose collection of villages. This includes the local settlements of Bold and Appleton. It is said that they owe their origin to the names of two influential families.

William Smyth of Peel House, Appleton (1460-1547) became Bishop of Lichfield and Coventry in 1496. In 1507 Bishop Smyth's link with Farnworth and Widnes was further strengthened when he endowed a sum of money to establish a grammar school at Farnworth. This was the original ancestor of Wade Deacon Grammar School. William Smyth was co-founder of Brasenose College, Oxford, and later became Bishop of Lincoln from 1514 to 1547.

The Industrial Revolution had its beginnings in Widnes between 1714 and 1830, and the birth of the chemical industry was between 1830 and 1865. Of particular significance was the making Sankey Brook navigable for coal barges from St Helens to Sankey Bridges in 1757. Soon after, a stretch of canal extended from Sankey Bridges to Fiddler's Ferry. The Sankey Navigation Canal was extended beyond Fiddler's Ferry to Widnes in 1833. The canal, like the railway, terminated at what is known as **Spike Island**. The name is probably derived from the word for cheap boarding houses that grew up around the factories on the island.

A new dock was constructed with sidings to facilitate the easy transfer of coal from the railway trucks on to flats (flat-bottomed sailing barges). By 1855, Spike Island and its immediate environment was the centre of a new chemical industry.

John Hutchinson (1820-65) was the founding father of the Widnes chemical industry. In his latter years he became a major landowner around Spike Island and Widnes Marsh. **William Gossage** (1799-1877) was initially an alkali manufacturer who was able to trap the great clouds of acid that poured from the chimneys. After 1835 he became a soap manufacturer. **Frederick Muspratt** (1825-1905) specialised in recovering copper and silver from the pyrite cinders which the alkali industry produced as a by-product. **Henry Deacon** (1822-76) manufactured soda by the ammonia process. John Brunner and Ludvig Mond are two other famous names and are best known for the introduction of the Solvay Process to replace the Leblanc Process.

The Leblanc Process was founded on the synthetic production of soda from common salt. Soda ash was of particular importance to the soap, glass and textile industries. However, the production of 'black ash' soda by the Leblanc process caused pollution by discharging choking hydrogen chloride into the atmosphere.

The railway bridge across the Runcorn Gap was officially opened on May 21 1868. The foundations had to be rooted in solid rock some 45ft (14m) below low-water mark. Pedestrians were also able to cross over the Mersey by walking on the railway bridge footway. A viaduct of 49 arches over Ditton Marsh was opened in 1868.

The Runcorn-Widnes **Transporter Bridge** was opened in 1905, and is one of only four built in Britain. In its first year it carried 187,000 passengers. It ran until 1961, when it was dismantled.

The roadbridge, by Mott, Hay and Anderson (1956-61), is a single steel arch rising elegantly in the air, carrying the roadway hanging beneath. The span is 1082ft (330m), the total length 1628ft (496m). The top of the arch is 306ft (93m) above high-water level. It was widened in 1975 to accommodate four lines of traffic and in 1977 was re-named the Silver Jubilee Bridge.

The **church of St Luke**, Farnworth, is situated in the northern part of Widnes. This ancient building of red sandstone has a large collection of painted hatchments, mostly showing the arms of the Bold family. These memorials were displayed outside the house of the deceased for the mourning period, usually a year, before being placed in the church.

The oak chancel roof of the 15th century is particularly notable. In 1431 the roof of the nave, north and south aisles and the tower were repaired. At the same time, Richard Bold was responsible for repairing the chancel roof. Today, only the large cross beams remain of this early work, the rest is later restoration work. The centre bosses depict a Griffin Passant with the initials of Richard Bold.

At the west end of the nave is a breach shelf. This was where bread bought with charitable donations was left for the poor to collect.

The first record of the Bold family of Bold township appears in 1154, in the reign of Henry II. The document mentions payment of 'scutage' which means paid for military services rendered.

Like many ancestral families, the Bold family name has been associated with a legend. The inhabitants of a village were losing all their cattle to a fierce griffin so the blacksmith volunteered to fight the beast. He covered himself with the skin of an ox and, armed with a sword and a dagger, lay in wait in the field. The griffin attacked and carried the smith over the treetops. The smith continued to stab the creature until it alighted, weak with loss of blood. The smith then drew his sword, cut off its head and returned with it to the village as proof of his brave deed. The blacksmith received the surname of Bold, as well as the grant of a large tract of land.

The first member of the Bold family to leave a memorial to the church was John de Bold who lived in the reign of Henry IV. In 1404 John de Bold was the commander of Caernarvon Castle, with a garrison of only twenty-eight soldiers. The defenders beat off an attack by a large force of Welsh and French led by Owain Glyndwr. For his efforts he was knighted and was also granted five thousand acres. He founded the Bold Chantry in Farnworth Church in 1406.

The Bold chapel is richly ornamented with exquisite pieces of sculpture. It lies at the east end of the north aisle and enclosed by three Gothic arches supported on columns with carved capitals. The memorial to Richard Bold, died 16 February 1635, and Anna Legh depicts the knight attired with ruffles and wearing a pointed beard. He bears a cuirass and carries a long naked sword. Anna is dressed in a farthingale with a cap on her head and a ruff round her neck.

Another memorial is a beautiful piece of workmanship by Pietro Tenerani to Mary Patten Bold, Princess Sapieha, who married Prince Eustace Sapieha of Dereczyn in Lithuania in the Bold Chapel on 21 December 1822 and who died of tuberculosis on 16 December 1824.

There is a monument by Chantry erected in 1823 to Peter Patten Bold, who died on 17 October 1819. It represents a female figure weeping over an altar. On the east end of the marble are sculptured a helmet and faces.

The church contains a King Charles II coat of arms dated 1661. In the south-east corner of the churchyard is the lock-up marked Bridewell, 1827. It is just a plain oblong building.

West Bank, Widnes, the bridgehead of the Mersey bridges has a planned grid layout which dates from 1860-70. A pleasant feature here is the riverside Victoria promenade. Facing the promenade is the **church of St Mary** (1908-10). Mrs Gossage laid the foundation stone on 14 May 1908. Her husband had been one of the benefactors of the fund for the buying of houses in West Bank and clearing them to build this, the second St Mary's Church. Mr F.H. Gossage gave a sum of £1000 and his firm, soap manufacturers, gave £3000.

This is a large and rather splendid sandstone church. It has a substantial west tower with the interior resting on huge east piers. The imaginative interior has aisles and high transepts and stone-work with inscription friezes. The chancel arch has large, round, panelled piers that complement the tower piers. The high organ chamber is situated on the north side, with a one-bay arch to the chancel. There is a Lady Chapel of three bays on the south side.

The **church of St Paul** (1883-4), Victoria Square, is a large brick building with the south-east tower added in 1907. It has a spacious exposed brick interior and a terracotta pulpit.

St Marie's Roman Catholic Church (1864-5) has a pretty bellcot and a polygonal apse. The interior is noted for its thin red sandstone columns. The top parts, or capitals, are typical of the architect E.W. Pugin.

North of Victoria Square, off The Kingsway, are the Municipal Buildings completed in 1967. There is a College of Further Education, 1961; swimming baths, 1961; and the Magistrates Court and Police Station (1966-7). The Magistrates Court is a low building faced with reconstructed marble and an attractive zigzag roof.

The **Catalyst Museum** is the museum of the chemical industry. This is located in Mersey Road, Widnes and was officially opened by Viscount Leverhulme on 14 June 1989. The Catalyst Museum offers a family day out, where science and technology come alive through a host of interactive exhibits and hands-on displays. From the rooftop observatory one can obtain panoramic views out across Cheshire.

Next to the Catalyst Museum is picturesque Spike Island, now reborn as a waterside park. There is an anchorage for fishing boats, a heritage trail and an opportunity to enjoy the riverside landscape.

Widnes Rugby League Football

Club was founded in 1878, although its origins can be traced back to 1873 when it was the Farnworth and Appleton Football Club. In 1974 the team beat Warrington at Wembley to take the Rugby League Challenge Cup. They won the Challenge Cup again in 1979. They also won the BBC Floodlit Trophy in 1979 and the John Player Trophy twice, as well as being Division One champions in 1977-8. Naughton Park, Lowerhouse Lane is the home of Widnes RLFC. It was reopened as Halton Stadium in February 1998.

WILDBOARCLOUGH [Macclesfield]

SJ9868: 6 miles (9km) E of Macclesfield

The village lies in a fold in the Pennine hill country of east Cheshire. The Clough Brook flows joyfully down its sequestered valley from its moorland source. One of the surrounding green hills is the guardian sentinel of Shutlingsloe, 1659ft (506m) above sea level. The area is a walker's paradise with a network of paths, tracks and old packhorse trails.

A little distance to the north stands the isolated **Cat and Fiddle Inn** – England's second highest hostelry at 1690ft (515m).

During the first part of the 19th century, an extensive water-powered cotton factory and bleaching, dyeing and printing works operated at Wildboarclough. The owner was George Palfreyman who had also built nearby Crag Hall.

By the mid-19th century, carpets had been made in the village. A local carpet was even exhibited at the Great Exhibition in 1851. By the late 19th century, production had ceased and most of the buildings were demolished in the 1950s.

The surrounding area was part of the

The old post office, Wildboarclough – said to have been, in its day, the largest sub-post office building in England *(Graham Beech)*

Earl of Derby's estate, and it is said that during the Second World War Winston Churchill paid secret visits to Crag Hall in order to enjoy the solitude of this remote hill country.

The large administration block of the old mill (c1770) once served as the largest sub-post office in England.

The **church of St Saviour**, built between 1901 and 1909, has a low west tower, a nave with a dormer and a chancel. The church lies in a beautiful setting on the east slopes of the wooded Clough Brook valley. The 16th Earl of Derby built this neat, handsome building with a simple interior as a memorial for the safe return of his sons from the Boer War. Craftsmen from the estate worked on the building using local materials.

Some time ago the village, and a smallholding in particular, was the setting for a TV production of a love story by H.E. Bates.

The **church of St Stephen**, Forest Chapel stands on high ground on the west slopes of the Tor Brook Valley, 2½ miles (4km) north of Wildboarclough. The

building, which is part of a tiny hamlet, was built in 1673, although the present church dates from 1834.

This remote place is a great favourite with ramblers, who come every year, on the first Sunday after 12 August, to attend the **rush-bearing service**. As in other churches, this ancient custom was intended to provide the churches with a warm and dry floor covering. Once a year, the old rushes were cleared out and fresh ones ceremonially brought in. In present times, Forest Chapel is decorated with plaited rushes, cut in an adjacent marshy hollow, which are interwoven with flowers. With such a large congregation, most of the service is conducted in the churchyard.

WILLASTON [Crewe]

SJ6653: 2 miles (3km) E of Nantwich

The village lies to the south-west of Crewe, with the housing development concentrated around the link road between the A534 and the A500. The

Crewe to Shrewsbury railway line runs through the village but there is no station. Much of the housing development of the village dates back over 100 years, when dwellings were built for the Crewe railway workers.

The community is noted for a special ceremony enacted in June each year. As part of the Willaston Summer Féte, the strange rite of worm-charming takes place, when competitors armed with garden forks attempt to 'charm' a metre square patch of ground. The rules insist that the worms may not be dug up, or that water may not be used. The creatures have to be persuaded and success is more likely if it is raining. Anyone taking part in these World Worm-Charming Championships will find the rules available in many languages. I wonder which language worms react to best?

Two trophies are awarded, one for the most worms collected and one for the heaviest worm. When daylight fades the worms are returned to the ground. Monies raised from the Summer Féte go towards a flourishing Community Association.

In the village, **the church of St Luke** was dedicated in 1965.

Willaston Hall stands just to the west of the village. The house is probably early Georgian and built of brick with substantial stone quoins. This two and a half-storey house was refronted in 1737, and lower wings were added to each side in the 1830s.

WILLASTON-IN-WIRRAL [Ellesmere Port]

SJ3377: 3 miles (5km) E of Neston

This village lies at the heart of the Wirral and close to the border between Cheshire and Merseyside. The community strad-

dles the B5133, Windle Hill to Hooton road.

The name of the settlement was described as 'Wilaston' in 1305 and is derived from a personal element – 'Wiglaf's tun'. Although not mentioned in Domesday, the settlement gave its name to the Hundred of Wilaveston or Wirral.

Christ Church, 1854, was designed by Fulljames and Walker. The building has a nave, chancel and a bellcot, with a north aisle added in 1926. The nave has a steeply pitched roof.

Willaston Hall is situated close by the village green. This manor house has an Elizabethan-style front with three tall gables and is built of red brick with stone dressings. There is a datestone over the door inscribed 'HB 1558' (the letters stand for Hugh Bennet). However, this is an unlikely date as the hall is situated in the centre of the house and is approached through a centrally-placed porch.

The Wirral Way is an unusual linear country park that runs for a distance of 12 miles (19km) between West Kirby and Hooton. The old railway trackbed provides an excellent amenity route passing along the Dee estuary and through attractive farmland. Train buffs will appreciate the retention of the former Hadlow Road Station, now restored to appear as it would have looked in the 1950s. The **Wirral Country Park** also includes nature trails, horse riding, fishing areas and picnic sites. There are car parks situated at various spots and a Visitor Centre located at Thurstaston.

WILLINGTON [Chester]

SJ5266: 8 miles (13km) E of Chester

The village, a near neighbour of Kelsall, nestles at the southern end of a sandstone ridge, below the Bronze Age hill fort of Kelsborrow. The community has remained rural, with its country cottages and attractive gardens looking over the Cheshire Plain towards Beeston and Peckforton. The scenic valley, known locally as 'Little Switzerland', leads down to the attractively situated hostelry, the Boot Inn. Off Chapel Lane stands a row of almshouses built by the Tomkinson family of Willington Hall.

The settlement was mentioned in Domesday as 'Winfletone'. In 1200 it was described as 'Wynlaton' and is probably derived from Old English women's names 'Winflaed's or Wynflaed's tun'.

Willington Hall was designed by George Latham of Nantwich and built in 1829 in the Jacobean style. A particular feature is the diamond pattern of brickwork with shaped gables. This handsome mansion is situated in impressive grounds.

Tirley Garth is a large house set in sequestered surroundings to the east of Willington Hall. It was designed by C.E. Mallows and built between 1807 and 1913: a product of the Arts and Crafts Movement with a high quality of craftsmanship. The gabled main front on the south side looks out to Beeston and Peckforton and contains a large bow window. The great hall runs through two floors, with an open timber roof and a gallery on three sides. The design for the formal and landscaped gardens was the joint imaginative product of C.E. Mallows and T.H. Mawson.

WILMSLOW [Macclesfield]

SJ8482: 4 miles (6km) NW of Macclesfield

Wilmslow lies on the banks of the River Bollin in north-east Cheshire and on the line of the A34. It has grown to the size of a town, becoming a large dormitory area with virtually nothing of the old settlement remaining. The Wilmslow conurbation extends to Handforth, which is close to the border with Greater Manchester.

Wilmslow has a station on the lines to Manchester via Gatley or via Stockport, and a modern shopping centre serves the needs of the neighbourhood. Wilmslow, in fact, is set in two river valleys – the Bollin and the Dean – and here were the lands of a family known as le Bolyns.

Domesday makes no reference to Wilmslow, but the name of the settlement became 'Wilmislowe' in 1260. The name is probably derived from 'Wighelm's hlaw or hlaew' – a low hill or mound. The mound could be a meeting place or burial place.

Wilmslow was specifically a farming community until the 18th century, when it branched out into a number of industrial activities including button moulding for the Macclesfield silk mills, jersey spinning and cotton mills. Cotton fustian became popular and long sheds or long rooms attached to houses were required for the job of cutting the cloth.

There is a commemorative plaque marking the site of a fustian cutting factory by the roadside at Stamford Court, Manchester Road.

Romany, the Reverend George Bramwell Evens, was a nationally known journalist, author and broadcaster on BBC Radio's "Children's Hour" in the 1930s and 1940s. His interest in nature led to a great following for his caravan, Vardo; dog, Raq; horse, Comma; and two companions, Muriel and Doris.

Romany moved to Wilmslow in 1939 to be nearer the BBC studios in Manchester. Wilmslow was chosen as it was then a leafy suburb with plenty of opportunities for studying wildlife. He died in

1943 and his ashes were scattered on a grassy hillock at Old Parks Farm, Glassonby, Cumbria.

Romany's caravan is located near to Wilmslow Library and can be visited on the second Saturday in the months from May to September.

The **church of St Bartholomew** is not mentioned in the Domesday Survey. All traces of the first church are lost and the existing fabric of the present church in Wilmslow is largely the remains of a re-modelling in the 16th century. The tower, with battlements and pinnacles, is possibly of the 15th century.

The remainder of the plan consists of the chancel, the nave with its clerestory and side aisles, and a south porch. Drastic 19th-century alterations and re-building removed the tomb of George Booth (1543) of Dun-ham Massey Hall from the Booth Chapel and many of the old furnishings, although some of the beautiful screens were saved.

In the chancel, a small door-way leads to a crypt below the altar. In the north wall of the chancel aisle are two sandstone effigies of Humphrey Newton, yeoman and landowner of Pownall Hall (1466-1536), and Elizabeth his wife. Humphrey's head lies on three tuns and Elizabeth's head is on a wheatsheaf. The chancel floor contains the earliest brass in Cheshire – a representation of Robert del Bouthe and his wife, Douce. Robert died in 1460 and his wife in 1453. Sir Robert del Bouthe was formerly Lord of Bolyn, Thorneton and Dun-ham.

Pownall Hall, Carwood Road, is a sandstone Georgian house dressed up in the early Tudor style (1830). Henry Bod-dington of the Manchester brewing fam-ily bought it. At Pownall he did little to the exterior but completely transformed the interior. He chose craftsmen from the Century Guild, specialists in furniture, metalwork, plasterwork, glasswork and art to decorate the rooms.

Boddington used his house for the most up-to-date work of the Arts and Crafts movement. His architects were Ball and Ilce of Manchester. A.H. Mackmurdo founded the Century Guild in 1882, its members included Selwyn

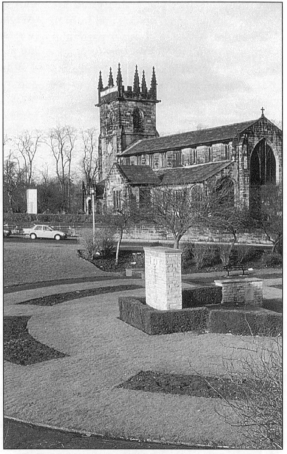

St Bartholomew's – Wilmslow's parish church
(Graham Beech)

Image, Herbert Horne and Benjamin Creswick. The oak carving was by Milsom of Manchester, the decorative painting by the Manchester artist John Dawson Watson. He was born in Sedbergh 1832, died Conway 1892. The stained glass was by the Gateshead Glass Company and Shrigley and Hunt of Lancaster. A particularly fine example of the latter's work are the signs of the zodiac in the hall windows. The Century Guild lasted as a group only until 1888 and the work of Pownall was its major commission.

WINCLE [Macclesfield]

SJ9566: 5 miles (8km) SE of Macclesfield

The soft red sandstone of the Cheshire plain gives way to harsh millstone grit; the old farms and barns are built of the same material and hedges give way to rough stone walls. Through this hilly area runs the delightful wooded valley of the River Dane, the county's boundary with Staffordshire.

This settlement was not listed in Domesday. In 1291 Wincle was 'Wynkehull' or 'Wineca's hill'.

In the latter part of the 19th century, roads in the district were in poor condition. However, matters improved when William Brocklehurst bought Swythamley Hall in neighbouring Staffordshire. Dane Bridge was rebuilt and widened in 1869. Swythamley Hall was burnt in 1813 and rebuilt by the Brocklehursts in the middle of the 19th century. Sir Philip Brocklehurst, the explorer, introduced llamas, yaks and wallabies to the Swythamley Park estate. In 1938 some wallabies escaped, and nowadays there are infrequent sightings of the species in the area of The Roaches in the Staffordshire Moorlands.

During the packhorse era many important cross-country trails passed close to Wincle.

The **church of St Michael** was rebuilt in 1882, except the tower which dates from around 1820. The burial ground has graves dating from the 1700s.

The **Ship Inn** at Wincle was named after the Liverpool vessel *Swythamley* which foundered off the Cape in 1862. Nearby, there is a trout farm and fishery along the banks of the River Dane.

The monastic farm of **Wincle Grange** is an unusual building with some pre-Reformation windows. The Cistercian monks of Combermere Abbey near Nantwich owned some of the surrounding land.

Cleulow Cross is situated on a mound surrounded by trees, a mile to the north-west of Wincle. The stone shaft has exactly the same markings as the ancient pillars that stand in West Park in Macclesfield and is also similar to the Saxon cross shaft in Leek (Staffs) churchyard. Stone pillars of this type acted as medieval crosses or waymarkers.

WINSFORD [Vale Royal]

SJ6367: 5 miles (8km) S of Northwich

The A54 from Chester descends into Winsford town, named from the ford over the River Weaver. The whole background of Winsford's prosperity is the mining of salt in the Weaver Valley. In fact, Winsford didn't exist until the 18th century, when, in 1721, the **Weaver Navigation Act** was passed allowing the river to be made navigable as far as Winsford Bridge. The River Weaver was canalised in 1731 to connect the salt field with the Mersey. After one full year's operation it carried 76,000 tons of material.

Documents recorded Winsford as 'Wyneford bridge' in 1334 and 'Wynsfurth brygge' in 1475. It is probably derived from a personal name 'Wine's ford'.

Four salt pans were working near the bridge when the Weaver Navigation Act was passed, but other works soon followed, together with the barges to transport the material The valley bottom was ideal for brine pumping and wild brine was pumped from the top bed of salt. As the salt works prospered, the areas where water entered the beds to become brine were eroding the salt. As a result of salt subsidence the **flashes** were formed. Today, the flashes are used for water sports.

By 1766 the Trent and Mersey Canal passed through Middlewich. It was kept away from Winsford for fear of competition on the River Weaver. Winsford's six boatbuilding yards have all closed down, but sailmakers turned their skills in canvas work to develop a marquee business.

By 1816, there was a great increase in population because of the salt works. Two beds of almost pure salt lie underneath the town. These were formed in the Triassic period around 200 million years ago. Shallow water in an inland sea was replenished by streams and tides and then continually being evaporated by the sun, leaving thick deposits of salt. The beds are separated by a layer of Keuper Marl, which is hardened desert sand, indicating that at that time of its formation there were no water supplies. No fossils have been found as the ancient sea was too salty for creatures to survive.

Today, the only **salt mine** continuing to operate is that of Meadow Bank, Winsford. Rock salt is mined primarily for road gritting in icy winter conditions and for the production of fertilisers. It is fascinating to realise that below ground there are roads big enough for large lorries, road signs, roundabouts and traffic lights; a world of **enormous caverns**, heavy machinery, drilling equipment and long conveyor belts.

Winsford salt contains a certain amount of sand so when it gets wet the outer surface forms a waterproof layer. This enables piles of salt to be stored outdoors without the need for a cover, in readiness for winter weather.

The modern town of Winsford includes a new shopping area with a large car park, a Civic Hall, the Dingle Recreation Centre and the library.

John Bradbury was born in the town in 1872 and lived there until he was the age of fifteen. He left the district and eventually became the Chief Cashier at the Bank of England, a position that he held at the time of the first issue of the ten shilling and one pound notes. Both of the notes bore his signature.

WINWICK [Warrington]
SJ6092: 3 miles (5km) N of Warrington

Winwick is situated on the Wigan road just north of Warrington and lies close to the Cheshire county boundary. Way back in time, the Winwick area was the frontier in the conflicts between the Saxon kingdoms of Mercia and Northumbria. Oswald, king of the northern part, is said to have died in battle at Winwick. The settlement is not mentioned in Domesday by name but an earlier church is recorded as lying in Newton Hundred. The church of the manor, St Oswald's, had an area of land which was exempt of all payments.

The surrounding countryside is listed as being heavily wooded and to contain hawks' eyries. Roger de Poitou owned the lands. The name was 'Winequic' in 1170 and 'Wynequic' in 1212 – it seems to be derived from 'Wineca's wic'.

The **church of St Oswald** is an amalgamation of periods from the early 13th century to the mid-19th century. During the latter time, Anthony Pugin designed a new chancel and some of his architectural drawings are preserved at the church.

One of Cheshire's notable families, the Leghs of Lyme Hall, was closely connected with St Oswald's, although the family seat lay some thirty miles eastwards. There is a fine memorial brass of Sir Piers Legh (1468-1527) and his wife. After his wife's death, Sir Piers became a priest and the brass plate shows him wearing priestly robes beneath his armour.

Resting in the Gerard Chapel is a large fragment of a Saxon cross, a reminder of the importance of this early Christian area.

WISTASTON [Crewe]

SJ6754: 2 miles (3km) SW of Crewe

Wistaston is a residential suburb to the south-west of Crewe. It stretches from the Wistaston Brook towards the village of Willaston. The A534 from Nantwich to Crewe threads its way through the housing development.

The settlement is mentioned in Domesday as 'Wistanestune', and the survey records meadowland, woodland and enclosures. It was described in 1241 as 'Wistanistone', and the name is derived from 'Wigstan's tun'.

The **church of St Mary**, 1827-8, was designed by the Nantwich architect, George Latham, and is basically a Georgian building. It is a brick structure with four divisions of arched windows and a narrow tower. In 1884 the chancel was increased in length and a transept was added.

WITHINGTON GREEN [Macclesfield]

SJ7970: 3 miles (5km) NE of Holmes Chapel

Withington Green is a small extended village made famous by the proximity of **Jodrell Bank** , which was opened in 1957 to house Manchester University's radio telescope. The 250ft (76m) circular metal dish, fully steerable, is supported on two 180ft (55m) metal towers. Nearby is Mark II, a 125ft (38m) paraboloid on a concrete frame. Mark III has a bowl of open one-inch mesh. There is a smaller telescope near to the control building, whose function is the tracking of space probes. This one has a bowl 50ft (15m) in diameter supported on a concrete frame. There is a fifth bowl of the same diameter with a massive concrete pillar.

There is an impressive visitor centre, many examples of 'hands-on' exhibitions, which are a great delight to children of all ages and Planetarium shows. There is an arboretum in the grounds with paths and tree trails, a children's playground and a picnic area.

WOODHEY CHAPEL, FADDILEY [Crewe]

SJ5752: 5 miles (8km) W of Nantwich

The village of Faddiley is a scattered collection of cottages and farmhouses. The chapel is situated in a remote and flat part of the county and stands alone in fields at the end of a farm lane. The supposed site of the old Woodhey Hall is a short distance away. This fine house, the residence of the Wilbrahams, was built by Lady Wilbraham around 1690. The hall replaced an earlier house of about 1600, but was demolished n the 1730s. The chapel is of red brick and has a portico with Roman Doric columns.

The family gallery was kept warm by two fireplaces. There is no altar but an elegant pulpit carved with foliage designs. The pews face inwards in the style of a preaching chapel. The chapel was restored in 1926.

Rookery Hall was originally a Georgian brick house belonging to William Cooke, who owned sugar plantations in Jamaica. Baron Wilhelm von Schroeder purchased the house and estate in 1867 and the building was altered into a more imposing style. The hall is now a luxurious restaurant and hotel.

WORLESTON [Crewe]

SJ6555: 3 miles (5km) W of Crewe

The scattered community of Worleston straddles the B5074, Nantwich to Winsford road. It lies in a rough triangle of agricultural land used mainly for dairy farming between the River Weaver, the Shropshire Union Canal and the Middlewich branch of that canal.

The course of a Roman road heading for Middlewich ran through the district, as supported by evidence discovered near Reaseheath Old Hall in 1920. The settlement was mentioned in Domesday as 'Werblestune', and it was described as 'Werliston' in 1260. The name is derived from a personal name – 'Werwulf's tun'.

The **church of St Oswald**, 1872, was designed by C. Lynam in the form of a cross and without aisles. There is a slender spire on the centre of the roof over the crossing. The interior contains examples of stained glass by C.E. Kempe dated 1872 and 1882. One particular window at the east end commemorates George Cotton, Bishop of Calcutta, who was drowned in the Ganges in 1866.

Reaseheath Hall, once owned by the Wilbraham family, was purchased in 1722 by the Tomkinsons of Dorfold. It was rebuilt in red brick in the gabled Queen Anne style in 1878. After being owned by the Cotton family, it became a School of Agriculture in 1919 and is now the home of the **Cheshire College of Agriculture**.

WRENBURY [Crewe]

SJ5947: 5 miles (8km) SW of Nantwich

The pleasant village of Wrenbury lies in the southernmost part of Cheshire, close to the Shropshire border. It is set in the most productive dairy farming area of the county and is renowned as the home of three varieties of Cheshire cheese. The settlement was listed in the Domesday Book as 'Wareneberie', when it was held by Karl, a free man. The lands were owned by William Malbank. Domesday mentions a sizeable area of woodland, two enclosures and a hawk's eyrie.

The village name became 'Wrennebury' in 1230 and possibly means 'old fort inhabited by wrens'.

Dating from the early 16th century, **the church of St Margaret** overlooks the village green. St Margaret of Antioch was a third-century martyr and the patron saint of expectant mothers. A church here was first mentioned in the 12th century as confirmed to Combermere Abbey. It became a chapelry of Acton church, which was also in the possession of Combermere Abbey, until the dissolution of the monasteries.

The church tower is a conspicuous feature with an embattled parapet and pinnacles. A stair turret protrudes from the south-east angle of the tower and terminates in a stone cupola. There is a five-bay nave with a clerestory and the nave roof belongs to the 16th century.

There are some interesting **box pews** and a number retain the painted crests of local families. The early Georgian pulpit no longer has its sounding board. There are monuments to the Cotton family of Combermere Abbey and the Starkey family of Wrenbury Hall.

An unusual feature in the church is the **'Dog Whipper's pew'** just inside the door. He was paid ten shillings a year in 1735, and in 1780 was uniformed in a blue gown and yellow tippet. In 1826 his title was changed to that of Beadle. His duties were to remove dogs that disrupted the service and also, it is alleged, to awake sleeping worshippers.

The exterior of the church displays a fine collection of grotesque gargoyles. Near the door are some curious cast-iron grave slabs dating from the early 19th century.

Set in the centre of the village, the green is overlooked by a number of houses, including timber-framed Elm House, which dates from the 17th century. This grassy area was once used for common grazing and for bear baiting. Now it is the location for village events such as the May Queen celebrations and the Summer Féte.

The Shropshire Union Canal was originally called the Ellesmere Canal. It was conceived by industrialists to link the River Mersey with the Dee at Chester and the Severn at Shrewsbury. Authorised in 1793, its chief engineers were Thomas Telford and William Jessop. The Ellesmere Canal later joined with the Chester Canal. Branches ran towards Newtown and Llangollen. The Wrenbury stretch of canal is characterised by a series of single-span timber bridges that are lowered and raised by counter-balancing beam weights. The road bridge is believed to be one of only two of its type in the country which carry road traffic. The canal, no longer used by commercial traffic, has a brisk trade in holiday craft every summer.

On the north side of the canal by the lift bridge is the former Wrenbury Mill, now the base for holiday hire canal cruisers. **Wrenbury Station** lies on the east side of the village on the Crewe to Shrewsbury line.

WYBUNBURY [Crewe]

SJ6850: 5 miles (6km) S of Crewe

Wybunbury is a small rural village set in a pastoral landscape of hedgerows and woodland to the south of Crewe. It is listed in Domesday as 'Wimeberie' in Warmundestrou Hundred. A priest was recorded as well as woodland and enclosures. The settlement was described as 'Wybbunburi' in 1276, and its name seems to be derived from an Anglo-Saxon personal element and a fortified manor – 'Wigbeorn's burg'. Wybunbury was formerly an important parish of 18 townships and one of the great medieval parishes of Cheshire. The usual form of pronunciation nowadays seems to be 'Winbury'.

The early builders of the **church of St Chad** unfortunately chose an area of ground that was unstable due to active underground springs, salt and sand. The tall, 96ft (29m), solitary **church tower** is the remaining part of the village's medieval church. The tower has survived due to its solid construction, but over the years began to lean away from its proper level. In the 18th century there was a local saying, 'as crooked as Wimberie steeple'.

The chancel was built in 1793 and in 1834 the whole body of the church was taken down and rebuilt under the supervision of the architect James Trubshaw.

Another building was erected in 1893, but again the fabric rapidly deteriorated. Finally, the body of the church was demolished in 1970 and the site around the tower is now a Garden of Remembrance.

The west doorway of the tower is deeply recessed with continuous mouldings. On either side of the west door and the great west window are canopied niches containing statues that probably represent bishops.

A memorable event took place on 26th March 1969, when the Revd Stanley Jones discovered a collection of antique silver in an iron chest while cleaning the tower. Amongst the items was a Charles II lidded tankard of 1677. Permission to sell was granted by a consistory court and the sum of £10,250 was raised for church funds. The other objects consisted of a George III private communion set of 1790; a George II chalice of 1728; a George I flagon dated 1726; a spoon from 1720 and a Queen Anne tazza (a saucer-shaped cup) dated 1702. These pieces are now secured in a bank vault and used only on special occasions.

A new **church of St Chad**, of brick construction, was built along the main road in 1978. This modern building was re-dedicated in a Service of Celebration by the Bishop of Chester in 1988. The new church contains a repaired effigy of Lady Katherine Delves Broughton and Rafe Delves of Doddington Hall, dated 1513. Other items from the old church include the reredos, two chests, the Bishop's Chair and a fragment of stained glass.

After the closure of the old church, the very fine alabaster memorial to Sir Thomas Smith of Hough and Dame Anne, his wife, daughter of Sir William Brereton of Brereton, is now resited in the south aisle of St Mary's Church, Nantwich.

To the north of the village lies **Wybunbury Moss**. This nature reserve covers some 10½ hectares (26 acres) and consists of a deep waterlogged hollow on which floats a layer of peat covered in sphagnum moss. Pine and birch trees have established themselves in this unique habitat and it is the home of many rare species of flora and fauna.

Bibliography

Acton Local History Group. *Acton – The History of a Cheshire Parish and its 17 Townships* (1995).

Angus-Butterworth, L.M. *Old Cheshire Families and Their Seats* Sherratt and Hughes, (1932), Morten Publ. (1970).

Audlem Local History Group. *The History of a Cheshire Parish and its Five Townships* (1997).

Bethell, D. *Portrait of Cheshire: Hale* (1979).

Brownsword-Hulland, D.J. *Historic Guide to Nantwich* (Guildmaster, 1996).

Cheshire County Council Information and Records Service. *Cheshire Gazetteer* (CCIRS, Chester, 1997).

Cheshire Federation of Women's Institutes. *Cheshire Village Memories* (CFWI, Tilston Court, 1952).

Cheshire Federation of Women's Institutes. *Cheshire Village Memories* (CFWI, Tilston Court, 1961).

Cheshire Federation of Women's Institutes. *The Cheshire Village Book* (Countryside Books, Newbury and the CFWI, Chester 1992).

Civic Trust in the NW *The Treasures of Cheshire* (Manchester, 1991).

Colin Jones, J. *The Remarkable History of Congleton* (Congleton Museum Trust, 1994)

Crosby, A. *A History of Cheshire* (Phillimore, 1996).

Darling, J. *Portrait of Warrington* (Sigma, 1989).

Dore, R.N. *Cheshire* (Batsford, 1977).

Ekwall, E. *The Concise Oxford Dictionary of English Place-Names* (Oxford, 1936).

Finn, R.W. *Cheshire* (Knopf, 1928).

Foster, A. *A History of Farnworth Church Its Village and Parish* (1981).

Hayes, C. *Widnes* (Sutton Publ. 1998).

Lake, J. *The Great Fire of Nantwich* (Shiva, 1983).

Lee R. *Portrait of Wilmslow, Handforth and Alderley Edge* (Sigma, 1996).

Longden, G. *The Industrial Revolution in East Cheshire* (Macclesfield and Vale Royal Groundwork Trust, 1988).

Manpower Series Commission. *Discovering Cheshire Churches* (1989)

Mclean M. and C. *The Dane Valley* (S.B. Publ. 1991).

Mee, A.. (Ed). *The King's England, Cheshire* (Hodder and Stoughton, 1949).

Morris, J. (Gen Ed.). *Domesday Book, Cheshire* (Phillimore, 1978)

Nantwich, Worleston and Wybunbury; A Portrait in Old Picture Postcards (Brampton Publ. 1987).

Pevsner, N. and Hubbard, E. *The Buildings of England, Cheshire* (Penguin, 1990).

Richards, R. *Old Cheshire Churches* (Morten, 1973).

Roberts, T.W. *Ellesmere Port* (Roberts, 1995).

Scholes, R. *Understanding the Countryside* (Moorland Pub. Co., 1985).

Simpson, R.C. *Crewe and Nantwich: A Pictorial History* (Phillimore, 1991)

Smith, G. *Bygone Widnes* (Cheshire Libraries, 1985).

Sylvester, D. and Nulty, G. (Eds). *The Historical Atlas of Cheshire* (Cheshire Community Council, 1958).

Tattenhall Local History Group. *The History of a Cheshire Village* (1977).

The Life and Labours of John Wedgwood.

Treuherz, J. and Figueiredo, P.de. *Cheshire Country Houses* (1995).

Wild, A. *Exploring Chester* (Sigma, 1996).

Wilson, R.J. *Knobsticks – Canal Carrying on the Northern Trent and Mersey* (Wilson Publ., 1974).

Index

A

abbeys
  Vale Royal, 57, 114, 123, 158, 160
Aldersey Hall, 15
Anderton Boat Lift, 26, 121
Anglo-Saxon crosses, 131, 137, 145, 169
Arley Hall, 20
Ashley Hall, 20

B

Backford Hall, 26
Barnston Monument, Farndon, 71
Barnston, Major Roger, 71
Battle of Rowton Moor, 28, 44, 49, 157
Beeston, Sir George, 37
Birkenhead, George, 26
Blomfield, Sir Arthur William, 105, 136
Blue Planet Aquarium, Ellesmere Port, 69
Bostock New Hall, Bostock Green, 33
Boteler, Sir William, 157
Boyd, Arnold, 19
Bradbury, John, 170
Bradshaw, John, 52
Brereton Hall, 33
Brereton Heath Park, 33
Brereton, Sir William, 22
Bridgemere Garden World, 42
Bridgewater, Duke of, 136
Brindley, James, 156
Bruen, John, 147
Brunner, John, 162
Buckley, William, 110
Buerton windmill, 36
Bunbury Locks, 38
Burton Hall, 39
Burton Manor, 39

C

Calveley, Sir Hugh, 36
canals
  Bridgewater, 77, 100 - 101, 103, 113, 154,
    156
  Ellesmere, 25, 67
  Macclesfield, 11, 30, 32, 53, 90, 93, 113,
    120, 129 - 130
  Manchester Ship, 67, 69, 94, 103 - 104, 113,
    137, 149 - 150, 154, 156, 159
  Peak Forest, 130
  Peak Forest, Disley, 62
  Sankey, 156
  Shropshire Union, 38, 48, 79, 107 - 108, 112,
    117, 127, 142, 152, 157, 172 - 173
  St Helen's, 126
  Trent and Mersey, 10, 32, 104, 108, 110, 121,
    132, 136 - 137, 155, 159, 170
  Weaver Navigation, 10, 85, 121, 159

Capesthorne Hall, 141
Carden Brook, 151
Carden Park House, Clutton, 50
Carroll, Lewis, 58 - 59
castles
  Beeston, 28
  Bolesworth, 87
  Chester, 45
  Halton, 82
  Mow Cop, 115
  Peckforton, 125
Checkley Hall, 42
Cheshire College of Agriculture, Reaseheath
  Hall, 172
Cheshire Workshops, 40
Chester Zoo, 46, 153
Chester, Rows, 44
Childe of Hale, 82
Chorley Hall, 14
Chorley, Robert de, 14
Chorlton Hall, 48
Christleton Hall, 48
Christleton Old Hall, 48
Churche's Mansion, 117
churches
  All Saints, Daresbury, 58
  All Saints, Glazebury, 77
  All Saints, Handley, 84
  All Saints, Harthill, 86
  All Saints, Marthall, 109
  All Saints, Saughall, 138
  All Saints, Siddington, 141
  Christ and St Mary, Chester, 44
  Christ Church, Alsager, 18
  Christ Church, Barnton, 26
  Christ Church, Croft, 56
  Christ Church, Crowton, 56
  Christ Church, Eaton, 65
  Christ Church, Ellesmere Port, 68
  Christ Church, Macclesfield, 105
  Christ Church, Wheelock, 160
  Christ Church, Willaston-in-Wirral, 166
  Congregational, Congleton, 53
  Holy Ascension, Upton-by-Chester, 153
  Holy Trinity, Bickerton, 28
  Holy Trinity, Capenhurst, 42
  Holy Trinity, Capesthorne, 142
  Holy Trinity, Culcheth, 58
  Holy Trinity, Hurdsfield, 93
  Holy Trinity, Little Bollington, 100
  Holy Trinity, Mossley, 113
  Holy Trinity, Rainow, 135
  Holy Trinity, Warrington, 157
  John the Baptist, Bollington, 31
  John the Baptist, Knutsford, 98

John the Baptist, Rainow, 135
Lud's, Allgreave, 17
Methodist Church, Brown Knowl, 34
St Alban, Macclesfield (RC), 105
St Alban, Tattenhall, 149
St Andrew, Tarvin, 147
St Bartholomew, Church Minshull, 49
St Bartholomew, Great Barrow, 78
St Bartholomew, Wilmslow, 168
St Bertoline, Barthomley, 27
St Boniface, Bunbury, 36
St Chad, Farndon, 70
St Chad, Over, 122
St Chad, Tushingham Cum Grindley, 153
St Chad, Wybunbury, 174
St Christopher, Pott Shrigley, 128, 6
St Columba, Newton (RC), 119
St Cross, Appleton Thorn, 20
St David, Wettenhall, 159
St Edith, Shocklach, 140
St Elizabeth, Ashley, 21
St Elphin, Warrington, 157
St George, Poynton, 130
St Helen, Northwich, 121
St Helen, Tarporley, 146
St James and St Paul, Marton, 109
St James the Great, Audlem, 25
St James, Christleton, 48
St James, Congleton, 53
St James, Gawsworth, 75
St James, Ince, 94
St James, Sutton Lane Ends, 144
St John Baptist, Guilden Sutton, 81
St John Evangelist, Alvanley, 19
St John Evangelist, Ashton, 21
St John Evangelist, Byley, 41
St John Evangelist, Congleton, 53
St John Evangelist, Great Sutton, 81
St John Evangelist, Lindow and Row of
    Trees, 100
St John Evangelist, Lostock Gralam, 102
St John the Baptist, Aldford, 16
St John the Baptist, Chester, 45
St John the Baptist, Hartford, 85
St John the Baptist, Smallwood, 142
St John the Evangelist, Cuddington and
    Sandiway, 57
St John the Evangelist, Kingsley, 97
St John the Evangelist, Norley, 120
St John the Evangelist, Toft, 152
St John the Evangelist, Walton, 155
St John the Evangelist, Weston, 159
St John, Burwardsley, 40
St John, Chelford, 43
St John, Cotebrook, 54
St John, High Legh, 91
St Jude, Tilstone Fearnall, 152
St Lawrence, Frodsham, 73
St Lawrence, Over Peover, 124
St Lawrence, Stoak, 142

St Leonard, Warmingham, 155
St Lewis, Croft (RC), 56
St Luke, Dunham-on-the-Hill, 64
St Luke, Goostrey, 77
St Luke, Holmes Chapel, 91
St Luke, Whitley, 161
St Luke, Widnes, 162
St Luke, Willaston, 166
St Margaret, Wrenbury, 172
St Marie's, Widnes (RC), 164
St Mark, Antrobus, 19
St Mary and All Saints, Great Budworth, 80
St Mary and St Helen, Neston, 118
St Mary Magdalene, Alsager, 18
St Mary of the Angels (RC), Childer Thorn-
    ton, 47
St Mary of the Angels, Hooton (RC), 92
St Mary, Acton, 9
St Mary, Astbury, 22
St Mary, Bosley, 32
St Mary, Bruera, 35
St Mary, Coddington, 51
St Mary, Disley, 62
St Mary, Dodleston, 63
St Mary, Eccleston, 66
St Mary, Hale, 82
St Mary, Halton, 82
St Mary, Handbridge, 83
St Mary, Lymm, 104
St Mary, Nantwich, 116
St Mary, Nether Alderley, 118
St Mary, Pulford, 134
St Mary, Rostherne, 136
St Mary, Sandbach, 138
St Mary, Thornton-le-Moors, 150
St Mary, Tilston, 151
St Mary, Weaverham, 158
St Mary, Whitegate, 160
St Mary, Widnes, 163
St Mary, Wistaston, 171
St Matthew, Haslington, 87
St Matthew, Stretton, 143
St Michael and All Angels, Middlewich, 111
St Michael, Burleydam, 38
St Michael, Burtonwood, 40
St Michael, Ditton (RC), 63
St Michael, Hulme Walfield, 93
St Michael, Macclesfield, 105
St Michael, Marbury, 108
St Michael, North Rode, 121
St Michael, Shotwick, 141
St Michael, Wincle, 169
St Nicholas Chapel, Cholmondeley, 47
St Nicholas, Burton-in-Wirral, 39
St Oswald, Aston Juxta Mondrum, 24
St Oswald, Backford, 25
St Oswald, Brereton Heath, 33
St Oswald, Lower Peover, 102
St Oswald, Malpas, 106
St Oswald, Winwick, 171

St Oswald, Worleston, 172
St Paul, Childer Thornton, 47
St Paul, Great Boughton, 79
St Paul, Helsby, 89
St Paul, Hooton, 92
St Paul, Over Tabley, 125
St Paul, Widnes, 164
St Peter, Aston-by-Sutton, 23
St Peter, Congleton, 52
St Peter, Delamere, 61
St Peter, Duddon, 64
St Peter, Elworth, 70
St Peter, Hargrave and Huxley, 85
St Peter, Little Budworth, 101
St Peter, Minshull Vernon, 112
St Peter, Oughtrington, 122
St Peter, Plemstall, 128
St Peter, Prestbury, 131
St Peter, Waverton, 158
St Philip, Kelsall, 95
St Saviour, Wildboarclough, 165
St Stephen, Forest Chapel, 165
St Stephen, Moulton, 114
St Thomas, Eaton-by-Tarporley, 66
St Thomas, Henbury, 90
St Thomas, Stockton Heath, 143
St Wenefrede, Bickley, 29
St Wilfred, Davenham, 60
St Wilfred, Grappenhall, 77
St Wilfrid, Mobberley, 112
Swettenham Church, 145
Unitarian Chapel, Knutsford, 98
Churton Hall, 50
Civil War, 29, 49, 79, 87, 111, 116, 148, 154, 158
Cleulow Cross, 169
Combermere Abbey, 38
Cotton, William, 73
Crewe Hall, 55
Crosfields Transporter Bridge, 156

D
Daffodil Dell, Swettenham, 145
Davenham Hall, 60
Davies Brothers, Bersham, 50, 66
Davies, Mary - the Horned Woman, 141
Deacon, Henry, 162
Dean Row Chapel, 60
Delamere Forest, 57, 60 - 61, 85, 96 - 97, 119 -
   120, 146, 154
Derbyshire Caving Club, 13
Dog Whipper's Pew, Wrenbury, 173
Dorfold Hall, 10
Douglas, John, 57

E
Eaton Hall, 65
Eaton Hall, Aldford, 16
Egerton, Lord Francis, 133
English Heritage
   Beeston Castle, 28

F
families
   Aldersey, 15
   Aston, 24
   Bold, 162
   Brereton, 107
   Cholmondeley, 103, 106 - 107
   Congreve, 40
   Davenport, 142
   Delves, 30
   Done, 54, 146 - 147
   Egerton, 63, 98, 135
   Grosvenor, 16
   Grosvenors, 46
   Leghs, 78, 105, 111, 171
   Leicester, 99, 103, 124
   Mainwaring, 124
   Mainwarings, 9
   Mallory, 112 - 113
   Masseys, 133
   Savage, 105
   Stanleys, 13 - 14, 105
   Tollemache, 117, 152
   Westminster, 63, 133, 158
   Wilbrahams, 9
Foden Motor Works Band, 70
Forest Centre, Delamere, 61, 120

G
Gallows Hill, Great Boughton, 79
Garner, Alan, 13, 141
Gaskell Memorial Tower, 98
Gaskell, Elizabeth, 98
Gawsworth New Hall, 75
Gawsworth Old Hall, 74
God's Providence House, Chester, 46
gooseberry shows
   Goostrey, 77
   Lower Withington, 103
   Marton, 110
   Swettenham, 145
Gossage, William, 162
Greg, Samuel, 144
Gritstone Trail, 62, 96, 106, 113, 144
Grosvenor Museum, Chester, 46

H
Hale Lighthouse, 82
Hamilton, Lady Emma, 117
Haslington Hall, 87
Haughton Hall, 88
Heber, Reginald, 107
Helsby Hill, 88
Henbury Hall, 90
hereditary foresters
   Davenport, 109, 142
   Done, 146, 154
High Legh Hall, 91
Hockenhull Platts, 149
Holford Hall, Lostock Gralam, 102, 127

Holly Holy Day, Nantwich, 117
Hooton Hall, 92
Horn of Delamere, 154
Hornby, A.N., 10
hotels
    Castle, Halton, 82
    Crown, Nantwich, 117
    Old Hall, Sandbach, 138
    Swan, Tarporley, 146
Hough Hole House, 135
Hutchinson, John, 162

J
James Mellor, 134 - 135
Jenkin Chapel, 96, 135
Jodrell Bank, 103, 171
Jones, Revd Stanley, 174

K
Kerfield House, 122

L
Lamaload Reservoir, 76
Leigh-Mallory, George, 113
Lindow Moss, 100
Little Moreton Hall, 34
Lower Carden Hall, Clutton, 50
Lyme Park, Disley, 62
Lymm Hall, 104

M
Macclesfield Forest, 105 - 106, 144
Maiden Castle, 34
Mainwaring, Sir William, 9
Malbank, William, 9
Malbank, William , 107
Marbury Hall, 108
Marbury Hall, Comberbach, 51
Mellor, James, 96
Memorial Stone, John Turner, Saltersford, 135
Merry Days, Marbury, 108
Middlewood Way, 30, 129
mills
    Adelphi, Bollington, 30
    Berisfords, Congleton, 52
    Bunbury, 37
    Clarence, Bollington, 30
    Congleton, 53
    Ginclough, 75
    Hankelow, 84
    Hough Hole, Rainow, 134
    Lumbhole, Kettleshulme, 96
    Nether Alderley, 119
    Paradise, Macclesfield, 106
    Quarry Bank, Styal, 144
    Stretton, Tilston, 151
    Wrenbury, 173
Mond, Ludvig, 162
Mottram New Hall, 114
Mottram Old Hall, 114
museums

Anson, Poynton, 130
Boat Museum, Ellesmere Port, 69
Catalyst, Widnes, 164
Forest Museum, Linmere, 61
Linmere Forest, 154
Museum of Primitive Methodism,
    Englesea-Brook, 27
Paradise Silk Mill, Macclesfield, 106
Salt Museum, Northwich, 121
The Railway Age Exhibition, Crewe, 55
Muspratt, Frederick, 162

N
National Trust
    Burton Hill, 39
    Helsby Hill, 89
    Little Moreton Hall, 34
    Maiden Castle, 34
    Quarry Bank Mill, Styal, 144
Ness Botanical Gardens, 117
Nixon, Robert, 123
Norton Priory, 83

O
Oakmere Hall, 57
Ormerod, George, 26
Oulton Park, 101, 147
Oulton Park House, Little Budworth, 101
Over Peover Hall, 124

P
Pace, George, 45
Pancake Bell, Tarvin, 149
Peel Hall, Ashton, 21
Peel Hall, Kingsley, 97
Plessington, John, 133
power stations
    Fiddler's Ferry, 127, 162
Pownall Hall, 168
Poynton Lake, Poynton, 129
prehistoric sites
    Billinge Hill, 154
    Eddisbury, 60, 120
    Helsby Hill, 89
    Henbury, 89
    Kelsall, 94
    Kelsborrow, 95, 167
    Norley, 119
    Pott Shrigley, 128
Pretty Pool, Whitegate, 160
public houses
    Bear's Paw, Frodsham, 72
    Bells of Peover, Lower Peover, 102
    Bhurtpore Inn, Aston, 23
    Black Bear, Sandbach, 138
    Boot Inn, Willington, 167
    Cheshire Cat, Nantwich, 117
    Combermere Arms, Burleydam, 38
    Davenport Arms, Marton, 109
    Duke of Portland, Lach Dennis, 99
    Greyhound Inn, Ashley, 20

Headless Woman, Duddon, 64
King's Lock Inn, Middlewich, 111
Legh Arms, Prestbury, 132
Pheasant Inn, Higher Burwardsley, 40
Ram's Head, Grappenhall, 78
Red Lion, Malpas, 106
Royal Oak Inn, Kelsall, 95
Ship Inn, Wincle, 169
Spinner and Bergamot, Comberbatch, 51
White Bear, Knutsford, 97
White Lion, Barthomley, 26
Puddington Old Hall, 133
Pugin, Anthony, 105, 171

R
railway viaducts
Congleton, 120
Holmes Chapel, 92
Ravenscroft Hall, 41
Redes Mere, 141
Risley Moss, 157
Risley Moss Country Park and Nature Reserve,
157
rivers
Bollin, 60, 100, 104, 131, 167
Croco, Brereton Heath, 33
Dane, 65, 92, 121, 136, 146, 169
Dane, Congleton, 52
Dean, 60, 75, 167
Dean, Bollington, 30
Dean, Rainow, 134
Dee, 63, 66, 70, 79, 118, 125, 133, 138, 140 -
141, 151, 166
Gowy, 36, 110, 127 - 128, 147, 149 - 150,
152
Mersey, 81, 93, 137, 150, 154, 156, 161
Weaver, 10, 49, 59, 72, 111 - 112, 115, 120 -
121, 145, 172
Wheelock, 138, 155, 159
Roe, Charles, 105
Roman Amphitheatre, Chester, 45
Roman roads, 60, 66, 95, 106, 110, 112, 115,
121, 143, 151, 155, 158, 172
Roman sites, 110, 155
Romany - The Reverend G B Evens, 167
Rostherne Mere, 135
Runcorn-Widnes Transporter Bridge, 162
Rush-bearing, 148, 165

S
Salt Mine, Meadow Bank, Winsford, 170
Salvin, Anthony, 100, 125
Sandstone Trail, 19, 41, 61, 74
Sankey Valley Park, 157
Scott, Sir Gilbert, 48
Scott, Sir Giles Gilbert, 45
'Scratch' Sundials, 78, 148
Shrigley Hall, Pott Shrigley, 129
Shropshire Union Canal, 25
Smyth, William, 161

Soul-Caking, 19, 51, 148
South Cheshire Way, 87, 108
Speed, John, 71
Spike Island, 162, 164
Staffordshire Way, 113
Stanlow, 68
Stapeley Water Gardens, 88
Stretton Hall, 143
Styal Country Park, 144

T
Tabley House, 99
Tattenhall Hall, 149
Tatton Hall, 98
Tegg's Nose Country Park, 104, 106, 144
The Cross, Lymm, 104
Thelwall Hall, 150
Thomasen, John, 148
Tirley Garth, Willington, 167
Toft Hall, Toft, 152
Tollemache, John, 125
Tunnicliffe, C.F., 144

U
Utkinton Hall, 154

W
Walton Hall, 154
Ward, John, 142
Warrington Rugby League Club, 157
Warrington Town Hall, 157
watermills, Audlem, 25
Weaver Navigation, 7, 23, 26, 56, 59
Weaver Navigation Act, 169
Well-dressing, 123
Wesley, John, 17
Weston Hall, 159
Whitegate Way, 57, 123, 160
Widnes Rugby League Football Club, 164
Wilbraham, Sir Richard, 9
Willaston Hall, 166
William Malbank, 115, 149, 172
Willston Hall, 166
Wincle Grange, 169
Wirral Country Park, 125, 166
Wirral Way, 125, 166
worm-charming, 166
Wyatt, Lewis, 98, 101
Wyatt, Samuel, 98
Wybunbury Moss, Nature Reserve, 174